SYRIA,
PRESS FRAMING,
—— AND THE ——
RESPONSIBILITY
TO PROTECT

Studies in International Governance Series

Studies in International Governance is a research and policy analysis series that provides timely consideration of emerging trends and current challenges in the broad field of international governance. Representing diverse perspectives on important global issues, the series will be of interest to students and academics while serving also as a reference tool for policy-makers and experts engaged in policy discussion.

SYRIA,
PRESS FRAMING,
AND THE
RESPONSIBILITY
TO PROTECT

E. DONALD BRIGGS
WALTER C. SODERLUND
TOM PIERRE NAJEM

WILFRID LAURIER
UNIVERSITY PRESS

LAURIER
Inspiring Lives.

Wilfrid Laurier University Press acknowledges the support of the Canada Council for the Arts for our publishing program. We acknowledge the financial support of the Government of Canada through the Canada Book Fund for our publishing activities. This work was supported by the Research Support Fund.

Library and Archives Canada Cataloguing in Publication

Briggs, E. Donald, author
   Syria, press framing, and the responsibility to protect / E. Donald Briggs, Walter C. Soderlund, Tom Pierre Najem.

(Studies in international governance)
Includes bibliographical references and index.
Issued in print and electronic formats.
ISBN 978-1-77112-307-5 (softcover).—ISBN 978-1-77112-308-2 (PDF).—ISBN 978-1-77112-309-9 (EPUB)

   1. Syria—History—Civil War, 2011– —Press coverage. 2. Syria—History—Civil War, 2011– —Mass media and the war. 3. Syria—History—Civil War, 2011– —Foreign public opinion. 4. Press—Moral and ethical aspects—Syria. 5. Journalistic ethics. 6. Journalism—Social aspects—Syria. 7. Mass media—Moral and ethical aspects—Syria. 8. Frames (Sociology). I. Soderlund, W. C. (Walter C.), author II. Najem, Tom, author III. Title. IV. Series: Studies in international governance

DS98.6.B75 2017   070.4ʹ49956910423   C2017-902147-8

Front-cover photo: News camera shoots bombing in Kobani, Syria. Credit: alfimimnill, iStockphoto. Cover design by Scott Barrie. Interior design by Angela Booth Malleau.

To Michael Bell—
student, colleague, diplomat, and scholar—
a true friend of the Middle East

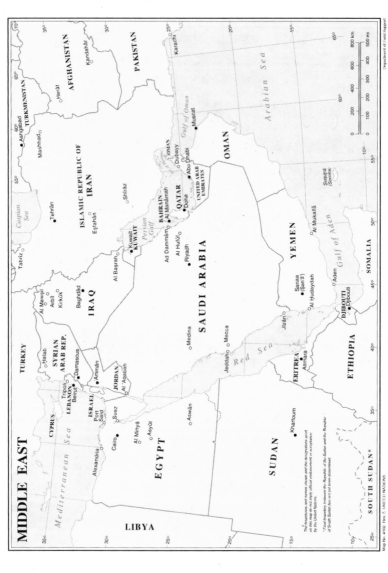

The Middle East, UN Map No. 4102 Rev. 5, November 2011, United Nations (http://www.un.org/Depts/Cartographic/map/profile/mideastr.pdf)

CONTENTS

LIST OF TABLES

ACKNOWLEDGEMENTS

As with all research, there are considerable debts to acknowledge. In this case, at the University of Windsor, Sarah Cipkar was instrumental in finding, retrieving, cataloguing, and organizing opinion pieces from the *The New York Times*, *The Guardian*, and *The Globe and Mail* newspapers—the 417 editorials and opinion pieces that form the data on which our quantitative and qualitative research is based. On the output side, Esme Prowse set up the SPSS file, input the data, and set up the analysis runs. Our profound thanks are extended to both of these talented young researchers—we see great futures for both. Our Windsor colleagues, present and past—Lydia Miljan, Blake Roberts, and Ronald Wagenberg—offered helpful comments on the manuscript. We would also like to thank Michael Siu, the Vice President of Research, and Marcello Guriani, Dean of the Faculty of Arts, Humanities and Social Sciences, who offered critical support and helped to see this project to completion.

Professor Elizabeth Smythe of Concordia University of Edmonton and Professor Jeremie Cornut of the University of Waterloo provided some very helpful suggestions on papers we delivered to the Canadian Political Science Association (CPSA) Meetings in 2014 and 2015, respectively—suggestions that have sharpened arguments in the book. In 2016, we subsequently published the paper, "Was R2P a Viable Option for Syria? Opinion Content in the Globe and Mail and the National Post, 2011–2013" (Najem, Soderlund, Briggs, & Cipkar, 2016).

This is the third book that we have published with Wilfrid Laurier University Press on the subject of media and international intervention, and in this case we wish to especially thank past and present directors Brian Henderson and Lisa Quinn for their patience as well as their encouragement in what has turned out to be a long, hard slog. Thanks as well to senior editor Siobhan McMenemy, managing editor Rob Kohlmeier, copy editor Colleen Ste. Marie, and indexer Elaine Melnick, all of whom greatly assisted in getting the manuscript over the final hurdles on the way to publication. The UN Map Library kindly allowed us to reproduce their map of the Middle East. Finally, we would like to extend our gratitude to the two anonymous reviewers whose thoughtful comments and suggestions prompted us to review the manuscript with an eye to strengthening each component. Shortcomings in the work remain ours alone.

E. Donald Briggs
Walter C. Soderlund
Tom Pierre Najem

Windsor, Ontario
January 2017

INTRODUCTION

Syria, Press Framing, and The Responsibility to Protect is predicated on the twin assumptions that in democracies public opinion matters with respect to government decision making, especially with respect to "large" foreign policy issues that may involve the commitment of significant financial or human resources, and that independent media outlets are important creators and/or reflectors of that opinion.

SCOPE OF THE RESEARCH

Research on decision making on serious public issues over more than half a century (see, for example, Snyder, Bruck, & Sapin, 1962; Rosenau, 1966; Allison & Zelikow, 1999; and, with specific reference to Syria, Goldberg, 2016) has confirmed that such decision making involves myriad factors, ranging from the configuration of the international system to the attributes of individual decision makers, with "societal variables" located somewhere in between (Rosenau, 1966). Prominent among the last are media and public opinion, reflected in "mood theory" (Almond, 1960; Caspary, 1970), which are recognized as playing an important part in establishing the viability of policy choices. (See, for example, Page & Shapiro, 1983; Soroka, 2003.)

Valuable as this research has been, it has not established a direct causal link between government decisions and media/public opinion, nor is it possible to do so short of revelations by decision makers themselves and/or the availability of historical records with respect to specific decisions. However, aggregate positions advocated by media form a domestic context within which decision makers must work, and the latter will have a more difficult task if they wish to move in a direction contrary to that being urged by public forums. It is therefore useful, on a case-by-case basis, to explore the correlations (or the lack of them) between actions taken by political leaders and the advice tendered to them by a media-influenced public opinion, and to form reasoned hypotheses therefrom. Over time, the accumulation of such studies may allow greater understanding of the relationship in general. The present authors have tried, in fact, to contribute to this accumulation by previous examinations of the positions adopted by media relative to international reactions to several significant humanitarian crises (Soderlund, Briggs, Hildebrandt, & Sidahmed, 2008; Sidahmed, Soderlund, & Briggs, 2010; Soderlund, Briggs, Najem, & Roberts, 2012; Soderlund & Briggs, 2014). The Syrian conflict consequently seemed to us to demand similar treatment, particularly as it had begun only weeks after the United Nations Security Council had invoked the new Responsibility to Protect (now familiarly known as R2P) principle to approve a NATO-led operation to assist Libyan revolutionaries against their government's overwhelming firepower.

Media Influence

Rarely has the importance of media coverage on public opinion been shown more graphically than by the photo of the body of Alan Kurdi, a three-year-old Syrian child, washed up on a Turkish beach in early September of 2015. He and his family had been attempting to flee the horrors of war in his homeland. In reality the toddler was but one of well over 220,000 Syrian deaths in the conflict up to that point—but media coverage made this one different. The photo served as a poignant visual representation of a situation gone horribly wrong, resulting in an epic refugee crisis that has shaken Syria, its neighbours, and the European Union to their cores. Once again, as had happened earlier with the famine in Ethiopia and the genocide in Darfur, media coverage ignited calls for the international community to "take action" and raised anew the agonizing question of whether the international community should, or could, have attempted to end the brutal war much earlier on.

As the research literature reviewed in Chapter 3 will show, especially with regard to "humanitarian interventions" where vital national interests are not prominent, the way in which such conflicts are framed by mass media is an important element in how the general public interprets them; indeed some suggest media coverage that is sympathetic to the victims of conflict ("empathy framing") is critical to creating "a will to intervene" (Chalk, Dallaire, Matthews, Barquerio, & Doyle, 2010). At minimum, either a *supportive* or *hostile* mass public becomes a significant part of the context in which decisions to intervene in a particular conflict are made (see Western, 2005).

A chemical weapons attack on a civilian neighbourhood outside Damascus on August 21, 2013 (widely believed to have been carried out by Assad's military), killed an estimated 1,400 people and impelled Great Britain and the United States to seriously consider military responses to what was indisputably a war crime, thus falling within the purview of R2P. With respect to these decisions, in the interaction between *media advocacy* and *government decision-making* (see Robinson, 2000), we know that the outcomes were that both countries backed away from military action. Specifically, in Britain, Parliament voted to reject the use of force, while in the United States, a plan for launching a series of air strikes against Syrian military targets was abandoned in favour of a Russian-brokered agreement to collect and destroy Syria's chemical weapons under international supervision.[1]

We now also know that these decisions were consequential. As it turned out, Great Britain and the US took Western military intervention off the table at precisely the time that the Islamic State of Iraq and Syria (ISIS) was building in strength and on its way to extending the reach of the war back into Iraq from whence it came, which it did in spectacular fashion some six months later in the spring of 2014. However, what is not as evident is the impact that opinion leaders writing in three leading Western newspapers may have had on public opinion during the two and a half years they counselled world leaders on appropriate policies to follow in Syria. Thus, with respect to media influence, we seek to provide readers with a detailed empirical examination of the way in which media opinion leaders in the United States, Great Britain, and Canada framed arguments for and against international intervention in Syria's civil war. As well, we offer what we believe to be reasonable interpretations regarding how this framing likely affected the context in which decisions *not to intervene* were made in Great Britain and the United States in the late summer of 2013.

The Responsibility to Protect

As of the beginning of 2017, multi-player warfare has been ongoing in the geographic centre of the Middle East for over six years. As mentioned, it has resulted in Syrian deaths estimated to be approaching a quarter of a million, and a refugee exodus that has created major ethical and economic problems for neighbouring states and European ones beyond. But it took a number of years for the conflict to attain such mammoth proportions. In its beginnings Syria looked much like the other challenges to oppression that the democratic world had been prematurely celebrating as the "Arab Spring"—for example, in Tunisia, Egypt, Yemen, and Libya, among others. All of these events caused concern and debate within liberal-minded governments about how far and by what means those who were assumed to be seeking justice and freedom should or could be encouraged or assisted. But most of these uprisings were resolved fairly quickly or did not result in extensive or prolonged public–government violence, such as might have given rise to serious consideration of physical intervention of some kind on the side of the would-be reformers. The exception was Libya, and there the international community felt compelled to undertake military operations on the grounds that civilians had to be protected from a government seemingly gone berserk; in mid-March 2011, the UN Security Council authorized a Chapter VII military intervention.

The Syrian outbreak quickly came to show every sign of equalling or surpassing Libya with respect to casualties, destruction, and durability, and looked to be politically more significant in relation to the ever-volatile Middle Eastern region. Yet, while there was no shortage of outrage concerning the actions of the Assad government in particular, this did not translate into a repeat of the Libyan precedent by the United Nations or into some action by a "coalition of the willing" during the early months of the conflict—when it is conceivable that the conflict might have been controlled before it became entrenched and complicated by the intrusion of a variety of radical forces. Not even the use of chemical weapons in August 2013 brought about any overt physical intervention, although it did cause Britain and the United States to seriously consider such a response.

It consequently seemed important to the authors to ask what positions prominent media outlets in major democratic countries adopted with respect to this "failure to protect":

- Did it occur despite the media's urging to the contrary? Or was media/ public opinion of one mind with political leaders?
- Were there significant variations in media attitudes to the crisis from country to country?
- What relevance was the ethical imperative of the recently minted Responsibility to Protect considered to have?
- And, finally, what consequences will the failure to save ordinary Syrians from the horrors of multi-sided savagery have for future humanitarian tragedies, and for the efficacy of the protection principle?

This volume, accordingly, has three objectives:

1. To provide a detailed review of how arguments concerning appropriate international responses to events in Syria were framed in leading newspapers in the United States, Great Britain, and Canada during the crucial early years of the civil war

2. To consider how such media counsel may have affected the domestic contexts in which American and British decisions were made not to launch forceful interventions of any kind following Assad's use of sarin gas in August 2013

3. To offer reasoned speculation concerning the relevance of R2P in future humanitarian crises in light of the failure to provide Syrians with effective protection

METHODS

To accomplish these objectives, the book examines every relevant editorial and opinion article focusing on Syria in *The New York Times, The Guardian,* and *The Globe and Mail* published between the outbreak of the conflict in March 2011 and the end of September 2013—over 400 items in all. The resulting data is subjected to both quantitative and qualitative analysis. Quantitative material tabulates the extent to which various types of international involvement in the ongoing tragedy (diplomatic pressures, the arming of Assad's opposition, the creation of a no-fly zone, or direct military intervention) were *encouraged* or *discouraged* by how they were framed by opinion writers. Tables track the comparative attractiveness of these options in the three newspapers over a two-and-a-half-year time period, as well as the perceived importance of affected or interested outside states in bringing the hostilities to a satisfactory end. Qualitatively, we have constructed what we have termed "opinion narratives" or story lines. Based on 82 per cent of total opinion items, these narratives briefly detail the specifics of the principal arguments presented concerning the various international response options. Combining quantitative and qualitative data in this manner illustrates not only what positions the papers adopted on the issues but also the reasoning behind those positions, thus giving readers a more complete picture over time of how the Syrian conflict was viewed in the context of international involvement.

ORGANIZATION

The book was planned and written primarily for two audiences: (1) those with an interest in the pros and cons of interventions by the international community in humanitarian crises, which is a controversial subject that has received growing attention since the 1990s, and seemingly culminated in the 2001 enunciation of the principle of the Responsibility to Protect and its subsequent adoption by the United Nations in a two-phased process in 2005 and 2006; and (2) those who focus on the influence of media on public opinion and government decision making.

The book is organized as follows:

- Chapter 1 provides an overview of the long- and short-term background necessary for readers to understand the complexity of Syria's problems.
- Chapter 2 reviews the origins of R2P, how it came to be adopted by the UN, what it actually is, and what it is often mistakenly assumed to be.
- Chapter 3 explains the role of the media in framing issues and considers the possible influence of this on public opinion and government

decision making; this chapter also details the research methods used in the study.

- Chapter 4 presents quantitative and qualitative data on conflict framing during the first nine months of the conflict, during which President Assad was widely expected to fall rather easily as had other authoritarian leaders in the early days of the Arab Spring.

- Chapter 5 reviews conflict framing over the full year of 2012, when press framing focused on various diplomatic strategies to remove Assad from office and on growing concerns about the character of his opponents.

- Chapter 6 picks up framing in 2013 up to the use of sarin gas on August 21, 2013. Quantitative data indicate that this period marked the first point in the study where international military action received more positive than negative commentary in any of the three newspapers.

- Chapter 7 reviews the critical period from August 22, 2013, to the end of September, when decisions were made in both Britain and the United States that first sought legislative approval for military strikes. This chapter also examines how the chemical weapons agreement, which ended the threat of American air strikes, was evaluated.

- The Conclusion offers a thematic summary of both tabular and narrative data presented in the previous four chapters as well as offering British and American data on public opinion on international intervention in Syria. It also addresses the possible effects that the lack of a robust international response to the Syrian crisis may have on the future effectiveness of the humanitarian protection ideal as expressed in R2P.

Much, of course, has changed in Syria since the September 2013 end of our study. There is no doubt that the situation there has become even more complex, more deadly, and with a greater number of parties involved than was the case during the conflict's early years. The Syrian civil war is now acknowledged to have created the greatest humanitarian catastrophe since the Second World War, and to have engaged the world's great powers in a UN-authorized, Chapter VII military intervention against ISIS in both Syria and Iraq. However, two intriguing questions still remain: Could or should greater effort been made by the international community to contain the violence at an earlier date? And how did media opinion leaders treat that issue?[2]

We hope that our efforts, as reflected in the following pages, will afford readers a better understanding of the complexities of the Syrian crisis and of the difficulties in deciding when and how to try to provide international solutions for states' inability to protect their citizens from grievous harm or, in this case, from active participation in perpetrating the harm. While we cannot assess the direct influence of media/public positions on the actions of government leaders, we hope to provide readers with information that will enable them to reach their own conclusions in that regard.

Eventually the Syrian tragedy will pass, but given the state of the world, the problems associated with trying to create a more humanitarian world will be with us for many years to come, as will the need to continue to try to understand the relationship between what governments choose to do and the opinions of the publics they serve.

Note on Spelling of Arabic Names

The English transliteration of Arab names varies a good deal, between American, Canadian, and British usage in general, and sometimes from writer to writer according to personal preferences. Every effort has been made in this book to use what seem to be the most common spellings and to be consistent with a single usage. However, when a different spelling is used in a quotation, the original spelling is retained as is customary. For example, the Syrian President's name is spelled "Assad" throughout the text except in a few quotations that use "Asad." Alternate spellings of "Alawi" and "Shia" also appear in a number of quotations.

CHAPTER 1

Understanding Syria's Civil War

When graphic photos showing toddler Alan Kurdi's body washed up on the Turkish shore were splashed on front pages across the world, *Globe and Mail* columnist Konrad Yakabuski was moved on September 10, 2015, to observe that Syria's anguish was "now the world's business" (p. 15). It would perhaps have been more correct to say that although the degree of public attention has waxed and waned as developments in the war have peaked or reverted to their destructive norm, the conflict has been the world's business since it became apparent that the anti-government protests that began in March 2011, and the violent response they generated, had deepened into entrenched and unrestrained mutual barbarity. It could scarcely have been otherwise. Any serious violent conflict is automatically the world's business because (a) there is always a real danger of such an occurrence becoming regional in scope through spill-overs to or from adjoining states; (b) "great powers" will almost by definition have interests to protect or to further in conflict zones—and if one power does respond, so too will others; (c) the United Nations is mandated to address such situations and has created various mechanisms for doing so; and (d) natural and universal humanitarian impulses ensure that, at least momentarily and to varying degrees, world attention is focused on situations that shock the conscience. All of these factors were, and are, particularly relevant to the Syrian case.

ANCIENT SYRIA

Modern Syria lies, of course, at what might be called the heart of the Middle East. In ancient times, the name (probably a corruption or variant of the Biblical "Assyria") was used to designate a swath of territory that included much of present-day Turkey, present Syria west of the Euphrates, as well as what is now Israel, Palestine, Lebanon, and Jordan (Bryce, 2014, p. 5)—more or less what is often referred to, and still claimed as a rightful historical inheritance, as *bilad ash-sham*. The region became part of a succession of empires: among them, Persian (Achaemenid), from 538 BC; Macedonian, from 333 BC; Seleucid, from 323 BC; Roman, from 64 BC; various Arab and Muslim regimes from the seventh century (Bryce, 2014, pp. 147, 150, 160ff., 221, 323); and, significantly, the Ottomans, from 1516 (Hopwood, 1969, p. 18). However, the region was rarely without clashing armies as personal and ideological rivals within each imperial regime continuously contested for power.

The area of contemporary Syria was never sought after because of the natural riches with which it was endowed; these were and are minimal compared in particular to the Middle Eastern oil states. But in pre-modern times, the area was important because its location placed it in the path of major caravan routes to the sought-after products of the Far East and because acquiring that area was a strategic necessity for those with territorial ambitions from Asia Minor to Egypt and beyond. The region was important, it might be said, less because of *what* it was than because of *where* it was. Remaining as it did merely a province of successive military regimes, the region, for instance, "never developed an autonomous ruling class" (Hinnebusch, 2001, p. 16) or any sort of individuality, let alone distinctive borders. For the most part, that remained true until at least World War I. Raymond Hinnebusch explains:

> Modern Syria has no history of statehood prior to its creation amidst the break-up of the Ottoman empire after World War I: as such, the political identities inherited by the new state focused not on it, but on smaller pre-existing units—city, tribe, sectarian group—or a larger community—the empire, the Islamic *umma* and, increasingly, the idea of an Arab nation. (2001, p. 18)

SYRIA IN WORLD WAR I AND BEYOND

The idea of an Arab federation, and the belief that European imperialists have been responsible for the failure to achieve this objective, has permeated the last 100 years of Syrian, and Middle Eastern, history. One of the Anglo-French objectives in World War I was the dismemberment of the Ottoman Empire, most immediately because it had opted to ally itself with Germany, but also because Britain and France, not to mention Russia, had long been agitated over Muslim occupation of the Holy Land and the treatment of Christians, particularly pilgrims, therein (van Dam, 1979, pp. 17–18). The British, already firmly entrenched in Egypt, were primarily responsible for the campaign against the Ottomans and, in exchange for assistance from Arab tribesmen under the nominal leadership of Amir Faisal bin Hussein, promised support for the creation of an Arab federation at the war's end. French demand for a share of the victor's spoils, however, was largely responsible for Britain's reneging on that promise. The Ottoman province of Syria thus came under French control, while Palestine and Jordan (the other parts of *bilad ash-sham*) became British-administered territories (Hinnebusch, 2001, p. 19).[1]

Under French Control

Arab nationalists, perhaps Syrians in particular, have neither forgotten nor forgiven this betrayal or the further wrongs visited upon them by the French or, later, by the Israelis and their American allies. Despite the demands for sovereign recognition by a Damascus-centred elected body called the Syrian National Congress, the League of Nations in 1919 confirmed French control under the mandate system. Paris then proceeded to rearrange the territory according to its own designs. One of its principal objectives was to protect and advance the interests of minorities in the region, especially the Maronite Christians in the Mount Lebanon area. To the latter end Paris detached from Syria "the ports of Tyre, Sidon, Beirut and Tripoli, the Biqa' valley, and the Shia region north of Palestine ... so as to create the State of Greater Lebanon" (Seale, 1988, p. 15; see also Quilliam, 1999, p. 33). Second, it ceded to Turkey large parts of the former province of Aleppo, as well as other areas deemed to have sizable Turkish minorities—perhaps to remove one potential source of trouble for their administration. Third, the Alawi mountains and the Druze mountains were given "independent" status—that is, treated as separate from the central administration, although Alawi at different times was called an "autonomous territory," a "state," and the "Government of Latakia." In sum, however, by the time the French finally departed in 1946 "Syria" had shrunk by nearly half—from 300,000 square kilometres to 185,000 square kilometres (Seale, 1988, pp. 15–16).

The sympathy that the French felt for those groups they saw as persecuted or discriminated against by the Sunni population of the territory was probably genuine enough, but it is also true that minority groups were likely to be seen as useful potential allies against the continuing unrest generated by Islamic nationalists. The French set out to bring the isolated, "backward," and impoverished mountain tribes under their control (something the Ottomans had never made much attempt to do) and singled out the Alawi for particular attention (Seale, 1988, p. 17). This group, perhaps 300,000 strong, was fiercely independent and religiously peculiar from the viewpoint of both Shia and Sunni branches of Islam, though claiming to be a part of the faith. The Alawi incorporated Shia, ancient pagan, Gnostic, and Christian elements in their worship, refused to practise the five duties required of every Muslim on the ground that they were mere symbols (the daily prayer obligation, for instance), and built no mosques to the glory of Allah because they preferred to worship in the open air. Above all, however, the Alawi considered Muhammad's son-in-law Ali to be literally a god as distinct from simply a venerated early Caliph (Ajami, 2012, pp. 15ff.). The last belief in particular made them extremists as far as the Shia were concerned and entirely heretical in the view of the Sunni. For the majority of Syrians, therefore, the Alawi were outcasts and they were disdained as such.

The Alawi did not accept French interference in their mountain retreats without resistance, however, and prominent among those who at first opposed the new rulers was one Ali Sulayman, grandfather of Syria's embattled current president. Second-class citizens, however, found it difficult to long resist the offer of a place in the sun and the material advantages that came with it, and most Alawi quickly "seized on the opportunity for self-improvement" (Seale, 1988, p. 17). Perhaps foremost among those opportunities was membership in the *Troupes spéciales du Levant,* the local disorder-fighting force the French put together from "reliable" minority groups. Young Alawi enthusiastically joined the *Troupes* because it was a rare opportunity for a steady income but also because the French sought them out for that purpose (Seale, 1988, p. 18), presumably because they were considered farthest removed from the Sunni/ nationalist troublemakers in the towns. This was the beginning of "an Alawi military tradition central to the community's later ascent" (Seale, 1988, p. 18).

French rule over Syria was punctuated by a series of revolutionary uprisings and their massive repression, during the 1920s in particular (Hinnebusch, 2001, p. 19). William Polk has observed that, in general,

> It is not unfair to characterize the impact of French rule thus: the "peace" the French achieved was little more than a sullen and frustrated quiescence; while they did not create dissension among the religious and ethnic communities, the French certainly magnified it, and while they did not create hostility to foreigners, they gave the native population a target that fostered the growth of nationalism. (2013, Dec. 10)

This is perhaps somewhat harsh, but certainly political ferment in Syria was not improved by French rule. Nor was it stilled by the achievement of independence on April 17, 1946, which ultimately came about as the result of British occupation of the territory in 1941 following continental France's fall to Nazi Germany.

Syrian Independence

Syria at independence was a society fragmented in a variety of ways: ethnically, the country was roughly 90 per cent Arab, with the remainder made up of Kurds, Armenians, Circassians, and Turkomans. The Arab majority, however, was further divided along sectarian lines, with Sunni Muslims making up about 74 per cent, and various offshoots of Shia Islam—Alawi, Druze, and Ismaili— totalling another 16 per cent. Christians of several different denominations comprised the final 10 per cent (Leverett, 2005, p. 2). The country was also saddled with a semi-feudal economy dominated by a landlord-merchant upper class, from which practically all leadership positions were filled (Hinnebusch, 2001, p. 23). These "notables," however, were united chiefly through a continuing resentment of the amputation of Lebanon, Jordan, and Palestine from the country's "historic" territory. The creation of the state of Israel in 1948 deepened this resentment and added new grievances to it. In the first instance the existence of the new state made the possibility of recovering the lost territories much more remote, but the 1948 war that followed also resulted in a dispute over three small, but strategically important, demilitarized zones, which the Israelis proceeded to grab for themselves by "sending in soldiers disguised as farmers to establish occupation" (Seale, 1988, p. 119). Then came the disaster of the Six-Day War of 1967. Deliberately provoked by the Israelis (see Seale, 1988, pp. 117–141), the war left the Golan Heights in Israeli hands, where the region remains to this day. Not surprisingly, its recovery remains a prime objective of Syrians specifically and Arab nationalists generally.

Partly as a result of these factors, it may be argued that Syria has never achieved real stability or, ironically, that it came closest to it under the harsh rule of the Assads from 1970 to 2011. According to one observer, for instance, between independence and the late 1950s Syria had twenty different cabinets, four constitutions, and three military coups during 1949 alone (Oxenreider, 2015, Sept. 7). More coups were to follow during the 1960s: in 1963, 1966, and 1970 (Ajami, 2012, p. 27).

The Harsh Rule of Hafez al-Assad

The last coup brought Hafez al-Assad, son of the Alawi and of the military, to power; remarkably, he was able to remain in office and provide the country with a restive near-peace until his death from natural causes in 2000. As Flynt Leverett observed, "Hafez al-Assad's most basic accomplishment as ruler of Syria was to transform the Syrian political order from a coup-ridden, postcolonial, semi-state into a veritable model of authoritarian stability" (Leverett, 2005, p. 23).

He accomplished this by three means: (1) by using the Ba'th Party (which had first come to office in Syria in 1963) as a "Leninist-style tool" to associate the population as a whole with his regime; (2) by constructing a broad alliance of the country's disparate social elements to support his rule; and (3) by establishing "a centralized and highly personalized presidential system supported by a strong cult of personality" (Leverett, 2005, p. 23; see also Seale, 1988, pp. 169–184).

To address these briefly in turn, Ba'thism was not only Assad's personal ideology, it was also in many respects an obvious instrument for mass unification. It was based on the idea that Arabs were a single nation that had been divided by a variety of imperialisms. The compelling objective, therefore, was ultimately to bring about the reunification of the Arab world. Until that could be accomplished, the aim should be to get rid of national scenes of decadence and injustice through state intervention and reform (Hinnebusch, 2001, p. 30). By definition, Ba'thism was secular in that it was above artificial divisions such as those between religious sects. It therefore provided a basis for urging people to unite in a common cause and behind a rule dedicated to that cause, and a foundation on which to construct mass organizations, including trade unions, youth organizations, and professional associations, to rally the mass population.

On the social and economic level, Assad sought to appeal to a wide cross-section of the Syrian population by undertaking much needed land reform in the countryside, by attempting to mobilize the middle class, and by reaching out to the urban Sunni population with concessions aimed at preventing the development of widespread opposition to his rule.

Finally, Assad consciously modelled his presidency on that of Gamal 'Abd al-Nasir of Egypt, with power centralized in the hands of a carefully selected inner circle whose members had personal ties to him (Leverett, 2005, pp. 24–26). As well, Assad glorified himself to the extent that "there were shades of North Korea in [the] Syrian regime. There were estimates of 3,000 statues of the Old Man by the time of his death" (Ajami, 2012, p. 43).

As successful as these tactics temporarily were, they were not completely so and, therefore, needed "to be consistently reinforced by a coercive police state apparatus and a willingness, on Assad's part, to exercise decisive brutality when needed" (Leverett, 2005, p. 25). One serious occasion when such brutality was considered necessary occurred between 1979 and 1982.

Islamists, like the Muslim Brotherhood, who agitated for a "purer" and more austere Muslim state, were never happy with the Assad regime. The tension between the two came to a head in the rebellion that began with the machine-gunning of up to 83 Alawi officer cadets at the Aleppo Artillery School in 1979 and that progressed to hit-and-run terrorism centred on both Aleppo and Hama, with the Muslim Brotherhood providing "the troops of this insurgency" (Ajami, 2012, pp. 39–40). In June 1980 an assassination attempt on President Assad led to "all restraints [being] pushed aside" and "one day after the assassination attempt … attack helicopters sent to the Palmyra desert prison gunned down 800 political [Muslim Brotherhood] prisoners in one bloody spree" (Ajami, 2012, pp. 40–41; see also Seale, 1988, p. 329, who puts the number killed at only 500). In early 1982, a full-scale insurrection broke out in Hama. The government response was to match savagery with greater savagery; as a result, the city was largely destroyed, with a loss of life of somewhere between 3,000 and 20,000 people (Seale, 1988, pp. 332–334). That largely ended the insurrection; hence, the government's response became the shining example of how to deal with such outbreaks and such extremists. In all probability, it was a lesson that was not lost on the young Bashar al-Assad.

Assad the elder was as practical and calculating in foreign policy as he was in domestic affairs. Pan-Arab revolution and the rebirth of the Arab Nation writ large might be a laudable objective, but it was unreachable in the short term. On a day-to-day basis it was necessary to engage in balance-of-power politics as dictated by existing circumstances. Above all this meant careful manoeuvring to contain what he saw as Israel's hegemonic aspirations, while also trying to improve Syria's standing and influence in the world (Leverett, 2005, p. 38). Doing those things in turn required maintaining Syria's hegemony in Lebanon, keeping up diplomatic and military pressure on Israel and the United States to negotiate the return of the Golan Heights, and avoiding being marginalized within the Middle East region—both for its own sake and for what that might mean for the Israeli connection (Leverett, 2005, pp. 37–50).

Assad's ambitions vis-à-vis Israel, mild as they were, together with his relatively close relationship with the Soviet Union/Russia, inevitably meant that there were varying degrees of friction with the United States. Assad was adroit at playing the two super powers against each other during the Cold War, but he was helped in this regard by the fact that he had value to both Moscow and Washington. Russian involvement in Syria, sometimes assumed to be a product of the East–West divide of that era, in fact goes back to at least the early nineteenth century when it grew out of rivalry with the Ottomans and concerns over the treatment of Christians in the area (see Hopwood, 1969). In more recent times, especially when post-Nasser Egypt gradually became an American dependency, Syria became the last outpost of Russian influence in the Near East, something Assad was able to use to ensure continued arms shipments from Moscow (Leverett, 2005, p. 53).[2] From the American point of view, Assad's policy with respect to Lebanon in particular was unacceptable. Nonetheless, while relations were often rocky, they did not break, largely because Washington was always aware that no general Middle Eastern peace could be obtained without Syrian participation and support (see Leverett, 2005, pp. 51–56).

More of the Same: Bashar al-Assad

The Syria that Bashar al-Assad inherited in 2000 was somewhat more settled and reconciled to Assad rule than it had been twenty years before, but, although the Muslim Brotherhood had never recovered from the crushing of 1982, a strong and persistent strain of Islamic revivalism remained among the Sunni population and continued "to reinforce the country's sectarian cleavages and add another layer of complexity to the maintenance of political stability by secular (and non-Sunni) rulers" (Leverett, 2005, p. 5). For more than a decade, however, the younger Assad was able to avoid major challenges to his author-itarian rule while he basically continued to pursue the regional and foreign policy directions established by his father: domination of Lebanon; support for the Palestinians battles with Israel; friendship with Iran to ensure supplies for Hezbollah; cordial relations with Russia; and problematic relations with the United States, which had placed Syria on its list of state sponsors of terrorism as early as 1979 (see Leverett, 2005).[3]

The Arab Spring

That relative peace came to an end, of course, when Syria followed other author-itarian Muslim states into the allure of the "Arab Spring"—an all-encompassing term that was coined to describe the series of supposedly popular uprisings that began in perhaps the least likely place of all: the North African country of Tunisia. The tipping point was the self-immolation of an impoverished young street vendor named Mohamed Bouazizi on December 18, 2010, in protest of his humiliating treatment by local officials and police (Byman, 2012, p. 25). His death served as a rallying cry for the Tunisian masses, which saw him as "a martyr in the face of a hopeless economic situation" (Seigneurie, 2012, p. 497). Protests spread quickly and became massive—there were rallies of tens of thousands of people in the capital of Tunis—and brought about the fall of the country's long-time dictator, Zine El-Abidine Ben Ali, in less than a month.

The success of the public protests–cum-uprising in Tunisia, which no one inside or outside the country would have thought possible (see, for instance, Gause, 2011, p. 81), was seized upon by those who suffered under similar repressive conditions elsewhere. These events were widely followed across the Arab world on satellite news and social media, resulting in what Marc Lynch and colleagues have called "the international diffusion of protest movements" (Lynch, Freelon, & Aday, 2014, p. 1). Suddenly, people saw that it was possible to challenge what had long been thought to be beyond alteration. Those who had chafed under the yoke of Hosni Mubarak in Egypt were the first to be energized by such thoughts, and generally peaceful public demands for change, beginning in January 2011, brought about his abandonment of office by early February. Mubarak's downfall was a far more important event than Ben Ali's overthrow. Tunisia was, after all, a small country at the far margins of the Arab world, and what happened there would probably not have significantly impacted countries with similar characteristics had it not reverberated strongly with Egypt's discontented. That it did so, and succeeded in the ouster of an established strongman from one of the largest and most influential states of the Arab region, one with a powerful military and the strong backing of the United States as well as regional powers like Saudi Arabia, could not but raise hopes for similar liberations wherever tyrants held sway.

Those events were watched by Western observers with the same kind of hope but also with wariness. President Barack Obama of the United States welcomed the fact that "across the region, those rights that we take for granted are being claimed with joy by those who are prying loose the grip of an iron fist" (as quoted in Byman, 2012, p. 25). But there was natural concern about the region's stability as well, especially since the initial uprisings had occurred in pro-Western client states, Egypt in particular being a linchpin for American regional objectives. There was, however, no inclination for Western involvement beyond diplomatic appeals for calm and restraint on the part of the besieged governments.

Libya changed that. While extensive bloodshed had not occurred in either Tunisia or Egypt, when Libyans launched protests against the autocratic (and erratic) regime of Colonel Muammar Qaddafi in mid-February 2011, the government responded with deadly force and casualties rapidly mounted. The Arab League became involved and, following Qaddafi's rejection of a ceasefire agreement, called on the UN Security Council to impose a "no-fly zone" in Libya. Ultimately, this resulted in the passage of Resolution 1973 on March 17, 2011, referencing the recently adopted doctrine of the Responsibility to Protect and authorizing NATO to enforce such a zone and protect the Libyan population (Dwomoh, 2015, pp. 19–27). Conceptually, no-fly zones are simple and minimally forceful, aimed simply at denying the target the use of air power in its military operations. In practice, however, doing so is easier said than done and, in any case, may be insufficient to provide much protection to civilians from other kinds of weapons, including ground-to-ground missiles. Whether for these reasons or because NATO command decided to "do the job right," the no-fly zone quickly morphed into the destruction of Qaddafi's fighting power and the creation of conditions conducive to his removal from office. Qaddafi was consequently captured, tortured, and executed by insurgents in October 2011.

Some observers, including Canadian General Lewis MacKenzie, felt that the NATO Libyan operation went well beyond what was appropriate for civilian protection (2013, June 25). Russia in particular was bitter that what it considered to be the limits of Resolution 1973 had been grossly exceeded and believed that Western leaders had misled it in acquiescing in its authorization. As the Russian Foreign Minister put it, his country "would never allow the Security Council to authorize anything similar to what happened in Libya" (Kuperman, 2015, p. 75). Many Westerners became disillusioned later when it was apparent that the intervention had not resulted in any smooth transition to democracy, or, indeed, to anything that could be regarded as a stable government.

The events in Libya had several repercussions for developments in Syria. In an interview with *The Wall Street Journal,* Assad dismissed the possibility that Syria might suffer a fate similar to that of Tunisia, Egypt, and Libya (Ajami, 2012, p. 69)—despite the fact that the country was vulnerable on almost every important basis.

> Unemployment was well over 20 percent, and 32 percent of its people lived below the poverty line. The country ranked 165th (out of 175 nations) in press freedom, 152nd (out of a sample of 152) on the index of democracy, and 19th (out of 22 Arab countries) in economic performance. Syrian universities and academic institutions were a shambles. (Ajami, 2012, p. 65)

In addition, the security apparatus had become increasingly oppressive during the ten years of Bashar's regime, famed for the riches amassed by the "children of authority" and, perhaps worst of all, the regime became alienated from the rural provinces. As the International Crisis Group observed, "The regime forgot its social roots, increasingly distancing itself from the peripheral areas from which it came" (as quoted in Ajami, 2012, p. 73).

Only Bashar al-Assad could have been surprised, therefore, when protests in Syria began on March 18, 2011, one day after the approval of Resolution 1973. They may or may not initially have been influenced by the Security Council discussions that led up to that decision, but they were in any case precipitated by an event eerily reminiscent of Mohamed Bouazizi's suicide in Tunisia. In the Syrian town of Dar'a (on the border with Jordan), fifteen schoolchildren, some as young as ten, were arrested and tortured for scrawling, on walls, "The people want to overthrow the regime" and other slogans referencing events in Tunisia and Egypt. One read, "It's your turn, Doctor," referring to Bashar al-Assad, who is a doctor specialized in ophthalmology. Adult protests of the children's treatment were rebuffed and the protests "quickly swelled and spun out of control as thousands joined" (Droz-Vincent, 2014, p. 1; Weiss and Hassan, 2015, p. 132; Ajami, 2012, pp. 73–74). Most authorities agree that the protests and demonstrations were initially essentially peaceful calls for reform (see Droz-Vincent, 2014, p. 6), and they were not primarily sectarian although an early report by the International Crisis Group acknowledged that there was "an Islamist undercurrent to the uprising" (as quoted in Cockburn, 2015, p. 84). This is scarcely surprising, however, since there has always been at least an undercurrent of religious dissention and intolerance in Syrian political affairs.

And it was that card that the Assad regime chose to play:

> From the outset, he … portrayed his opponents, even those who were only calling for modest economic reforms, as al-Qaeda terrorists, hirelings

of the United States, Saudi Arabia, Qatar, and Israel—surely one of the most elaborate coalitions of the willing in modern history. (Weiss and Hassan, 2015, p. 134)

Phillippe Droz-Vincent concurred: "The regime ... depicted all mass protests as violent, led by Islamist-leaning criminals, and supported by foreign countries plotting against Syria" (2014, p. 6). While it is possible, or perhaps even probable, that the struggle would have become overtly sectarian in character in any case, the position adopted by the government assured that it did so. Protesters were in effect pushed to take up arms in order to legitimize the violence the regime wished to use against them. It is also true, however, that anti-government activists may have deliberately courted violence in the hope of forcing international intervention on their behalf. That sort of tactic has been used even without as clear and recent an illustration as Libya. However that may be, the end result of government and activist escalations has been that Syria "has descended into a nightmarish sectarian civil war as the government bombs its own cities as if they were enemy territory and the armed opposition is dominated by Salafi-jihadist fighters who slaughter Alawites and Christians simply because of their religion" (Cockburn, 2015, p. 81).

Could this appalling development have been prevented? If so, when? By whom? And by what means? On the face of it, it would seem that if the slaughter of Libyans by their own government was a justification for invoking what had so recently been declared to be an international responsibility to provide protection for the innocent and the vulnerable, the same should have been true for Syria. The volatility of Syrian and Middle Eastern affairs, particularly after 9/11 and the beginning of the "War on Terror," plus the wave of insurrections that had already occurred, should surely have forewarned even the casual observer of the dangers inherent in public agitations against a government not known for its restraint in such circumstances. Why not intervene, in the name of the Responsibility to Protect, as soon as demonstrations began to develop into armed clashes? Why not intervene before the number of players exploded, their nature shifted in incomprehensible directions, and all positions hardened beyond compromise? These are the questions we will address in the following pages, beginning with an examination of what the Responsibility to Protect is and what it is not.

Evolving Norms of International Involvement in Domestic Conflicts: The Responsibility to Protect

In the years since the publication of *The Responsibility to Protect* (R2P), the 2001 report of the Canadian-created International Commission on Intervention and State Sovereignty (ICISS), professional commentators on world affairs have enjoyed a feast perhaps second only to that occasioned by the emergence of the United Nations itself. Conferences, books, and articles have proliferated on the subject to an almost amazing extent (see Reinold, 2010, p. 56); two international organizations, the International Coalition for the Responsibility to Protect (ICRtoP) and the Global Centre for the Responsibility to Protect, have been founded to further the doctrine's aims; and the position of special advisor to the secretary-general of the United Nations has been created to promote its implementation (Bellamy, 2009, pp. 117–118). Indeed, in the view of one authority, R2P has become "an industry" to the extent that it may have "deflected attention from potentially useful avenues of research and … advocacy" (Hehir, 2012, p. 5).

The jury is still out, however, on whether R2P is, or could be, the greatest single advance in the pursuit of a more ordered world in history or merely, at best, an overhyped moral exhortation of no substantial relevance to political reality—or something in between. At the negative extreme, in fact, there are some who consider R2P a dangerous overreach by emotion-driven utopians. But it is noteworthy that it cannot be ignored, even—perhaps particularly—by those who think it most iniquitous. On the other hand, crises like the Libyan and Syrian chapters of the Arab Spring have provided real and contrasting tests of its practical effectiveness.

To a large extent, the doctrine's attractiveness comes from its apparent simplicity and its appeal to the most basic human instincts. It invites endorsement and forbids rejection in principle. Who is willing to say that political authorities at either the state or the international level do not have a responsibility to protect their people from egregious suffering as far as possible? Who is willing to say that every effort should not be made to combat genocide and similar massive crimes against humanity? As Thomas Weiss observed with respect to the discussions that led to the endorsement of R2P by the 2005 World Summit, "nowhere did a substantial number of people argue that intervention to sustain humanitarian objectives was never justified" (2012, p. 109). But such general agreement in principle does little to clarify where that responsibility lies in specific circumstances, or where and how the concept should be operationalized. One of the ironic difficulties is that the basic idea of R2P is so appealing that its most enthusiastic supporters are tempted to overlook the details and qualifications that the ICISS built into its report.

PREVENTION, REACTION, AND REBUILDING

The main components of the report are sufficiently familiar that it is unnecessary to repeat them in detail here. What is notable is that R2P came about because of dismay at the perceived inadequacies in responding to humanitarian crises during the 1990s, Rwanda and Bosnia being the most frequently cited examples. The ICISS sought to respond to that discontent by building on the concept of "responsible sovereignty" originally advanced by Francis Deng in 1996 (Evans, 2008, p. 36; Hehir, 2012, p. 69). R2P was foreshadowed to some extent by the drafters of the Constitutive Act of the African Union in 2000 (Puley, 2005, p. 8). The drafters of this act enunciated the now familiar principle that when states are unwilling or unable to protect their citizens from serious harm, the responsibility devolves to the international community. There are, in fact, three interrelated responsibilities the ICISS asserted: (1) to *prevent* humanitarian crises from arising by providing assistance whenever their development appeared likely; (2) to *react* with appropriate measures when prevention is unsuccessful; and (3) to *rebuild* as necessary following efforts to mitigate crises. The commissioners emphasized that, of the three, they considered *prevention* the most important.

The Responsibility to Prevent

Prevention has not, however, received significant attention from commentators anywhere, and for fairly obvious reasons. First, the idea of prevention lacks immediacy and specificity—it's a long-term and generalized project that has difficulty competing for attention against the many very real and urgent crises occurring at any given moment. No one is likely to dispute the contention that it is better in principle, and cheaper, to deal with a threat of humanitarian disaster than its actual occurrence. That, after all, is merely the international application of the old adage "an ounce of prevention is worth a pound of cure." But knowing which of many potential sites of large-scale violence affecting ordinary people will actually materialize is far from easy. Similarly, since all such potential humanitarian crises cannot be given full attention, determining where prevention resources should be concentrated is difficult at best. As the present authors pointed out in *The Independence of South Sudan*, "while state failure and large scale violence are often correlated, they are not necessarily the same," and "states can in fact exist in a state of 'failure' for significant periods of time without the eruption of devastating violence" (Soderlund & Briggs, 2014, p. 21; see also King and Zeng, 2001, pp. 654–655).

Zimbabwe is frequently cited as the classic example of a state where all the factors normally identified as conducive to massive unrest and violent repression have long been present, but where such extremes have so far been avoided. While this suggests how problematic predicting state failure or the outbreak of unconscionable criminal actions is, another possibility also exists: that, in the case of Zimbabwe, international diplomatic pressures have been sufficient to maintain the situation at below boil-over temperature. That is another of the difficulties with the concept of prevention: it is impossible to know whether or when you have been successful. Failures, of course, are blatantly obvious, though what is frequently seen as "failure" is not always for want of international effort.

The Rwandan genocide, for instance, is now firmly established as the quintessential example of international failure to respond adequately to unthinkable human tragedy. What most people seem to have forgotten, however, is that the resort to genocide was in many respects the outgrowth of international efforts to end the ongoing civil war and reconcile the rival "ethnic" groups in that country—in other words, to prevent further, or more serious, bloodshed. It was the fact that significant elements in one group could not accept the power-sharing arrangements worked out under well-intentioned external pressures that precipitated, or at least hastened, resort to a "final solution." This is not, of course, to suggest that the effort to reconcile Tutsi and Hutu should not have been made, but merely to point out that even when serious efforts at prevention are undertaken the results are uncertain, perhaps especially where there are deep-seated ethnic or sectarian divides. Indeed, such efforts can sometimes even be counterproductive.

The Rwandan example also demonstrates that preventing major humanitarian tragedies has been part of international and individual government repertoires since long before R2P. Other examples include Kosovo in 1999 (prior to the military campaign) and Sudan (with respect to both the North–South conflict and Darfur). States with extensive international interests and significant outreach capacity have always tried to prevent crisis development whenever they could for the simple reason that, apart from humanitarianism per se, such occurrences are disruptive in a variety of ways, not least of which is in providing nesting places for terrorists; this is particularly true in recent decades. That is not likely to change, and it is unclear what more can be expected of either individual states or the international collective in this regard.

Frank Chalk and colleagues believe, however, that Canada and the United States in particular should make the prevention of mass atrocities a priority "as a vital national interest" (2010, p. 5). In the case of Canada, this could be accomplished partly by appointing a senior minister of international security, who would have the responsibility (as well as "the gravitas and the experience") of forging "a coherent policy between the different levels of government and across departments, [and] coordinate defense, diplomacy, and development policy" (p. 84). A realist would probably respond that neither the creation of such a "super ministry" nor the seconding of everything else to an atrocity prevention campaign is likely in Canada or elsewhere. The interests of human-itarianism would likely be better served by focusing on what may be within the realm of possibility. And while coordination among government ministries could undoubtedly be improved in the interests of many worthy causes, it is probably not the principal problem as far as the prevention issue is concerned.

In any case, all of the above mainly addresses prevention in the short term. But long-term prevention must also be considered. As Gareth Evans has put it,

> Achieving *good governance* in all its manifestations—representative, responsive, accountable, and capable—is at the heart of effective long-term conflict and mass atrocity prevention.... Both individual states themselves and the wider international community have mutually sup-portive roles to play in developing the institutions and processes—leg-islative, executive, and judicial—of effective government. (2008, p. 88; italics in original)

This, of course, has been the essential rationale behind developmental aid going back at least to the 1950s. It was assumed that if wealthy nations provided financial assistance and technological expertise to those who were less fortu-nate, such as the newly independent states of Africa, this would prevent, in the long term, poverty-engendered discontent that could build into ethnic and sectarian explosions. As is now widely admitted, such development aid has not been wildly successful, however, perhaps particularly with respect to Africa. The reasons for, and the extent of, that failure are complex and still controversial, and are in any case beyond the scope of this study. But two points are worth making. First, there is no means of determining whether the world would now be better or worse off had developmental aid never existed; and, second, however ineptly or selfishly it might have been administered, aid was a genuine attempt to prevent inhuman suffering on the one hand and disorder in the international system on the other. The extent to which the attempt failed is an indication of both the difficulty of the task and the naïveté with which it has been approached.

In both the long and the short term, therefore, significant efforts have been made to prevent intrastate atrocities and the like from developing, and there is no reason to think that will not be a continuing preoccupation. But the success of such efforts will always be uncertain, and the efforts themselves will rarely grab headlines or be much noted by people at large, partly because they will normally extend over a considerable period of time, and partly because most will be conducted largely in as private a manner as possible. It should also not be forgotten that they may sometimes have to take a back seat to the more critical and immediate demands of crises that have arisen despite the efforts that have been made to prevent them.

The International Commission on Intervention and State Sovereignty (ICISS) may have stipulated that the responsibility to prevent is "the single most important dimension of the responsibility to protect" (2001, p. xi), but it may not really have been the commission's primary concern. The ICISS's members undoubtedly did believe that prevention is to be preferred to reaction, but the impetus for the commission's formation, as was previously mentioned, was distress over the inadequacies of the humanitarian interventions launched, and not launched, during the last decades of the twentieth century. Secretary-General Kofi Annan repeatedly stressed that it was essential to do better in this regard (Bellamy, 2009, pp. 27–32; Evans, 2008, pp. 37–38; Weiss, 2012, pp. 104–107), and Canadian Prime Minister Jean Chrétien's organization of ICISS was in direct response to Annan's challenge. The commissioners themselves must have been aware that they were dealing with a delicate issue. *Intervention* (usually thought of in military terms) in "sovereign" territories was a frightening concept to many, including some of the permanent members of the Security Council. The word could all too easily be interpreted as authorization for great power neo-imperialism. As a result, the ICISS had to tread carefully, and the commissioners may well have decided that one of the ways to do that was to emphasize the primacy of prevention over seemingly more intrusive approaches to the problem. The fact that "prevention figured prominently in the 2005 World Summit's endorsement of R2P" (Bellamy, 2009, p. 98) provides some support for that speculation.

However that might be, it is certainly the responsibility to react that has become virtually synonymous with R2P. The commissioners were careful with this provision also. They made it abundantly clear that reaction was not another term for "sending in the marines," although commentators frequently overlook this and assume, in situations like Syria for example, that if military means have not been used no appropriate reaction has occurred and that R2P is consequently a "failure." This assumption is perhaps understandable when there is a compelling, conscience-wrenching need for human protection that is perfectly obvious to all and about which nothing is being done. The fact is, the use of armed force is definite and unambiguous and, therefore, emotionally satisfying in such circumstances; other means of persuasion are less visible, at least to the general public, and may easily be mistaken for lack of humanitarian commitment. However, the following is what ICISS actually posited:

> When preventive measures fail to resolve or contain the situation and when a state is unable or unwilling to redress the situation, then interventionary measures by other members of the broader community of states *may be* required. These coercive measures may include political, economic or judicial measures, and in extreme cases—*but only in extreme cases*—they may also include military action. As a matter of first principles, in the case of reactions just as with prevention, less intrusive and coercive measures should always be considered before more coercive and intrusive ones are applied. (ICISS, 2001, p. 29; italics added)

In addition, the commission specified six criteria that must be considered before military intervention is to be undertaken:

1. There must be just cause: large-scale loss of life "actual or apprehended," or large-scale ethnic cleansing (Par. 4.19, p. 32).
2. There must be right intention: "The primary purpose must be to halt or avert human suffering" (Par. 4.33, p. 35).
3. It must be the last resort: "Every diplomatic and non-military avenue … must have been explored" (Par. 4.37, p. 36).
4. Proportional means must be used: "The scale, duration and intensity of the planned military intervention should be the minimum necessary to secure the humanitarian objectives in question" (Par. 4.39, p. 37).
5. There must be reasonable prospects of success: "Military intervention is not justified if actual protection cannot be achieved or if the consequences of embarking upon intervention are likely to be worse than if there is no action at all" (Par. 4.41, p. 37).
6. It must be launched by the right authority (Par. 4.17, p. 32).

The last point will be discussed further below.

R2P could not have made its appearance in less auspicious circumstances— December 2001 was a scant three months after 9/11. Nor was its receptivity improved by the 2003 invasion of Iraq, justified *ex post facto* on humanitarian grounds. As Neil Macfarlane and colleagues expressed it, "In a post-September 11 and post-Iraq world, many people and states are having second thoughts about the importance and risks of humanitarian intervention. Does anyone care any longer?" (2004, p. 977) Among those who had serious reservations on the subject was the United States:

> At the Security Council's annual private retreat in May 2002, the ICISS recommendations were discussed with the commission's two chairs. The US was unenthusiastic about R2P. The Bush administration does not and will not accept the substance of the report or support any formal declaration or resolution about it. (Macfarlane et al., 2004, p. 983)[1]

Not surprisingly, an array of concerns was raised about the brash new doctrine. Some of them were predictable, such as the extent to which the doctrine constituted an erosion of sovereignty and/or was a euphemism for American or great power hegemony (see Funk and Fake, 2009). Some of them were simply cynically dismissive of "a clever twist of words" without substance, or a disparaging of humanitarian intervention in general because, as David Rieff expressed it, no such action has ever "actually kept a single jackboot out of a single human face" (as cited in Macfarlane et al., 2004, p. 980). Some humanitarian non-governmental organizations (NGOs) were also hesitant about the doctrine. Human Rights Watch, for instance, strangely worried that R2P might divert attention from caring for refugees in their countries of asylum to treating them in their countries of origin (Macfarlane et al., 2004, p. 980). The Non-Aligned Movement (NAM) flatly rejected R2P, going so far in late 2002 as to block a Canadian attempt to have the General Assembly commit itself to discussing the report. The Group of 77 was more divided on the matter but agreed that the report needed substantial revision (Bellamy, 2009, pp. 68–70). Both Russia and China were essentially negative as well.

Canada nonetheless conducted a tireless campaign for acceptance of R2P, joined enthusiastically by Australia and, to some extent by Britain, and occasionally supported by France and Germany. Canadian diplomats lobbied for it in a determined manner, and Prime Minister Paul Martin used his opportunity to address the General Assembly in 2004 to urge its approval (Bellamy, 2009, p. 73). But up to that point there seemed little possibility that anything of the sort would happen. One of the main sticking points was that the report left open the possibility that in exceptional circumstances military intervention for humanitarian purposes could be undertaken without the prior approval of the Security Council—as it famously, and controversially, had in Kosovo in 1999 (see Lynch, 2006; Jackson, 2006; Groom & Taylor, 2000):

> We have made abundantly clear our view that the Security Council should be the first port of call on any matter relating to military intervention for human protection purposes. But the question remains whether it should be the last. In view of the Council's past inability or unwillingness to

fulfill the role expected of it, if the Security Council specifically rejects a proposal for intervention where humanitarian or human rights issues are significantly at stake, or the Council fails to deal with such a proposal within a reasonable time, it is difficult to argue that alternative means of discharging the responsibility to protect can be entirely discounted. (ICISS, 2001, Par. 6.28, p. 53)

That undeniably left an opening would-be imperialists might gleefully exploit.

In the negotiations to build support for the R2P principle, and to get it on to the agenda of the World Summit scheduled for 2005, the Canadian government and its allies, including Secretary-General Kofi Annan, backed down on this wording, quietly allowing that the Security Council was the sole "Right Authority" for sanctioning military operations on behalf of humanitarian principles (Bellamy, 2009, pp. 73–74). These, and a few other concessions, were sufficient not only to get R2P on the agenda of the World Summit but to achieve the endorsement of a version of it, thanks to "persistent advocacy by sub-Saharan African countries led by South Africa ... [and] ... by Latin American countries. Above all, what carried the vote over the line was some very effective last-minute personal diplomacy by Paul Martin, the Canadian Prime Minister ..." (Evans, 2009, pp. 20–21). Paragraph 139 of the World Summit Outcome Document thus contained the following:

> The international community, through the United Nations ... has the responsibility to use appropriate diplomatic, humanitarian, and other peaceful means, in accordance with Chapters VI and VII of the Charter, to help to protect populations from genocide, war crimes, ethnic cleansing, and crimes against humanity. In this context, we are prepared to take collective action, in a timely and decisive manner, through the Security Council, in accordance with the Charter, including Chapter VII, on a case-by-case basis and in cooperation with relevant regional organizations as appropriate, should peaceful means be inadequate and national authorities are manifestly failing to protect their populations from genocide, war crimes, ethnic cleansing, and crimes against humanity. (quoted in Evans, 2008, pp. 48–49)

This repetitive language was presumably adopted to leave no possible misunderstanding of what was intended—no unilateral, regional, or "coalition of the willing" military action undertaken on supposed humanitarian grounds would be considered legitimate.

It should be noted that two other summit objectives of R2P's advocates likewise fell by the wayside. They had hoped, first, to see approval for the principle of establishing a just-cause threshold—the crossing of which would automatically trigger Security Council intervention; and, second, they had hoped to reach agreement that the veto would not be used in cases of humanitarian emergencies (Hehir, 2012, p. 49). However, neither of these proposals had any traction at the summit. As might have been expected, the permanent members of the Security Council (P5) were not inclined to relinquish the privilege of the veto nor to allow themselves to be locked into any sort of automatic response—note the careful emphasis on "a case by case basis" in the Outcome Document's stipulation of when "collective action" might be undertaken.

The result was undoubtedly disappointing to the most optimistic of R2P's disciples, although they consoled themselves that something was better than nothing, or they rationalized that most of the differences between the original ICISS document and the summit's version of it were either positive or of little significance (see Evans, 2008, pp. 45–49). Others, however, such as noted authority Thomas Weiss, considered the summit document "a step backward … R2P lite" (as quoted in Hehir, 2012, p. 49) or an opportunity for real reform "squandered" (*New York Times* editorial, no date, as quoted in Weiss, 2012, p. 121). However that may be, the only formulation of R2P that has any legal or political standing in current international affairs is that approved by the World Summit, and later by the Security Council and General Assembly (see Bellamy, 2009, p. 196).

In operational terms that formulation translates to a moral exhortation and little more. As Simon Chesterman has put it, "By the time R2P was endorsed by the World Summit in 2005, its normative content had been emasculated to the point where it essentially provided that the Security Council could authorize … things that it had been authorizing for more than a decade" (2011, p. 280). But at least in principle it is an exhortation with near universal approval—the General Assembly resolution endorsing it was passed with four abstentions and no negative votes—but that is a little like saying everyone agrees that motherhood is a good thing and life is worth preserving. Organizationally, neither the machinery nor the procedures for coping with human tragedies at the international level had changed, apart from adding a Special Advisor's office responsible for R2P to that which already existed for genocide, and the emergence of a number of specifically dedicated NGOs to the many that already lobbied on behalf of human rights in a more general sense. Such dedicated advocates are no doubt useful because they increase the likelihood that deteriorating situations will not slip under the radar or be quietly ignored by state or international decision makers. However, lack of awareness of the type of massive violation of civilized behavior that R2P addresses has never been a major problem, and these additional bodies will not alter the bases on which Security Council, or individual state, decisions are made.

To R2P devotees this merely means that sustained efforts are required to make military coercion in relief of large-scale human suffering, when necessary, the unquestioned operational principle that conscience demands it should be. To some, the secret to achieving this is to mobilize mass public opinion behind the principle, in order to create a "will to intervene," and reorganize domestic governmental machinery to reflect and prioritize that will (Chalk et al., 2010. No intervention will occur unless there is a will, or wills, to do so, but to the extent that the "will to intervene" slogan suggests that national selfishness or lack of commitment to humanitarianism is the chief barrier to the assured rescue of grievously suffering people, it does not do justice to the very real, practical problems involved in such matters—not a few of which the ICISS commissioners themselves pointed out. It is, for instance, not only useless but clearly counter-productive to intervene in situations where nothing positive can be achieved. In those instances one would hope for a will not to make matters worse than they already are.

Determining whether conditions allow for a successful protection mission or not will take place on a case-by-case basis, and that determination is something about which even the most altruistic statespersons will often differ. On the individual government level, moreover, each must decide whether, how, and to what extent it is able to contribute to any possible military operation. Part of that calculation, of course, is determining what resources can be spared from other immediate needs, and/or what costs it is politically feasible to devote to the cause in question. There will inevitably be internal differences of opinion about these matters as well. As President Obama warned with respect to the Libyan operation, "America cannot use our military wherever repression occurs. And given the costs and risks of intervention, we must always measure our interests against the need for action" (as quoted in Chesterman, 2011, p. 283). "Our interests," it should be noted, include domestic as well as international concerns.

There is no need for any state to apologize for such a position. Governments are elected to protect the lives and interests of their inhabitants (as R2P itself emphasizes), and they would be remiss—and held accountable by publics who are not especially charitable in such matters—if they seconded those to the interests of strangers, however endangered. In the words of Aidan Hehir, "If a state concludes that to intervene would imperil national security and/or domestic welfare, it is entitled to decide not to do so, and cannot reasonably be criticized for so doing" (2012, p. 139). Such choices will never be easy to make, especially for those who are blessed with resources and are burdened with, or aspire to, world leadership, but national interests and international humanitarian interests should never be thought of as an either-or proposition.

It should not be forgotten, in any case, that "the use of military power can be a blunt instrument and that its capacity to protect is shaped by a host of context-specific factors" (Bellamy, 2011, p. 14).

Although Hehir also has a good deal to say about the importance of "will" with respect to both the authorization and the adequate execution of humanitarian interventions (see, for example, 2012, pp. 218–221, p. 230), he also has his own, more legalistic, suggestions for furthering human protection objectives in the world at large. He maintains that R2P itself has been less than helpful in this regard because it "adopted a strategy which has ignored systematic reform for moral advocacy" (p. 119) when "the only viable solution to the near perennial problem of how we should respond to man-made intra-state humanitarian crises is a strengthening of international law involving significant reform of the United Nations" (pp. 3–4). He believes two major innovations are required: "the establishment of an international judicial body and a standing UN army" (p. 232).

The first of these is necessary because of "the evident unwillingness of the P5 to respond to intrastate crises on the basis of need, due to the pervasive influence of their respective national interests...." An "alternative body" should therefore be established "with the power to judge how to respond to a particular intra-state humanitarian crisis." Hehir goes on to emphasize that "this judicial body would *not be more powerful than the Security Council* but rather would operate as an alternative when the P5 are paralyzed." In that instance, and on the basis of evidence gathered from UN bodies, NGOs, and national intelligence services, the body would make two judgments: (1) whether one or more of the four R2P specified crimes was being committed, and (2) the appropriate response to the situation—which might or might not be military. The advantages of this "independent judgment," he believes, would be to increase pressure on the Security Council to do its duty (although he admits that the new body's recommendations might simply be ignored) and provide a basis on which "individual states could decide to intervene without the P5's explicit approval,... [but with] ... *a defensible claim to legitimacy and legality*" (2012, pp. 232–233; italics added). The body, similar to the International Criminal Court (ICC), should consist of a panel of 12 judges, elected for three-year terms by UN members "on the basis of 'one state one vote' ... [and having] ... at least one member from each continent.... The body would have no national affiliations and would be independent of existing UN organs and institutions, though the body would be accountable to the General Assembly" (p. 235). How independence and accountability are to be reconciled here is not entirely clear.

A standing UN army is required because even if the new independent judicial body were to find evidence of heinous crimes and were to recommend military intervention, it is possible that neither the Security Council nor individual states would be willing to answer the call:

> It would be untenable, and highly embarrassing, for a judicial body to determine that intervention was necessary if no intervention subsequently occurred. Likewise, it would be ridiculous to create a standing UN army which could only be deployed by the Security Council as the spectacle of inertia would be even more pronounced than at present. (Hehir, 2012, p. 234)

Accordingly, if neither the Security Council nor individual states respond adequately to the new judicial body's recommendation, it "*could deploy the UN standing army*" (Hehir, 2012, p. 235; italics added). Deploying the force would not often be necessary, however, because its very existence would act as a deterrent (p. 236).

In any case, the army, Hehir tells us, would not have to be large or need to possess heavy weapons, such as tanks, because it "would not be used to defeat an opposing army but rather to halt atrocities and repel further attacks … [as a rapid reaction force] … designed and equipped to engage in the type of robust peacekeeping missions currently deployed" (2012, p. 235). The force would be comprised of soldiers who joined the UN command directly, rather than being seconded by member states as is currently the practice with peacekeeping undertakings, and would have bases on each continent to facilitate rapid deployment to trouble spots as required. Such a force would be funded through UN member states' fees. Hehir estimates that a force of 5,000–10,000 troops would cost $500 million to establish and $200 million per year to maintain (p. 236).[2] He does not explain how such a small force could be effective, especially if faced with multiple crises at the same time. Indeed, much larger forces have been unable to achieve much over the past twenty-five years, including in the Democratic Republic of the Congo, Somalia, Darfur, and, most recently, South Sudan.

One cannot help but wonder if Professor Hehir fully realizes just how radical, and idealistic, his proposals are (although he does admit that some may find them "fantastical") (2012, p. 205). He is by no means the first to advocate the establishment of a UN interventional force, of course (see, for instance, Cooper and Kohler, 2009; and Pattison, 2008), although the idea has usually been confined to the sort of ready-at-the-airport group that could be dispatched at a moment's notice as a precursor to whatever full force has been authorized; and as far as the present authors are aware it has never before been suggested that such a force might operate without a specific Security Council mandate.[3] Even in this limited sense, however, the idea inches the UN from international toward supranational organizational status and has, accordingly, received far more academic than state attention to date. It would be surprising, moreover, if many serious academics would be prepared to endorse the idea in the form proposed by Hehir, and even more surprising if any government, let alone the principal powers, would give it a second glance. It is a proposal that is simply inconsistent with the world as it now is.

That is doubly true of the additional "judicial" body that Hehir contemplates. He maintains that such a body would "not be superior to the Security Council." Yet it would be able to circumvent that body, in effect acting like a domestic court of appeal (a Supreme Court?), and sanction actions that the Security Council, in whole or in part, disapproved. One has to ask: What possible reason is there to think that the P5 in particular would ever countenance such a creation? Or that other states would be willing to trust in the independence and impartiality of a body with ultimate decision-making powers, even without, but especially with, an army at its disposal? Keep in mind that the ICC, despite careful efforts to avoid such a possibility, has come under attack by African states for "Western bias" because it is perceived as focusing too frequently on the sins of African political leaders—in other words, politics has intruded into ostensibly impartial judicial proceedings (see Mills, 2012). Hehir maintains, however, that the mere creation of the ICC "shows that, under certain circumstances, sovereign states are willing to cede aspects of their sovereignty to a higher authority" and might be willing to do so with respect to something like his proposed body because the present "reluctance of states to support a more interventionist Security Council" is due to "the absence of a legitimate higher authority" to protect them from abuses of power by the P5 (2012, p. 205).

Ultimately, then, an authority that is "higher" than the Security Council (Hehir, 2012, p. 205), but not "more powerful" than it (p. 232), is needed to hold the world's most powerful states in check. It is difficult to follow this logic, although it would appear to be based on the assumptions that "law" will always trump "politics" and that if only the politics of the Security Council could be escaped all would be well. What this logic seems to overlook is that law consists of what can be politically and socially agreed upon and is, therefore, enforceable and that even if an additional "judicial" body were to be created for the world's states, it would scarcely be immune from political pressures. Nor could such a body base its decisions (nor should it try to) on anything but political realities, chief among them world distributions of power and prevailing attitudes among world leaders. Such a body, in other words, would not make approaches to humanitarian crises less political but merely politically different and perhaps even more contentious. For example, the United States would be unlikely to cooperate with such a creation when it, through a number of administrations, has so far remained steadfastly aloof from the ICC, a body with significantly fewer far-reaching powers than the one proposed by Hehir, and has also pressured other states to do the same (see Forsythe, 2002; Johansen, 2006a).

Both the Chalk and Hehir formulas suffer from essentially the same defect: they operate on the implicit assumption that the realities of the world can be ignored in the effort to improve them. In comparison, placing one's faith in the moral exhortations of the Responsibility to Protect doctrine at least appears more logical in that it accepts that the world is not easily transformed; in effect, it appeals to those responsible for operating in it merely to observe it through a different, more human-friendly, lens than in the past. The doctrine's greatest virtue may be that it does not seek to transform the world overnight, even if its more enthusiastic exponents sometimes yield to the temptation to treat it as though it does. Gareth Evans, the former Australian Foreign Minister who was co-chair of ICISS and remains one of R2P's strongest advocates, has warned of the dangers of extravagant or mistaken claims for the principle that might undermine it entirely:

- *That R2P is just another name for humanitarian intervention.* Evans maintains that this is not the case because "above all, R2P is about effective preventive action" and because reaction to the failure to prevent need not be military (2008, pp. 56–57).

- *That "extreme cases" always mean use of coercive military force.* This is not true because "it is necessary for a case to be really extreme for coercive military force to be an option, but the fact that it is extreme is not in itself sufficient to conclude that such force *should* be applied" (2008, p. 59; italics in original).

- *That R2P applies only to weak states.* While it is true that "there will always be some countries too militarily powerful for military action against them to do more good than harm," nevertheless, "no major country in the world, however big and powerful, is today wholly immune from peer group pressure" (2008, p. 63).

- *That R2P applies to all human rights issues.* While "one can argue, linguistically and as a matter of good public policy, that the international community has the responsibility to protect people from the ravages of AIDS … nuclear proliferation and … climate change," R2P's focus is on mass atrocities and that needs to be maintained so that the principle is not hopelessly defused (2008, pp. 64–65).

- *That Iraq was an example of R2P in operation.* Iraq "was in fact nothing of the kind, and—quite apart from its botched implementation— stands rather as a classic example of how *not* to apply the R2P norm" (2008, p. 69; italics in original).

There is much good sense in these clarifications—and perhaps a bit of wishful thinking. Because the idea of people having a right to protection from serious hazards is simple and appealing, it is bound to be evoked whenever such a danger is identified. Those who concern themselves with trying to prevent or contain genocide, or the like, will undoubtedly be irritated to hear that climate change, for example, has been placed on the same plane. This idea probably will have little effect, however, on international reactions to humanitarian crises when they arise. Similarly, states throughout history have frequently claimed some form of moral justification for their self-interested forays into other countries, and it would be surprising if the Responsibility to Protect were not seized upon for that purpose on some occasions. When it is used to justify actions such as those in Iraq, the validity of the claim will simply have to be weighed and evaluated, as it was in that instance. But that sort of thing should not happen often, and should not constitute a real danger to the integrity of the R2P principle in the long run.

But it is both to prevent false claims of that sort, and to make Security Council decisions easier and more consistent, that efforts are made to promote the adoption of precise threshold criteria for launching military efforts to contain mass atrocities. This idea received little support at the 2005 World Summit, and it is little short of anathema to those like the United States who would be compelled to bear the cost of such near automatic operations. But in the view of some analysts the idea is an inherently bad one in any case. Alan Kuperman, for example, has underlined the dangers not only of such a rigid structure but by implication also of R2P in its present configuration. His argument in general terms is relatively simple: if discontented groups within a state—national, ethnic, or religious minorities, for example—calculate that they are unlikely to be able to obtain their political objectives by peaceful means, or on their own by violent ones, they may deliberately court even severe repression if they believe that international forces will come to their rescue. Bosnia and Kosovo, Kuperman maintains, "illustrate how the moral hazard of humanitarian intervention has fostered suicidal rebellion since the end of the Cold War" (2006, p. 9). The more certain that would-be rebels can be of forcing intervention on their behalf (and there is a tendency always to consider that virtue resides with those who rebel), the greater the temptation to do whatever it takes to bring such intervention about. A definite threshold for rescue missions, therefore—so many thousand killed or made refugee or the apparent deliberate targeting of a distinguishable group or some such—would increase the likelihood of violent upheavals that might not otherwise materialize. Even R2P in its present form, in that it tends in the direction of more certain reaction to gross humanitarian transgressions, provides a degree of the same temptation.

What do we then conclude about R2P? Is it "much ado about nothing," a major advance in international thinking, or something in between? A case can be made for each of those positions, but the last is probably closest to the truth. As mentioned earlier, the doctrine isn't all that its advocates had hoped for, and it can't be all that the most enthusiastic of them imagine it might become—short of the kind of world reconstruction that would make the concept unnecessary. But R2P is not a "nothing," either, because, as at least a slogan and a desired objective, it has resonated strongly with many people. Even in the words of Theresa Reinold, who suggests the "much ado about nothing" possibility, "rejecting the concept altogether has become politically untenable" (2010, p. 63). Indeed, the ideas of sovereignty as being limited and conditional and there being a universal responsibility for the well-being of people everywhere have now been clearly enunciated and widely disseminated. In practical operational terms, the Security Council has made a number of references to R2P in resolutions and thus "has now set a precedent that it will not be inhibited *as a matter of principle* from authorizing enforcement for protection purposes without host consent" (Bellamy, 2011, p. 264; italics in original). That in itself constitutes progress.

The full implications of R2P are of course still being worked out. It is one thing to say that there is such a thing as a responsibility to protect and quite another to specify on whom or what that responsibility rests. It is one thing to say that there is such a responsibility and another to specify the conditions under which it can be fulfilled. To move forward and consolidate R2P into an established norm of international behaviour it will be necessary to accept that protection may not always be possible, even when attempted, and that failure to do so in one instance does not mean that the basic principle has died. It *could* die of course; not all infant norms make it to adulthood (see Fennimore & Sikkink, 1998). But at this point that does not appear very likely. The doctrine now seems to be a firmly entrenched, if vague and variously understood, concept that media usage over time will have much to do with refining. That is why it is useful to consider how R2P was presented to publics in the context of a major crisis, such as the Syrian civil war, especially as there appeared to have been significant differences in how it was perceived in that instance and in the overlapping case of Libya.

CHAPTER 3

The Role of the Press in Framing Conflict

In a series of studies starting in 2008, the present authors examined Western mass media treatment of a number of intra-state conflicts, most of which occurred in Africa (Soderlund et al., 2008; Sidahmed et al., 2010; Soderlund et al., 2012; Soderlund & Briggs, 2014). The particular focus of these studies was the extent to which international humanitarian intervention was thought to be necessary and/or appropriate to deal with such conflicts, or, on the contrary, to question such intervention on such bases as cost or likely effectiveness. The 2008 study in particular confirmed the relationship between extensive media coverage and the strength of international responses to humanitarian crises.[1]

Numerous authors have emphasized the importance of both the volume and the direction of media reporting with respect to government decision making regarding intervention in grave humanitarian situations. Frank Chalk and colleagues, for instance, maintain that

> [t]he "fourth estate"—the news media—exerts a powerful influence on government. The "CNN effect" is credited with persuading the US and Canadian governments to intervene in Somalia in 1992, Bosnia in 1995, and Eastern Zaire in 1996. Policy experts argue that the process of "policy by media," or formulating policy in response to media coverage, is a contemporary phenomenon that arises from the government's sensitivity to media coverage. While news media reports influence policy, the reverse is also true: an absence of reporting on mass atrocities in a particular country removes the pressures on the American and Canadian governments to act on their "responsibility to protect." (2010, p. 48; see also Thompson, 2007)

This suggests, perhaps somewhat too strongly, that what matters is the "volume of coverage" and implies that governments act only when pushed to do so by the "fourth estate." It may reasonably be argued that there is little likelihood that media will ignore mass atrocities when they occur, or that governments depend on media to alert them to such events. Moreover, in such cases governments do not rely entirely on media or public opinion to tell them what to do. The relationships between media and public opinion, and between media/public opinion and government decision making, are complex and multidirectional and less than clearly understood despite extensive attention by analysts over the past half-century. Part of the difficulty in that respect is the prior necessity of understanding the processes of government decision making, which, despite significant similarities, may differ to a greater or lesser extent from country to country.

Jon Western (2005) has impressively addressed the decision-making issue with respect to the United States in his book *Selling Intervention and War*. He uses what we may term a theory of liberal decision making to review six cases in which military intervention was a possibility for the country in question.[2] For him, liberal decision making implies the following:

- That states are not unitary decision makers
- That states' interests cannot "be assumed from a set of fixed preferences"
- That state preferences will vary according to "the nature of state-society relations and the specific domestic, international and social context"
- That "state action is the result of the push and pull of social actors operating within a particular liberal ideological and institutional context" (Western, 2005, pp. 5–6)

In short, decisions, including those concerning the use of force in situations of humanitarian crisis, are the outcome of implicit and varying competition(s) among "advocacy groups," both within government (see Allison & Zelikow, 1999, Chapters 3 and 5), and within society at large, to mobilize support among the mass public for their particular positions. This process determines, in effect, what interpretation of the "national interest" will achieve primacy in any given situation.

Assuming this to be an accurate description of what occurs within the American system, to what extent does it also describe decision-making processes in other liberal states? There are of course many similarities between the governmental systems of the United States and, for example, Britain and Canada. Each has a highly developed representative political system wherein non-fraudulent elections determine the composition of their governments; each features institutionalized freedom of association and of the media; and each enjoys advanced economic development, to mention only three of the most important points of comparison. But that does not mean that their decision-making processes are identical. The fusion of executive and legislative functions in the parliamentary systems of Britain and Canada contrasts sharply with the strict separation of these in the United States.[3] This means, at minimum, that intra-governmental processes of decision making in the first two are likely to be less complex and adversarial than in the last, particularly if the government in power holds a legislative majority. It probably also means that the precise process by which the two systems relate to their publics differs somewhat. The important thing, however, is that positions taken by media and public advocacy groups are crucial for both systems.

Governments in liberal states cannot often, or for very long, pursue policies that are strongly opposed by significant segments of their citizenry. At the same time, governments themselves are perhaps the most powerful advocacy groups of all and, hence, are always in a strong position to win debates concerning the appropriate policy to adopt. Jon Western found, in fact, that the US government made significant attempts to manipulate media to influence public opinion in each of the cases he studied, and most of these were successful (Western, 2005, chapters 2–6). Moreover, when such attempts are not successful, he suggests it is because of the public's "general mood," which he terms "latent public opinion" (2005, pp. 21–22). As we will discuss further in the following chapters, this factor appears to have played an important role in both British and American decision making regarding a military role in Syria during the first two and a half years of the civil war. But whether this factor is in play or not, the fact is that elite public opinion, as expressed primarily in the media, is a crucial part of the decision-making process in liberal states. This is perhaps especially true when decisions may result in significant cost in lives and/or material.

MEDIA AND AGENDA SETTING

But questions remain, including the following:

1. How is public opinion formed?
2. Does media construct public opinion or reflect it?
3. To what extent is government influenced by, or able to influence, either media or public opinion?

Research to date has not provided definitive answers to these questions, but one might hazard generalized, common-sense answers, at least with respect to the first two.

Public opinion in the most general sense is surely formed by the interplay of a large number of societal forces and circumstances, which will vary in significance from country to country and from time to time. It is not possible, therefore, to be precise about how public opinion is formed across even very similar countries. Obviously, opinion will be formed on the basis of the information that is available, and media, especially in liberal democracies, are primary sources of information about the world at large. At the very least, media "set the agenda" for public discourse and provide the beginning point "in the formation of public opinion" (McCombs & Reynolds, 2002, p. 1), and advocacy groups do in fact "seek to harness the perceived potential of the news media to facilitate humanitarian action" (Robinson, 2000, p. 613).

Much earlier than these observations, pioneer media observer Walter Lippmann similarly drew attention to press reports creating "pictures in our heads" (1922), and Bernard Cohen famously claimed that media might not tell people what to think, but they are enormously successful in telling them "what to think *about*" (1963, p. 14; italics in original). Beginning with a study of voting in the US presidential election of 1968 (McCombs & Shaw, 1972), an impressive body of work has confirmed the reality of the agenda-setting phenomenon: a strong correlation between media coverage and issues that mass publics think to be important (for an overview of this research, see Rogers & Dearing, 1988; McCombs & Shaw, 1993; Rogers, Dearing, & Bergman, 1993; McCombs, Shaw, & Weaver, 1997; McCombs, 2005; and Weaver, 2007).

At the same time, reporters, commentators, and editors, being human, are bound to be influenced in the information that they present, and in the manner in which they present it, by the prevailing attitudes and opinions of the public—the "latent public opinion" referred to by Western. The only reasonable answer to question 2, above ("Does media construct public opinion or reflect it?"), is therefore "It does both," but we cannot expect the relationship to be either constant or consistent. Most of the time, media probably do influence opinion more than the other way around, but the balance will depend on the specific issue and the extent of prior public familiarity with it.

MEDIA FRAMING AND PUBLIC OPINION

It is worth revisiting here the distinction that Cohen drew between the attention media give an issue and the actual content contained in media coverage. Many in fact suggest, to varying degrees, that media *do* tell the public *what* to think. Gadi Wolfsfeld, for one, argued that reporting consists of two elements: (1) "hard news," which deals with the who, what, where, and when of an event; and (2) the "framing" of that event, which either implicitly or explicitly tells the audience how it should interpret the event—i.e., what is really going on, who is responsible, and, at a minimum, what options there are for dealing with it (Wolfsfeld, 1997, pp. 31–36; also see Entman, 2007). Vincent Price and colleagues make a more explicit claim, arguing that

> how events and issues are packaged and presented by journalists can … affect how readers and viewers understand those events and issues…. By

activating some ideas, feeling and values rather than others ... news can encourage particular trains of thought about political phenomena and lead audience members to arrive at more or less predictable conclusions. (Price, Tewksbury, & Powers, 1997, pp. 482–483)

Karen Callaghan and Frauke Schnell add that "by promoting a particular frame, political elites, the media, and other players *can alter how an issue is understood and how to shift public opinion.* In other words, political elites can effectively use frames to promote their own political ends" (2001, p. 186; italics added).

There is nothing necessarily nefarious or deliberate or even conscious about framing. In its simplest form, it is nothing more than placing events for target audiences in a context they might more easily understand or relate to. To a large extent, then, framing is unavoidable—even when no specific axe is being ground; consequently, there is little doubt that it is important to the issue of media influence on public opinion.

A research study published in 2014 clearly demonstrated the reality of framing effects. The study was based on an experiment to test for the unconscious transfer "of positive and negative emotions," which the authors termed "emotional contagion" (Kramer, Guillory, & Hancock, 2014, p. 8788). In the study, newsfeeds were sent to 689,003 Facebook users. However, the number of positive and negative words used in the text were altered, and then the positive and negative outlooks expressed in the recipients' subsequent posts were examined. The results confirmed the reality of "emotional contagion": a reduction in positive words in newsfeeds led to "a larger percentage of words in people's status updates [that] were negative and a smaller percentage [that] were positive. When negativity was reduced, the opposite pattern occurred" (2014, p. 8789).[4]

Research specific to international issues has also demonstrated framing effects. Adam Berinsky and Donald Kinder examined the impact of pro- and anti-intervention framing with respect to the 1999 crisis in Kosovo. They suggest that citizens "organize and retain information" through "cognitive processes" that utilize clues supplied by media (2006, pp. 640–641). As in the Facebook study, they found that even subtle manipulation of story content—"highlighting the risks of intervening" as opposed to "emphasizing the humanitarian aspects of the crisis"—led to predictable results. Subjects receiving pro-intervention content, in fact, "were more likely to favor US intervention, *not only in Kosovo but elsewhere around the world*" (2006, p. 653; italics added). Berinsky and Kinder further describe a framing process whereby citizens "organize and retain information" by linking media cues to "cognitive processes" (2006, p. 653).

In addition to the "emotional contagion" concept, some suggest that framing works through a process of "persuasion via belief change" (Nelson, Oxley, & and Clawson, 1997, p. 223); others contend that the process is one of "audience responses" to "media stimuli," whereby the latter lead to audience selection from a range of pre-existing beliefs. Specifically, "the mode of presentation of a given piece of information (i.e., its frame), makes it more or less likely for that information to be processed using a particular schema" that audience members have stored in their minds (Scheufele & Iyengar, 2011, p. 1). Kimberly Gross studied the impact of episodic (emotional) versus thematic (cognitive) framing and concluded that "framing effects on policy opinion can operate through both affective and cognitive channels" (2008, p. 169).

Research methods other than those based on experimental design have also produced similar conclusions regarding framing effects. Using survey data from a US National Election Study, Shanto Iyengar and Adam Simon found a modest but significant (0.03) correlation between watching news coverage of the 1990–91 Gulf War, which was event-oriented and focused on military operations, and support for military as opposed to diplomatic responses to the Iraqi invasion and occupation of Kuwait (Iyengar & Simon, 1993, p. 381).

Whatever the precise influence mechanism at work, few if any media analysts question that what is important in the media–public opinion connection is the slant or frame that information is situated in when it is conveyed. Moreover, media influence clearly is likely to be most powerful when framing takes the form of open advocacy, such as may be found in editorial and other overtly opinion material in newspapers, as opposed to what Sean Aday has termed the "objectivist framing" normally found elsewhere in straight news reporting (Aday, 2006).

THE IMPACT OF MEDIA FRAMING

How important is public opinion or media framing to government decision making? This crucial question has received a variety of answers over the years. At one extreme is Cohen's concept of the "CNN effect" referred to by Chalk and colleagues (see above). Cohen's (1994) argument was that in at least some instances media can all but dictate foreign policy decisions to government, with the American intervention in Somalia in 1992 most often cited as evidence for this claim. Most analysts, including the current authors, would today consider Cohen's position an overstatement but would agree that when there is a persistent media/public clamour for "something to be done" about a conscience-rending situation, a government may find it difficult to resist responding in some fashion. Democratic governments, after all, are supposed to be responsive to the wishes of their people; and, in any case, government officials themselves are unlikely to be immune to the human atrocities that appear on their TV screens and that are described day after day in their newspapers.

We should keep in mind a number of points, however. First, unanimous or near unanimous or even substantially uniform media/public demands for some kind of action in response to even an event as horrendous as the Rwandan genocide are rare. And such universal demands are becoming, we would suggest, even more uncommon as experience demonstrates how complex such situations are and how difficult it is to determine what an effective response to them might be.[5] A second point to remember is that media advocates of "doing something" are often less than specific about what that something should be. Therefore, on the basis of the superior information available to them, governments are almost inevitably free to adopt the response that they consider most appropriate. In other words, if media can back a government into a corner, it is a very broad corner with much room for manoeuvring. The final point to keep in mind is that media and governments should not be treated as entirely independent of one another, even in liberal democracies. Freedom of the press is no doubt quite real in such countries, but what government officials—particularly presidents or prime ministers or ministers of foreign affairs or the like—choose to say publicly is *always news* and is guaranteed to receive extensive coverage in media of all kinds. Governments themselves thus are key players in the influence game simply by performing their normal functions. Beyond that, they are quite capable of deliberately affecting how issues are framed in the media, should they consider this to be necessary.

The relationship between media advocacy and government policy is thus less simple and unidirectional than is sometimes supposed. Piers Robinson has recognized some aspects of this complexity. Assuming that media coverage is sufficient to place a possible intervention on the decision-making agenda, he offers what he calls a "policy-media interaction model," which postulates that the impact of media advocacy on decision making will depend on the following:

- Whether the government has a *clear and firm policy* for dealing with the crisis at hand (that policy can be either pro- or anti-intervention)
- Whether there is a *consensus* within the government regarding that policy
- Whether in its *framing* of the crisis, media coverage is either supportive or critical of government policy (Robinson, 2000, pp. 614–617; see also Robinson, 2002)

Robinson further argues that mass media have little influence on policy when a government has a clear and firm idea of how to respond to a crisis and is internally united in that course of action. In the longer term, however, he suggests that government policy may come under media scrutiny if "elite dissensus," rather than consensus, develops. It is, in any case, where "policy uncertainty" exists that "policy-makers ... can be forced to intervene during a humanitarian crisis due to media-driven public pressure or the fear of *potential* negative reaction to government inaction" (2000, p. 614; italics in original).

Robinson's case studies (Bosnia, 1995, and Kosovo, 1999) dealt with hard news coverage as well as editorial and opinion pieces. In that "journalistic norms regarding 'objectivity' preclude journalists from making explicit prescriptions (other than in editorials)," Robinson had to go beyond identifying media positions that were explicitly supportive or critical of government policy. To deal with this problem he opted for examining what he termed "empathy framing" (that which identifies with suffering victims) and "distance framing" (that which seeks to create an emotional divide between the audience and victims of the crisis). For Robinson, these are the two journalistic constructions that "*pressure for a particular policy outcome, without explicitly calling for a particular course of action*" (2000, p. 616, footnote 3; italics added).

In that all data for the present study deal with editorials and opinion articles, there was no lack of legitimate calls for greater involvement in or for remaining aloof from the Syrian conflict. Quite to the contrary, such advice dominated opinion commentary. Hence, while empathy and distance framing were part of what we looked for, in most cases policy advice was far more specific, leaving little doubt as to what course of action editorial boards or opinion contributors wanted the three governments (or the international community more broadly) to pursue with respect to Syria.

In that there will rarely, if ever, be policy certainty with respect to the appropriate response to complex humanitarian emergencies in distant, marginally understood societies, one might argue on the basis of Robinson's model that there will usually be ample room for media influence. On the other hand, it would be a mistake to assume that media will generally be more certain than government leaders about what to do, so there may well be uncertainty on the part of both. With respect to the third point of Robinson's policy–media interaction model (whether in its framing of the crisis, media coverage is either supportive or critical of government policy), the conclusions suggest that the relationship between media and government decision making is inevitably symbiotic and fluid, but that, to one degree or another, media are always potentially relevant to government decision making. Consequently, it is important to try to understand the nature of the relationship in each crisis situation. It is that conviction that motivates and informs our study.

RESEARCH METHODS

The research presented in the following four chapters focuses on the role of the media in framing the Syrian conflict, and particularly on the extent to which robust international intervention was promoted or discouraged. To accomplish this, the editorial and opinion content of three elite Western newspapers—*The New York Times* (US), *The Guardian* (UK), and *The Globe and Mail* (Canada)—during the first 31 months of the civil war was studied. The research thus covers the period from the beginning of the protests against President Bashar al-Assad in March 2011 until the UN Security Council's September 2013 approval of an agreement to remove and destroy Syria's chemical weapons under international supervision following the Syrian government's use of nerve gas against its civilian population a month earlier. The end date is significant because it effectively closed consideration of any immediate Western military intervention in the civil war.

The newspapers selected for the study are all considered highly influential in shaping elite views in their respective countries, either those of political leaders directly or indirectly through the shaping of public opinion.[6] All relevant editorials and opinion pieces published during the study period were included, resulting in a database of 417 items: 163 from *The Times*, 170 from *The Guardian*, and 84 from *The Globe*. Of these, 135 were editorials and 282 were opinion articles.[7] Our decision to restrict analysis to overtly opinion material was prompted by the fact that the overall coverage of Syria was extensive—one of the criteria Robinson specifies for significant media influence. The Syrian situation simply commanded so much media attention that in order to have a project of manageable proportions, it was not only possible but necessary to restrict our analysis to the type of material most likely to contain relevant advocacy frames.[8] Given the substantial volume of that material, we are confident that such a highly focused approach allows us to accurately reflect the framing performance of the three papers during the conflict's critical early period, one that culminated in the first explicit decisions regarding military responses in Britain and the United States.

Quantitative Analysis

The research combines quantitative and qualitative content analysis. Quantitative analysis is based, first, on the frequency with which principal actors in the conflict—the Syrian government, the Syrian president, and the "opposition"—were mentioned, combined with assessments of whether their actions were framed positively or negatively with respect to ending the civil war and/or achieving a democratic outcome. Key global actors, such as the US, Britain, Russia, Canada, the UN, the international community in general, and NATO, as well as regional actors, such as Iran, Saudi Arabia, Turkey, Israel, the Arab

League, and Hezbollah, were also coded for mentions and for whether their actions were framed as helpful or unhelpful with respect to a satisfactory ending of the crisis. Assessments as to whether opinion content was positive or negative were based on specific descriptive words or phrases used and our judgment as to how these would reflect on their subject. In all cases, the possibility of ambiguous assessment was left open.

Also assessed quantitatively was press framing of key issues raised by the war, including possible forceful intervention in the name of the international community. The following dimensions were coded:

- Optimism vs. pessimism about the likely success of diplomatic initiatives

- Optimism vs. pessimism about the likely success of three possible types of international intervention: arming the opposition, creating a "no-fly zone," and using direct military action

- Whether the government or the opposition was seen to be "winning" the civil war

- Whether an item promoted or discouraged the international community "to do something" about the crisis (i.e., its role in "creating a will to intervene")

- Whether the long-term outcome for Syria was likely to be positive or negative with respect to achieving democracy

Changes in these evaluations were tracked over four time periods.[9] Finally, following the announcement on September 10, 2013, of a proposed agreement to remove and destroy Syria's chemical weapons, opinion material was coded as to whether the agreement was likely to have a positive or negative effect.

Qualitative Analysis

While such quantitative analysis is useful in summarizing how such events as the Syrian civil war were presented to media audiences, it cannot, and should not, be expected to tell the complete story. In order to provide a more complete understanding of the crisis and the international response to it, we have constructed what we have termed qualitative "opinion narratives" (or coherent storylines) for each newspaper for each year of the study. These narratives, presented in conjunction with the quantitative data in chapters 4, 5, 6, and 7, are based on the arguments and analyses presented, and/or policies advocated or discouraged, in 82 per cent of the opinion-leading material that was included in the qualitative tables. Items were selected on the basis of their contributions to understanding international involvement in the crisis. Particular attention was given to possible media inputs to the August/September 2013 decisions on the part of Great Britain and the United States to pursue direct military action in response to the Assad government's chemical weapons attack, followed by the abandonment of these policies: in one case, due to legislative rejection; and in the other, in favour of an agreement to destroy Syria's chemical weapons.

One of the study's goals is to provide as complete and nuanced a description as possible of three different Western media perspectives on the issues involved in the Syrian civil war, the character of its participants, and, most importantly, the problems of determining an appropriate international response to what all acknowledged was a horrendous humanitarian crisis. Also, among other factors that will be discussed in the book's conclusion, as we indicated in the introduction, we will pay particular attention to the relationship between media framing and mass public opinion and how this relationship contributed to the context in which governmental decisions were made in the late summer of 2013 on whether a military intervention was an appropriate international response to the Syrian crisis.

CHAPTER 4

Conflict Framing in 2011

INTRODUCTION

During the first nine months of the Syrian conflict, opinion-leading material in the three Western newspapers under study focused on the following themes:

- Placing the conflict in the context of "the quest for democracy" theme, which was characteristic of the early days of the Arab Spring—largely peaceful protestors confronting repression from a brutal regime
- Evaluating the possibility that the government of Bashar al-Assad might initiate a program of political reforms sufficient to satisfy the demands of protestors
- Examining the likely outcomes, both domestically and regionally, should Assad fall
- Assessing possible international actions, including an R2P-type military intervention, such as the one the Security Council had authorized for similar circumstances in Libya, to bring about a satisfactory outcome

While by the fall of 2011 there was some concern that the situation in Syria had developed from uncoordinated protests to something approaching a civil war, opinion writers did not, by and large, recognize that they were witnessing only the beginning of what was to become a prolonged and devastating military and social conflict. Their assessments with respect to all of the above issues tended to be mixed and conflicting, although each newspaper approached these issues in its own unique way—as they all did throughout the period of our study.

QUANTITATIVE FINDINGS

As indicated in Table 4.1, initial opinion material on Syria in all newspapers was firmly focused on the domestic situation, with 94 per cent of items commenting on the government of Bashar al-Assad and 56 per cent on his opposition; *The Guardian* in particular was focused on the latter, mentioning it in fully 80 per cent of opinion items. In addition to an understandable emphasis on the role of the US, *The New York Times* led in commentary on the international and regional implications of the conflict, especially the roles of the international community, the UN Security Council, Russia, Turkey, and the Arab League. *The Globe and Mail* was the only newspaper where opinion material addressed a possible role for Canada in Syria,[1] and it was somewhat more concerned than the other newspapers about Iran's role in the conflict.

Table 4.1   Salience of Domestic Combatants, Major Global and Regional Actors, 2011, by Newspaper (Per Cent of Opinion-Leading Items)

	Times N=31	Guardian N=35	Globe N=21	Total N=87
Domestic Combatants				
Syrian government*	96.8	100.0	81.0	94.3
Syrian opposition	45.2	80.0	33.3	56.3
Global Actors				
US*	54.8	34.3	14.3	36.8
International community	35.5	17.1	33.3	27.6
Russia*	25.8	14.3	9.5	17.2
UN (Security Council)	22.6	0	19.0	12.6
NATO	0	14.3	9.5	8.0
UN (General)	3.2	8.6	4.8	5.7
Britain*	0	11.4	0	4.6
Canada*	0	0	14.3	3.4
Regional Actors				
Turkey	25.8	25.7	14.3	23.0
Arab League	25.8	11.4	14.3	17.2
Iran	12.9	14.3	19.0	14.9
Saudi Arabia	16.1	14.3	0	11.5
Israel	12.9	11.4	9.5	11.5
Hezbollah	9.7	14.3	4.8	10.3

* Includes references to respective leaders: Presidents al-Assad, Obama, and Putin; Prime Ministers Cameron and Harper.

Data in Table 4.2 show similarities as well as some obvious differences in how the newspapers evaluated the various actors. Chief among the former, the Syrian government was overwhelmingly condemned by all papers (overall in 86 per cent of opinion items), while the opposition received far more positive than negative appraisals in all papers (35 per cent to 3 per cent). The opposition was especially well received in *The Guardian*, where just over half the items (51 per cent) were positive. Material in *The Times* was uniquely supportive of the role of the US (23 per cent), and critical of the roles of Russia (26 per cent) and the Arab League (13 per cent). *The Guardian* led in commentary critical of the US (23 per cent) as well as in that favourable to the role of Turkey (14 per cent). In *The Globe*, opinion material was most positive regarding the roles

Table 4.2　Evaluation of Domestic Combatants, Major Global and Regional Actors, 2011, by Newspaper (Per Cent of Opinion-Leading Items—Ambiguous Items Omitted)

	Times N=31		Guardian N=35		Globe N=21		Total N=87		Percentage Difference
	Pos	Neg	Pos	Neg	Pos	Neg	Pos	Neg	
Domestic Combatants									
Syrian government*	0	90.3	0	91.4	0	71.4	0	86.2	−86.2
Syrian opposition	29.0	0	51.4	5.7	14.3	4.8	34.5	3.4	+31.1
Global Actors									
US*	22.6	3.2	8.6	22.9	4.8	4.8	12.6	11.5	+1.1
Int. community	3.2	9.7	2.9	8.6	9.5	9.5	4.6	9.2	−4.6
Russia*	0	25.8	2.9	8.6	0	0	1.1	12.6	−11.5
UN (Security Council)	3.2	12.9	0	0	0	14.3	1.1	8.0	−6.9
NATO	0	0	0	0	0	14.3	0	2.3	−2.3
UN (General)	0	3.2	2.9	2.9	0	4.8	1.1	3.4	−2.3
Britain*	0	0	2.9	5.7	0	0	1.1	2.3	−1.2
Canada*	0	0	0	0	0	0	0	0	0
Regional Actors									
Turkey	12.9	3.2	14.3	2.9	9.5	0	12.6	2.3	+10.3
Arab League	0	12.9	2.9	5.7	14.3	0	4.6	6.9	−2.3
Iran	0	3.2	0	5.7	0	14.3	0	6.9	−6.9
Saudi Arabia	6.5	0	0	8.6	0	0	2.3	3.4	−1.1
Israel	0	3.2	0	5.7	0	0	0	3.4	−3.4
Hezbollah	0	3.2	0	2.9	0	0	0	2.3	−2.3

* Includes references to respective leaders: Presidents al-Assad, Obama, and Putin; Prime Ministers Cameron and Harper

Table 4.3   Optimism vs. Pessimism toward Conflict-Ending Strategies, 2011, by News-paper (Per Cent of Opinion-Leading Items—Ambiguous and Mixed Items Omitted)

	Times N=31		Guardian N=35		Globe N=21		Total N=87		Percentage Difference
	Opt	Pess	Opt	Pess	Opt	Pess	Opt	Pess	
Strategies									
Diplomacy	25.8	6.5	8.6	11.4	38.1	9.5	21.8	9.2	+12.6
Arming the opposition	0	0	2.9	0	0	0	1.1	0	+1.1
Imposing a no-fly zone	0	0	0	5.7	0	14.3	0	5.7	−5.7
Military action	0	6.5	2.9	22.9	0	19.0	1.1	16.1	−15.0

of the Arab League (14 per cent) and most critical of the actions of the UN Security Council, NATO, and Iran (14 per cent for each).

With respect to possible conflict-ending strategies, data in Table 4.3 indicate that while *The Globe* and *The Times* saw reasonable hope for diplomacy (38 per cent and 26 per cent of opinion items, respectively), *The Guardian* featured slightly more negative (11 per cent) than positive (9 per cent) items. At this point there was little mention of arming the opposition or creating a no-fly zone, but direct military action was seen as particularly unhelpful by all of the newspapers, with *The Guardian* offering the most negative assessments (23 per cent).

As data in Table 4.4 tell us, not surprisingly, most early predictions regarding who was winning the struggle in Syria tended to be ambiguous, and this was the case for all newspapers (overall 24 per cent). As well, however, all newspapers had more commentary pointing to a victory by the opposition (14 per cent) than by the government (1 per cent). In *The Guardian,* 26 per cent of items saw the opposition to be winning, as compared to much lower figures in the North American papers (7 per cent in *The Times* and 5 per cent in *The Globe*).

Table 4.5 assesses the extent of initial support for the idea that the international community had a "responsibility to do something" about the Syrian

Table 4.4   Side Seen to Be Winning, 2011, by Newspaper (Per Cent of Opinion-Leading Items)

Times N=31			Guardian N=35			Globe N=21			Total N=87		
Gov't	Ambig	Oppos	Gov't	Ambig	Oppos	Gov't	Ambig	Oppos	Gov't	Ambig	Oppos
3.2	19.4	6.5	0	28.6	25.7	0	23.8	4.8	1.1	24.1	13.8

Table 4.5   The International Community "Should Do Something," 2011, by Newspaper (Per Cent of Opinion-Leading Items—Ambiguous Items Omitted)

Times N=31		Guardian N=35		Globe N=21		Total N=87		Percentage Difference
Pro	Anti	Pro	Anti	Pro	Anti	Pro	Anti	
3.2	9.7	8.6	17.1	4.8	9.5	5.7	12.6	–6.9

Table 4.6 Positive or Negative Outcomes for Democracy, 2011, by Newspaper (Per Cent of Opinion-Leading Items)

Times N=31			Guardian N=35			Globe N=21			Total N=87		
Pos	Ambig	Neg	Pos	Ambig	Neg	Pos	Ambig	Neg	Pos	Ambig	Neg
12.9	19.4	12.9	17.1	11.4	11.4	4.8	14.3	19.0	12.6	14.9	13.8

conflict. Data provide little in the way of evidence that early on the press was helpful in creating "a will to intervene," as framing that distanced the international community from the conflict predominated in opinion-leading material in all three newspapers. Interestingly, material in *The Guardian* was both most strongly opposed to an international involvement (17 per cent) and also the most supportive (9 per cent). Overall, there were twice as many opinion-leading items opposed to international involvement than were supportive of any such action.

Data in Table 4.6 point to important differences in how opinion material in the three newspapers initially saw the ultimate outcome of the Syrian conflict. *The Guardian* was both the most optimistic (17 per cent) and least pessimistic (11 per cent), while *The Globe* was the least optimistic (5 per cent) and the most pessimistic (19 per cent). *The Times* had equal percentages of positive and negative appraisals (13 per cent). Overall, optimism, ambiguity, and pessimism were nearly equally distributed: 13 per cent, 15 per cent, and 14 per cent, respectively.

QUALITATIVE FINDINGS

The New York Times' Opinion Narrative

The New York Times began its opinion narrative with background material relative to the Arab Spring–type protests that were taking place in a number of Syrian cities. On March 27, 2011, British author Simon Sebag Montefiore offered an opinion article focused on revolutions of the Arab variety. He linked the severity of rule by a regime to the ease of its overthrow: "the more moderate the regimes," the easier they were to overthrow, while "the more brutal the police state," the more difficult it was "to bring down." Significantly, both Libya under Muammar Qaddafi and Syria under Bashar al-Assad were counted among the latter. Sebag Montefiore also examined possible regional implications of a protracted conflict in Syria: the encouragement of rebellion in Iran and the consequent liberation of "Lebanon from Hezbollah" (2011, Mar. 27, p. 11).

Professor David Lesch, author of a book about the Syrian president, provided assessments of whether he was likely to opt for repression or reform in response to the growing protests. Following a series of interviews with Assad at the time of his elevation to the presidency in 2000, Lesch saw him as "evolving into a confident and battle-hardened president." While there were signs that "he had begun to equate his well-being with that of his country," Lesch's overall evaluation of Assad was that "he had good intentions, if awkwardly expressed at times." He saw the Syrian president as having the ability to "change the course of Syria by giving up that with which he has become so comfortable." On balance, his judgment was that Assad "could go either way" (Lesch, 2011, Mar. 30, p. 27).

Moreover, to those who sought regime change, Lesch counselled restraint: "Syria is ethnically and religiously diverse and, with the precipitous removal of central authority, it could very well implode like Iraq." As a consequence, he claimed that "the Obama administration wants him to stay in power even as it admonishes him to choose the path of reform" (Lesch, 2011, Mar. 30, p. 27). Long-time Syrian writer and activist Yassin al-Haj Saleh also held out hope that reform might work. Citing broader support for the Syrian regime than had been the case in Egypt, he argued that "this is a source of strength" that should not be squandered. Time, however, was running out: "If the regime is to keep any of its deeply damaged legitimacy, it will have to answer the protesters' demands and recognize the popular longing for freedom and equality" (Al-Haj Saleh, 2011, Apr. 11, p. 25).

A few days later, *Times* columnist Thomas Friedman was more pessimistic. Describing Syria as a country "fractured by tribal, ethnic and religious divisions," he argued that while "a gradual evolution to democracy" might have been possible, "it is probably too late now.... Even if the iron fist of authoritarianism is lifted, civil strife could easily trample democratic hopes" (Friedman, 2011, Apr. 13, p. 25). In an article a month later, Friedman was more specific: "to embrace the downfall of these dictators—as we must—is to advocate leveling a rotten building with no assurance that it can be rebuilt" (Friedman, 2011, May 15, p. 10). Earlier, toward the end of March, Friedman had sketched out the dilemma facing the United States in Syria in one mind-twisting sentence:

A regime we don't like ... could be toppled by people who say what we like, but we're not sure they all really believe what we like because among them could be Sunni fundamentalists, who, if they seize power, could suppress all those minorities in Syria whom they don't like. (2011, Mar. 30, p. 26)

Friedman also drew distinctions between American support for the overthrow of Libya's Muammar Qaddafi and the situation facing the US in Syria. Friedman praised Mr. Obama's decision to confront the Libyan colonel, even though he predicted "that any kind of decent outcome there will require boots on the ground"—although he hoped these would not be American. Syria, however, had to be looked at differently "because the situation ... is just not as clear as we'd like and because Syria is a real game-changer. Libya implodes. Syria explodes" (Friedman, 2011, Mar. 30, p. 27).

Times columnist Nicholas Kristof supported what he termed "a humanitarian intervention" in Libya, and pointed out that in a process of "cherry-pick[ing] our humanitarian interventions" Syria had been ignored. While not addressing the reasons why this was the case, Kristof argued that it was "better to inconsistently save some lives than to consistently save none." Although the NATO mission in Libya was still in its early days, Kristof also expressed hope that it "may help put teeth into the emerging doctrine of the 'responsibility to protect'"—the first specific mention of R2P in the paper's opinion narrative (Kristof, 2011, Apr. 3, p. 12).

An end of April *Times* editorial offered a comprehensive assessment of the Syrian situation. While there was a decided lack of optimism, the door was not seen to be closed to the possibility that reforms might somehow work. Assad, however, was clearly moving in the wrong direction, described as "appear[ing] determined to join his father in the ranks of history's blood-stained dictators." He also appeared uncommitted to follow through on the reforms he had proposed and was "fast losing all legitimacy" (*NYT*, 2011, Apr. 29, p. 26).

On the international side, the US and its president were described as pushing Assad toward reforms. This push was presented as "a start, but it is not nearly enough." The US and its allies needed to "rally international condemnation" and implement a regime of "tough sanctions." Moreover, the Arab League and the UN Security Council needed to be pressured "to take strong stands." On this point the Security Council was criticized for not having "even been able to muster a press statement." The International Criminal Court (ICC) was also called upon to "investigate regime abuses." The final outcome of the struggle was seen as resting in the hands of Syrians. And, while Assad commanded "a powerful security establishment ... he cannot stifle the longing for freedom forever" (*NYT*, 2011, Apr. 29, p. 26).

A May 20 editorial was impressed that "the [Obama] administration is finally getting tougher with Syria," noting that it had placed sanctions on the Syrian president and six of his associates. However, the paper was more pessimistic both about the possibility of reform and the likelihood of Assad's stepping down than it had been a month earlier. While Mr. Obama had indicated that Assad could "lead the transition, or get out of the way," the editorial was skeptical that "Mr. Assad can produce reform even if he wants to. But insisting that he leave power isn't realistic, although continued pressure could change that" (*NYT*, 2011, May 20, p. 22).

Two days later, Thomas Friedman assessed the regional implications of the conflict, arguing that the possibility of either "democracy or breakdown in Syria would change the whole Middle East overnight." In that Friedman didn't "see how Syria's president ... can last," one or the other of these outcomes was likely. Impacted would be Lebanon (controlled by Syria since the mid-1970s); Israel (which "has counted on Syria to keep the peace on the Golan Heights since 1967"); Iran (which had been using Syria as a "platform for exporting revolution into the Arab world"); as well as Hezbollah and Hamas, both dependent on Syrian support (Friedman, 2011, May 22, p. 8). Friedman asked what has turned out to be "the million dollar question hanging over the Syrian rebellion, and all the Arab rebellions: ... Can the people really come together and write a social contract to live together as equal citizens—not as sects—once the iron fist of the regimes is removed?" For Friedman, there was no clear answer (Friedman, 2011, May 22, p. 8).

By the beginning of June, Assad was clearly no longer seen as part of the solution. *Times* columnist David Brooks described the Syrian regime as "depraved," and, as such, it "can never be part of a successful negotiation." As a consequence, "it's necessary, as everybody but the Obama administration publicly acknowledges, to see Assad toppled" (Brooks, 2011, June 3, p. 23). In response to what was termed "perhaps the most vicious counterattack of the Arab Spring," an editorial a day later called upon the US and Europe to press the Security Council for a "robust" package of sanctions "and dare Moscow and the others to side with Mr. Assad over the Syrian people." While some in the international community still believed that it was possible for Assad to implement reforms, the newspaper's editorial board was not among them: "Arguments that Mr. Assad is the best guarantor of stability and best way to avoid extremism have lost all credibility" (*NYT*, 2011, June 4, p. 20). In mid-June another editorial criticized President Obama, claiming that he "has done too little to rally international pressure" to force Assad to leave office, and calling upon him "to find better ways to punish [Assad] and his cronies." Importantly, military action was not presented as an option: "Washington needs to mount

an all-out campaign to pass a tough United Nations Security Council resolution condemning Syria and imposing sanctions" (*NYT*, 2011, June 18, p. 18).

An editorial a month later reiterated the conclusion that "Mr. Assad has
lost all legitimacy." Moreover, it was time to stop sending "mixed messages" to
the Syrian president regarding the possibility of reform, as it was claimed both
the Americans and the French were still doing. Although "*a foreign military
intervention is out of the question*," an expanded regime of sanctions, to be
imposed by the West, Turkey, and the Arab League, was called for. It was clearly
time for Assad to go, and without international pressure, he "will believe he can
hang on" (*NYT*, 2011, July 19, p. 22; italics added). Citing the legacy of Syria's
colonial experience, Bassma Kodmani, executive director of the Arab Reform
Initiative, reinforced anti-intervention framing: "In Syria, anyone who calls
for outside interventions is likely to be branded a traitor; any Western threat
of military action would therefore hurt the opposition more than the regime"
(Kodmani, 2011, Aug. 1, p. 21).

Two further editorials in August explored the international response to the
Syrian conflict. On August 9, the UN Security Council was damned with faint
praise for issuing "a statement condemning 'widespread violations of human
rights and the use of force against civilians by the Syrian authorities'—but
with no threat of sanctions." More needed to be done—by the UN (approval
of sanctions and referral to the ICC for war crimes) and by the US and Europe
(more severe sanctions, plus "no new investments in Syria's energy sector"). As
well, Turkey needed to step up pressure on Assad, while what was described as
the "cowardly Arab League" was called upon "to stand with the Syrian people"
(*NYT*, 2011, Aug. 4, p. 24). Another August 9 editorial commented favourably on Saudi Arabia's King Abdullah's statement calling on Assad "to stop the
killing machine and end the bloodshed." This was seen as evidence that Assad
was "destabilizing the region … [and that eventually he] … will be brought
down." In this context, Syria's connection to Iran (a country feared by Arab
leaders), was highlighted. The entire international community was encouraged
to "keep up the diplomatic pressure and broaden sanctions … until those
enabling Mr. Assad—the military and the business community—force him
out" (*NYT*, 2011, Aug. 9, p. 22).

Vali Nasr, the dean of Johns Hopkins School of Advanced International
Studies, explored the impact of sectarianism on outcomes in Syria and the
Middle East in general, arguing that "the region's history points to darker outcomes" than at first promised by the Arab Spring. In Syria, the split between
the ruling minority Alawi (part of the Shiite tradition) and the majority Sunni
population posed the "risk of setting off a regional dynamic that could over-
whelm the hopeful narrative of the Arab Spring itself, replacing it with a much
aggravated power struggle along sectarian lines." The Shia-Sunni divide within

Islam pitted Iran (and its allied Lebanese militia, Hezbollah) on one side, and Saudi Arabia, Qatar, and the Arab League on the other. Syria was seen to be "particularly important because Sunnis elsewhere see the Alawite government as the linchpin in the Shiite alliance of Iran and Hezbollah." The future did not look good for either "democracy or American interests," but Nasr suggested that the US "has little leverage and influence in Syria" (Nasr, 2011, Aug. 28, p. 4).

An editorial at the beginning of September commented positively on the Arab League for its call on Assad to "'end the spilling of blood and follow the way of reason before it is too late.'" The League was urged to "impose strong sanctions, now," as were Turkey and the European Union (EU). In addition, Assad's international "enablers"—chiefly Russia and China—were called out for "shameful" behaviour in blocking UN Security Council sanctions (*NYT*, 2011, Sept. 1, p. 28).

Autumn brought more of the same message. The UN Security Council was "paralyzed" by Russian and Chinese vetoes of a resolution "condemning Syria's brutal crackdown." The position of the two countries was explained in terms of loss of arms sales for the former and "fears of any popular movement" for the latter. However, the editorial in *The Times* in October claimed that, for popular consumption, their vetoes were justified by the fear that the US and Europe "would use the resolution to take military action against Mr. Assad just as they had against [Libya's Colonel Muammar Qaddafi]." Europe and the US were called upon to "keep stepping up the pressure, robustly enforc[ing] their own sanctions." It was important that Assad not think "that the failed United Nations vote was the last word" (*NYT*, 2011, Oct. 11, p. 26).

A November editorial noted the failure of an Arab League initiative calling for the "release of political prisoners" and the start of talks dealing with political reform. The League was called upon to do more: eject Syria from the organization and "urge the United Nations Security Council to condemn Mr. Assad and impose international sanctions against the regime." Turkey, in particular was called upon to impose "tough sanctions." As for the Syrian opposition, "it still needs to translate its campaign into a coherent vision of governance after Assad and what that will mean for the country's Sunni, Alawite and Christian communities" (*NYT,* 2011, Nov. 9, p. 30). A week later, it was clear to *The Times* editorial board that the Syrian president was "willing to destroy his country to maintain his hold on power.... International pressure for his removal is finally building—but not fast enough." Regional neighbours—Jordan, Saudi Arabia, and Turkey, plus the Arab League—needed to do more; Russia and China needed to "stop their enabling and agree to tough sanctions on Mr. Assad and his cronies in the military and business community." It was again suggested that the Security Council "refer Mr. Assad and his henchmen to the [ICC] for prosecution for crimes against humanity" (*NYT*, 2011, Nov. 17, p. 30).

Thomas Friedman's end of November opinion article continued to express his earlier skepticism. He was "deeply worried that the longer the fighting continues … the less chance that any stable democratizing order will emerge anytime soon." As well, Friedman broached the possibility that "Syria could disintegrate into civil war." He again reviewed the impact of what he termed "a big Lebanon-like brawl" on the region as a whole, and he explained the thrust for a democratic transition in the region in terms of "a generational rupture": insiders vs. outsiders, "the privileged old guard versus the disadvantaged young guard,… Salafists vs. modernists" and "entrenched military/crony elites … [vs.] … the masses." The future was at best uncertain, and Friedman noted that the international community would not be around to help: "There will be no impartial outside midwife to guide the transitions." This was an argument that he would restate in a number of articles that followed (Friedman, 2011, Nov. 27, p. 11).

The final *New York Times* editorial in 2011 again rebuked Russia and China for obstructing action by the Security Council and stressed the need for sanctions to be applied by the US, Europe, and the Arab League. The editorial reiterated that "Mr. Assad has left no doubt that he is willing to destroy his country to maintain his hold on power" (*NYT*, 2011, Dec. 23, p. 30).

The Guardian's Opinion Narrative

The Guardian's 2011 opinion narrative began with a business-like analysis of what the future held for Syria's president in the context of the unfolding Arab Spring. In so doing, the newspaper pessimistically predicted that Assad would not be able to head off more bloodshed even if he accepted a package of political reforms.

Shortly after the protests began, veteran journalist and author David Hirst predicted that the "51-year-old 'republican monarchy' looked the next most logically in line of candidates to succumb to the Arab uprising." While Assad proclaimed that his regime was "stable,… the people want the overthrow of the regime." Hirst pointed to "the weaknesses and divergences of the traditional Syrian opposition," and these, along with an army and police that were predicted to "never abandon the political leadership as they did in Egypt and Tunisia," led him to suggest that Syria's uprising "will be more like Libya's" (Hirst, 2011, Mar. 22, p. 36). *The Guardian's* first editorial also focused on the Arab Spring connection, arguing that "its momentum [is] unstoppable [and] its consequences will be neither uniform nor predictable." However, for Assad, the future did not look good. His anti-American stance would not be enough to buy him "insurance against some of the issues his people have with him and his family: political repression and crony capitalism" (*Guardian*, 2011, Mar. 23, p. 34).

By the end of March, a second editorial suggested that Assad, in a speech delivered to the Syrian Parliament, had "missed his moment" by not offering a program of political reforms in response to the protests. The editorial pointed out, however, that Assad did have some positives to build on: closeness in age to the protestors and foreign policies that enjoyed some support. As well, it was noted that "the regime does offer some protection to minorities, Kurds excepted." It was now clearly up to the Syrian president to do something beyond repression: "If he wants to be seen a part of the solution and not as part of the problem, he will soon have to offer the detailed, convincing measures he signally failed to produce yesterday." The title of the editorial captured its overall argument: "Syria—A Lost Opportunity" (*Guardian*, 2011, Mar. 31, p. 34).

On March 30, Rana Kabbani, a Syrian writer and broadcaster living in the UK, wrote a scathing opinion piece in *The Guardian* on the Assad regime, characterizing it as a "Totalitarian State." She argued that the regime was seen by "many Syrians as an internal colonialism that ... has robbed them and bombed them and impeded them from joining the free peoples of the world." She wrote at length about the brutal nature of the regime, which she referred to as "a vindictive family mafia, monopolising business and power with the crudest of propaganda machines and the most lethal of security services." At the same time, she referred to the Syrian protestors in positive terms: "Syrians have come out en masse to demand rights they have been denied for so long ... [claiming] ... they are resolved to change their country for the better, whatever it may take" (Kabbani, 2011, Mar. 30, p. 30).

In another article on the same day, Haytham Manna, a Syrian scholar, human rights activist and leader of one of the main secular oppositions groups, not surprisingly adopted a decidedly pro-opposition position, along with clear optimism for

> a democratic future for Syria: Youth are demanding a new politics that ushers in a genuine democracy,... the tide of democratic change had become irreversible,... [and] ... the future can only be better than the past." He argued that there was still time for reform to work, but that if the regime did not change, it was "going to be changed." (Manna, 2011, Mar. 31, p. 31)

In mid-April Patrick Seale, a leading Western scholar on Syria, wrote an extensive piece examining the geopolitical implications of an overthrow of the Assad regime. His argument was that regime change in Damascus would have far-reaching consequences for its neighbours as well as for the general balance of power in the region. Iran, Hezbollah, and Hamas were placed among the losers, while Israel could see either advantages or disadvantages depending on what kind of government replaced Assad's. As for Turkey, it would "continue to cultivate its friendship with Syria whatever the nature of its regime." Seale pointed out that demands of protesters had escalated from political reforms to "a change of regime," and he agreed with *The Guardian*'s editorial board that Assad had "missed a historic opportunity to assert his leadership and pull things back from the brink" (Seale, 2011, Apr. 12, p. 28).

At the end of April, Professor Salwa Ismail of the School of Oriental and African Studies added another key piece of the Syrian conflict to *The Guardian*'s opinion narrative—that being sectarianism—and she did so in an unusual way. Ismail challenged the widespread idea that the Syrian regime unduly privileged Alawi (comprising 12 per cent of the population), claiming that "in fact Alawis neither rule nor benefit, as a group, from the regime." Rather, she argued that they, like most Syrians, "remain economically disadvantaged." Her main argument was that "the regime is raising the threat of sectarianism ... [and using it] ... to counter the opposition." She pointed out the danger that "the regime, in desperation to hold on to power, will seek to turn its warnings of sectarian conflict into reality" (Ismail, 2011, Apr. 29, p. 36).

A *Guardian* editorial on April 21 brought the first mention of possible international involvement in Syria, and it recommended restraint. Advice offered by those who counselled "that fomenting dissent in Syria is a risk worth taking," was not seen as helpful; in fact, it was described "as folly in any part of the Middle East, but particularly for a country with Syria's borders." The editorial ended with the observation that not only had foreign intervention not nurtured the Arab Spring, it threatened to kill it (*Guardian*, 2011, Apr. 21, p. 40). A week later, an opinion piece by well-known media commentator Tariq Ali endorsed the anti-intervention position, arguing that no one among Syria's opposition "wants western military intervention. They don't want a repeat of Iraq or Libya." Moreover, he maintained that "the opposition is not under the control of Islamists. It is a broad coalition that includes every social layer apart from the capitalist class that remains loyal to the regime." Ali commented as well that "the Israelis and the US would prefer Assad to stay ... but the dice are still in the air" (Ali, 2011, Apr. 30, p. 36).

Further on the international side, a May editorial focused on a "singularly unconvincing" speech given by President Obama. He had declared the status quo in Syria to be "untenable ... [but] ... many aspects of his policy maintain it." The editorial's conclusion was that "the US is not on the side of reform if to be so conflicts with a core strategic value" (*Guardian*, 2011, May 20, p. 36).

Sorbonne University professor Burhan Ghalioun, who in August 2011 would be named the head of the Syrian opposition Transitional National Council, contributed another harsh condemnation of the Assad regime. The article also addressed the issue of a possible international response quite differently than had earlier contributions. First, it emphasized the opposition's "intention to persist in their struggle until they achieve their demands for freedom— whatever the cost" and then went on to argue that the Syrian government "is wagering on a weak international stance," in part because of Russian and Chinese opposition to any action by the UN Security Council. Ghalioun held out hope that Assad had placed the wrong bet. In language suggestive of the spirit of R2P, he maintained that "the regime must be awakened to the fact that the international community will no longer allow a ruling junta to wreak havoc on its people without having to bear responsibility for its actions before the international system" (Ghalioun, 2011, May 31, p. 28). A few days later an editorial also struck an R2P chord by noting that "pressure is growing on the UN to hold Assad and key members of the security apparatus accountable for crimes against humanity." As well, Syrian dissidents were proposing "a UN Security Council resolution, similar to the one passed on Libya, which would allow an investigation by the International Criminal Court" (*Guardian*, 2011, June 2, p. 32).

The issue of international intervention was again addressed in a June 13 editorial that took issue with a long-held Western assumption that "better a Middle Eastern strongman than Middle Eastern anarchy." First, there was a real question as to how strong President Assad actually was. Beyond that issue, the crisis was seen as moving past Syria's borders, and, to date, the world's response had been less than adequate. The editorial also noted the consequences for "having pretended that Assad was somebody else's problem." In spite of this, the piece argued that while the mere threat of repressive violence by Muammar Qaddafi had been enough to "unleash NATO's firepower," in the face of a far more dire situation in Syria, "*military action is not realistic.*" In the end the editorial demanded the application of a "full range of diplomatic, financial and legal sanctions" that were being held up in the Security Council by Russian and Chinese obstructionism (*Guardian*, 2011, June 13, p. 26; italics added).

Author and journalist Robin Yassin-Kassab reviewed Assad's performance in dealing with the crisis and graded it a clear failure, claiming that prior to the protests Assad "may well have won" an election; however, his brutal response to protests, which initially "didn't aim for regime change,… destroyed the regime's legitimacy." Unfortunately, "the chances of the regime's bowing out gracefully are close to zero." While some sort of Turkish intervention was seen as possible, "Western intervention [was] improbable. NATO is overstretched and a Syrian adventure requires a commitment to potential regional war—and—wouldn't be welcomed by Syrians anyway." The author agreed with Professor Ismail on the impact of sectarian cleavages, predicting that "sectarian war appears unlikely" (Yassin-Kassab, 2011, June 17, p. 36). An editorial a few days later likewise saw the Syrian situation as beyond repair, as the opposition had indicated that "a point of no return has been reached." As for Assad, he "can still inflame passions, but no longer has the ability to quench them" (*Guardian*, 2011, June 21, p. 30).

An editorial written about four months into the uprising argued that the Assad regime had miscalculated badly in its response to calls for reform and by so doing had hardened these into calls for his overthrow. The case of the protests in the city of Hama and their repression was reviewed in detail; the result was that "from now on … there will be no talks. The regime, they say, must go." The editorial claimed that Assad "has lost even the bare minimum, the sullen acquiescence of his people, to govern." However, it also acknowledged that the opposition did not have the institutional or structural pieces in place to replace Assad and govern Syria and that, should his regime fail, these "would have to be built from the bottom up … [and] … done in an atmosphere of sectarian mistrust" (*Guardian*, 2011, Aug. 2, p. 28).

Two days later Ali al-Bayanouni, former head of the Muslim Brotherhood in Syria, also set out to refute the claim that Syria suffered from sectarian tensions, a position put forth, he argued, by the Assad regime and unfortunately believed by the international community: "The international community's mute response implies that there are some who see as credible … [Assad's] … claim that he is defending the country from 'sectarian divisions.'" Bayanouni maintained that "the time has come to reject this myth. Like his father, Hafez, before him, Assad has violated the rights of all Syrians, regardless of religious or sectarian identities." He also dismissed the notion that Syria would fall apart if Assad were removed: "The fear that Syria will descend into chaos if the regime falls is unjustified." Bayanouni went on to argue that it was time for the international community to say "that Assad's regime has lost all legitimacy. That is what the Syrians want—no more and no less." He then put forth a plan that called for an international conference to be convened that would enable "Syrians to develop a collective national alternative." He predicted that once Assad departed, the Syrian opposition and all Syrians "would rally round a civil, plural state based on power sharing, free elections and a modern civil constitution in which all citizens—men and women—are equal. This is what the Syrians want, and what they are on course to achieve" (Al-Bayanouni, 2011, Aug. 4, p. 30).

The Guardian's first editorial to focus on regional power dynamics, including the strategic competition between Saudi Arabia and Iran and long-standing tensions between the Saudis and the Syrians, was occasioned by a speech by Saudi Arabia's King Abdullah that was critical of Syria's ruler. The editorial noted that "the King's public condemnation went beyond the discreet tones in which the oil-rich kingdom normally conducts its business … [and warned that] … Syria risks isolation in the Arab world." The uprisings were spreading, and with regional powers openly condemning the regime, this confirmed that the Assad government was in trouble. The increasingly open Saudi (and its Arab allies) criticism of Assad was a clear sign of their support for the opposition and how they viewed Syria in the wider regional power struggle (*Guardian*, 2011, Aug. 9, p. 28).

A second article written by Rana Kabbani presented another strong case against the regime, laying out both its historic and current brutality. In addition to wishing to show the regime's vicious nature, she attempted to counter the notion that the regime was fighting a sectarian war against salafi fighters or, as she put it, the "salafi bogeymen." Rather, she argued that regime propaganda to this effect was simply untrue and that "every single minority and ethnicity across Syria has risen in revolt, repelled by the war crimes it has been witness to." She concluded by predicting that the end of the regime was near and that the country would be a better place (Kabbani, 2011, Aug 10, p. 26).

An editorial on August 19 observed that the international community, led by the US and Europe, had given up on Assad, claiming that "he is too sullied and compromised to be part of any solution in Syria." It further maintained that Assad's policy of "crackdown first, top-down reform later was never a viable option." Room was left for a compromise with the regime—one, however, that included the removal of Assad. It was hoped that "elements of the regime will have the common sense to realize that the only way out of the impasse, and the only chance of even a qualified fresh start, is to shed the leader identified with policies which may have achieved momentary physical control but have irrevocably alienated large parts of the population" (*Guardian*, 2011, Aug. 19, p. 30).

In an article at the very end of August, *Guardian* executive editor Jonathan Freedland reviewed possible roles for the international community in the conflict. The article was supportive of the opposition ("impossibly courageous people continu[ing] to brave bullets and rocket-propelled grenades, as they work to topple the pitiless Assad regime") and highly critical of the Assad government. Its main focus, however, was on the question of military intervention and whether there was a middle ground between what was described as "a crude binary choice: either we bomb the hell out of a wicked despot or we do nothing." He argued that "that dichotomy might be false. A further range of options might be available." As to what these options might be, he cited the advice of British diplomat Carne Ross: "Rather than waiting for an uprising to begin,… outsiders could embark on any combination of these three steps, depending on the circumstances: 'Boycott, Isolate, Sabotage.'" He noted that Syria was "no cold, academic inquiry. Lives are at stake. Even if there is to be no military help for the people of Syria, that does not mean we have to do nothing. We can act—and we surely must" (Freedland, 2011, Aug. 31, p. 27).

A member of the Coalition of Free Damascenes for Peaceful Change (writing under the pseudonym Abdur Rahman al Shami) reported that while the

Syrian opposition was reconsidering its rejection of foreign intervention, it was still opposed to Western intervention. What was needed was a regional intervention; specifically "an Arab-Turkish pre-emptive force to protect the people in Syria.... It could preserve the unity of the country and prevent chaos and violence" (Al Shami, 2011, Sept. 1, p. 31).

Later in September, journalist George Monbiot addressed the role of international sanctions in overturning the Assad regime and reviewed both their positives and negatives. There was little doubt that foreign companies were "enriching a government that is violently repressing peaceful protest," but Monbiot noted that the Syrian people were divided on the issue of sanctions. He laid out the respective arguments, pro and con; however, in light of the complexities surrounding the issue, he did not endorse one position over the other (Monbiot, 2011, Sept. 20, p. 31).

In early October, foreign affairs columnist Simon Tisdall registered his dissatisfaction with President Obama's policy on Syria: "[He] talked the good fight from the sidelines," with the result that he was ignored in Damascus while "a fracturing Syria accelerates towards the abyss" (Tisdall, 2011, Oct. 4, p. 28). Long-time journalist David Hearst focused his criticism on the international community more broadly, charging that, for different reasons, Iran, Saudi Arabia, Israel, and the United States were not committed to the success of the Arab Spring, which signalled the emergence of democracy in the region. He charged that "between them, they could kill off the Arab spring, just as its first fragile shoots are beginning to poke through" (Hearst, 2011, Oct. 14, p. 41).

The Guardian's November 1 editorial confirmed that Syria was indeed engulfed in a civil war and maintained that President Assad was "in denial." The editorial made two additional points: (1) that the outcome in Syria had far-reaching regional implications (at minimum, "Lebanon, Iraq and Iran would all be shaken to the core if the majority Sunnis in Syria returned to the ascendency"); and (2) that international intervention, specifically a no-fly zone, was not a good option: "As we are all now witnessing in Libya, a no-fly zone does not protect civilian lives.... Nor is its aim to force dictators to negotiate. As UN mandates have been interpreted [in Libya] no-fly zones are a cover for regime change." The solution to the crisis was a realization on the part of Assad that he was finished "and that his only hope for survival is to agree to a transitional government and free elections" (*Guardian,* 2011, Nov. 1, p. 32).

In a November 5 opinion piece, director of Conflicts Forum Alastair Crooke took aim at the Western strategy of supporting Sunni extremists in order to weaken the Iranian/Hezbollah/Syrian axis that was seen as the major challenge to Western hegemony in the region. Citing the consequences of earlier support for the mujahedeen in Afghanistan, Crooke warned of the danger involved: "the fruits of this new attempt to use radical forces for western ends will yet again backfire … [because] … the radical armed elements used in Syria as auxiliaries to depose Assad may well have a bloody and very undemocratic agenda of their own" (Crooke, 2011, Nov. 5, p. 42).

Jonathan Steele, *The Guardian's* former chief foreign correspondent, criticized the Arab League, and its Gulf State members in particular, for taking sides in Syria, which he described as "on the verge of civil war." In the face of fears of sectarian violence, Steele proposed a solution that offered the Assad family "amnesty," while introducing "a democratic transition that would include guarantees of status and protection for all minorities, including the Alawites from whom the ruling elite comes." He offered the power-sharing agreement that ended the Lebanese civil war in 1990 as an example of what might work if the international community, Saudi Arabia in particular, adopted a mediatory role (Steele, 2011, Nov. 18, p. 47). An editorial in mid-December, on the other hand, pointed to a radically different example of what the future might hold for Syria: "It could be Iraq in 2006" (*The Guardian,* 2011, Dec. 14, p. 32).

The final *Guardian* editorial in 2011 proved to be prescient in its assessment of where Syria fit within the wider Arab Spring, a movement that was described as "at a crossroads":

> If [Assad's] blood-stained regime falls, and the country stays in one piece and avoids a sectarian civil war, there is nothing to stop the revolution from moving onwards and eastwards…. But if Syria disintegrates, it would quickly become a regional battlefield, fed by the rival interests of its neighbours…. And then the Arab spring would well and truly have come to a halt. (*Guardian,* 2011, Dec. 24, p. 36)

Especially pertinent to future developments for the region was the report that "jihadi websites in Anbar province, in neighbouring Iraq, have been full of calls to go to the rescue of the Sunni brothers in Syria…. Parts of Iraq which are moving out of control of the dictatorial Shia-dominated government in Baghdad could easily form a human reservoir for the conflict in Syria" (*Guardian,* 2011, Dec. 24, p. 36).

The Globe and Mail's Opinion Narrative

During the first month of the protests in Syria, a *Globe and Mail* editorial pointed the finger at Iran as the likely culprit in preventing President Assad from adding political reforms to some economic ones he had already enacted. Whatever the case, political reform was seen as long overdue for a regime holding "the world's record for the longest state of emergency"—48 years and running. Dismissing Assad's claims of a Western conspiracy to be at the root of the unrest, the editorial argued that "the Syrian authorities brought the protests on themselves." With "the Soviet-style entrenchment of the leading role of the

Baath Party," Syria was portrayed as far from a democracy (*Globe*, 2011, Mar. 31, p. 22). The vicious nature of the Syrian government was stressed in a second editorial that claimed that "a regime that fires on unarmed mourners ... is sending a message that it will stop at nothing to hold power and rule as it sees fit" (*Globe*, 2011, Apr, 25, p. 10).

In that "the stage appear[ed] set for a prolonged conflict with escalating bloodshed," *The Globe's* editorial board deemed the situation appropriate for the "invocation of the responsibility-to-protect doctrine." The board saw, however, serious complications in implementing this. In that "the West is tied up in Libya," the UN had no "plausible means to apply that principle ... [and] ... no clear way forward" (*Globe*, 2011, Apr, 25, p. 10). Another editorial picked up on the connection to concurrent events in Libya, arguing that the UN/NATO military operation there was "undermining ... the international community's attempts to respond to the bloodshed and repression in Syria." This editorial claimed that NATO's "overstretched interpretation—and application" of the Security Council's resolution on the use of force in Libya left Russia, among others, skeptical of approving a similar resolution for Syria. It suggested that the "mission creep" in Libya needed to be reversed by enforcing "a no-fly zone as originally planned" (*Globe*, 2011, June 21, p. 16). Lloyd Axworthy, University of Winnipeg president and former minister of External Affairs, suggested that the West had "more tools at our disposal than just the NATO-type intervention that's taking place in Libya," with one of these being the International Criminal Court (ICC). Specifically, Axworthy called upon the UN Security Council to "direct the ICC to investigate whether Mr. al-Assad is guilty of crimes against humanity as a result of his government's violent crackdown against civilians peacefully calling for democratic reform" (Axworthy, 2011, July 7, p. 17).[2]

Yet another editorial attempted to explain the failure of the Security Council to address the Syrian situation under the R2P doctrine. While national interests might explain the reluctance to act on the part of Russia and China, the emerging democracies (India, Brazil, and South Africa) were singled out for failing "to condemn violence against demonstrators for democracy" (*Globe*, 2011, Aug. 4, p. 14). University of Waterloo professor Bessma Momani pointed out that even if the Security Council did authorize an intervention, the reality was "that few of the cash-strapped Western nations are apt to finance or support another NATO military intervention" (Momani, 2011, p. 15). An end-of-August editorial also conceded that "the NATO nations that took part in the Libyan intervention ... have no appetite for another such mission so soon." Nor, it noted, should they, as the "circumstances and terrain" in Syria differed widely from those in Libya (*Globe*, 2011, Aug. 29, p. 10).

Momani, along with fellow academic Heather Roff, explained in detail the nature of these differences: a significantly larger population (only 40 per cent of which was seen as opposing Assad); a far larger and stronger military to engage (eight times the size of Qaddafi's); "no identifiable rebel group occupying and controlling territory"; the location of Syria's population ("tucked in or along-side mountainous terrain, complicating any tactical strategy"); and a location farther away from NATO's European bases (which had been used effectively in the bombing of Libya). While the Syrian president's tactics constituted "a clear violation of human rights," the authors concluded that ending the repression would be difficult "without putting boots on the ground." The stark reality was that "unless Western powers … are prepared for an on-the-ground invasion, we will continue to merely deplore what the Syrian regime is doing against its own people" (Roff & Momani, 2011, Oct. 25, p. 17). In spite of these serious problems, Lloyd Axworthy had not given up on R2P, arguing that following Libya, "the next serious step is to find the means to end the tyrant Bashar al-Assad's bloodshed in Syria" (Axworthy, 2011, Aug. 23, p. 22). In the one opinion article that addressed a possible Canadian response, former Canadian diplomat Paul Heinbecker made it clear that a Security Council authorization would be needed prior to any Canadian action (Heinbecker, 2011, Nov. 22, p. 15).

For *The Globe and Mail,* not only was an R2P-type military response unlikely, the sectarian fragmentation of Syria's population did not bode well for a peaceful outcome to the conflict. Lebanon-based journalist Rami Khouri explained the seriousness of the Syrian situation: Assad's brutal attacks on the city of Homs "seemed designed to inflame the destructive passions between the majority Sunnis and the minority Alawites who dominate the ruling elite." Khouri argued that sectarianism was the default mechanism of self-defence in poorly governed societies: "Stable societies that are neither democratic nor economically and socially productive are decaying societies that end up being machines of mass corruption and dehumanization, which inevitably pushes citizens to seek refuge in their sect or tribe" (Khouri, 2011, July 26, p. 13). Former Canadian diplomat Michael Bell reviewed three possible outcomes to the Syrian situation—(1) the survival of the Assad regime (seen as most likely),[3] (2) a victory by the opposition, or (3) the breakup of Syria into "a series of contesting micro-states"—but, whatever the outcome, he foresaw "no happy ending." The reality was that "Syria's population is highly fragmented along ethno-religious lines"—Alawi, Druze, Kurds, and Christians, along with the dominant Sunni—with each possible outcome affecting the power relationships among these groups. While Bell cautioned that "it would be simplistic to argue that ethnicity rules all,… the power of identity and narrative should never be underestimated in the Middle East" (Bell, 2011, Aug. 12, p. 13).

Two additional themes that ran throughout *The Globe's* first-year opinion narrative were confidence in the efficacy of sanctions and the power of example.

Sanctions needed to be imposed both by the West (Kingston, 2011, June 23) and the Arab League (Khouri, 2011, Nov. 16; *Globe*, 2011, Nov. 29). With respect to positive examples, Turkey was singled out as a model of secular democracy toward which Syria should aspire (*Globe*, 2011, Apr. 25), while Egypt was held up as an example for Syria's military to follow in dealing with protesters (*Globe*, 2011, Nov. 17).

DISCUSSION

The initial *New York Times* 2011 opinion narrative presented background material on President Assad, on the complexity of the domestic situation, on how Syria fit into the wider Arab Spring phenomenon (Egypt and Libya, in particular), and on the possible impact of a regime change on Syria's neighbours. Both optimistic and pessimistic scenarios were presented; in the first months that Assad might navigate the country toward reform, especially if he were pushed in that direction, certainly appeared to have been possible.

By early June, however, the possibility of reforming the regime had ceased to be a viable option and was replaced by continuing calls for tough and meaningful sanctions to be imposed by a host of actors: the UN Security Council, the US, the EU, Turkey, and the Arab League. Russia and China (often linked in the same sentence) were singled out for criticism for their blockage of Security Council action. Throughout the remainder of the year, Assad's removal, rather than his reformation, became a focus of the newspaper's opinion material. His removal, however, was not to be accomplished by international military intervention, which was never considered a possibility, not even by columnist Nicholas Kristof, who, some eight years earlier, had been a tireless advocate of such action in Darfur. Rather, Assad's removal would come about through increasingly severe sanctions imposed on the domestic groups that were supporting the president, especially the military and the business community.

It was evident that, if not contained, the Syrian conflict had the possibility of disrupting the entire region. Moreover, while such events would likely not be favourable to US interests, in that a military intervention was not an option, the Western super power was portrayed as having limited means to affect events on the ground. In such circumstances, the US needed to mobilize the international community to impose strong sanctions to force Assad from power, although what was to follow his removal was far from clear.

With respect to *The Guardian's* opinion narrative, our first observation is that many opinion pieces were written by political activists and academics associated with the Syrian opposition, including both secular and religious (i.e., Muslim Brotherhood) contributors. In light of this, it is hardly surprising that virtually all editorials and opinion articles were highly critical of Assad and, dare we say, overly optimistic with respect to democracy taking hold in Syria under the auspices of Assad's opposition. There was also a clear attempt to counter the fear of sectarian warfare, which tended to be dismissed as regime propaganda designed to portray Assad as the country's only possible saviour from that grim eventuality. However, as time passed, opinion material began to acknowledge the probability that if the war continued, sectarian conflict did indeed lay in Syria's future and that creative solutions were needed to prevent this from happening. Also, opinion material noted that regional instability was a likely outcome of prolonged conflict in Syria. Perhaps most importantly, virtually all opinion material offered during the first nine months of the conflict, for a number of different reasons, argued strongly against direct Western military intervention in the conflict.

Of the three newspapers studied, *The Globe and Mail* was the only one that initially argued that the situation in Syria called for a Libya-type, R2P military intervention by the international community. However, the overextension of the UN's Libyan mandate by NATO made this impossible because Russian and Chinese vetoes in the UN Security Council would assure that there would be no authorization for similar international action in Syria. Also contributing to the problems entailed in any intervention was the high degree of Syria's ethnic and religious fragmentation, and the extension of these cleavages into regional geopolitics focused on the role of Iran. These realities pointed to a situation where even an intolerable Assad might look reasonable when compared to his possible successors. In any event, the country faced a number of negative outcomes.

In the final six months of 2011, *The Globe*'s opinion attention to the Iranian connection faded, and while the misdeeds of Mr. Assad continued to be documented, these were not highlighted to the extent they had been earlier. What did continue to receive major attention, however, were the problems associated with any international response under the R2P doctrine. Indeed, both editorials and opinion pieces made it clear that a Libya-type intervention was highly unlikely in Syria and that if one occurred, it would not enjoy the swift success seen in the overthrow of Colonel Qaddafi. In spite of this, some hope was expressed that the imposition of sanctions (by the West and the Arab League) along with the examples set by Turkey (by way of a model of secular democracy) and Egypt (by way of the behaviour of its military and security forces in the removal of President Mubarak) would prove helpful in resolving the Syrian conflict.

CHAPTER 5

Conflict Framing in 2012

INTRODUCTION

In 2012 the following themes figured prominently in the opinion pages of our three selected newspapers:

- The increased regionalization of the civil war as Syria's neighbours became involved by supporting both sides
- The growing concern that among Assad's opponents lurked various "extremist" elements, some of which were linked to al-Qaeda
- The urgent need for a diplomatic settlement, with or without Assad, stressing the importance of Russian leadership
- The possibility of Western intervention in the war in the form of "no-fly zones" or what were referred to as "humanitarian corridors."

By the beginning of 2012, the realization had set in that Syria was indeed caught up in a civil war. Moreover, that Syria's neighbours were actively supporting both sides was the issue that dominated opinion commentary. In assessing the impact of this outside involvement, the West could hardly feel reassured as Hezbollah (the Lebanese Shia militia, supported by Iran) had forces in the field helping Assad's army while, perhaps even more troubling, Sunni extremist groups (including an offshoot of al-Qaeda supported by Saudi Arabia, Qatar, and other Arab states) were increasingly appearing in the ranks of Assad's opposition. This of course aggravated the sectarian cleavages within Syria, which had been downplayed in 2011 by *Guardian* commentators in particular.

The character of the opposition, and the kind of government it might establish should it prevail, had also become a major issue of concern. As a result, there was some rethinking among "Assad must go" advocates: a number argued that to avoid a post-2003-Iraq type of power vacuum, a negotiated settlement would have to include the Syrian president; others favoured a "Yemeni solution"—that is, getting rid of Assad while keeping parts of his regime in place.

In terms of resolving the conflict, 2012 saw a vigorous debate regarding the utility of positive and negative diplomacy. On the hopeful side, Russia's Vladimir Putin was seen as the key to any negotiated settlement, and an Arab League observer mission and peace plans associated with Kofi Annan and Lakhdar Brahimi were also seen as helpful. Others placed more faith in the application of strong and effective sanctions. Various strategies of intervention on the part of the international community were also debated; most prominent were arming the opposition and imposing no-fly zones or creating humanitarian corridors to protect fleeing refugees. Importantly, direct military intervention was still not seen as a viable option. This was at least partially attributed to war weariness in the West, although Syria's stock of chemical weapons was identified as a potential problem that might force the international community to engage the in conflict more directly.

QUANTITATIVE FINDINGS

While in 2012 Syria's domestic combatants continued to dominate opinion-leading material, data in Table 5.1 also point to a greater focus on both global and regional actors in the conflict. Although reduced from the extraordinarily high attention it received in 2011, the Syrian government continued to elicit the most commentary of all actors (80 per cent), followed by the Syrian opposition (56 per cent), which remained the special focus of *Guardian* commentary (75 per cent).

Opinion material in *The New York Times* remained focused on the role of the US (62 per cent) and showed significantly increased attention to Russia (50 per cent) and to the international community (33 per cent). *The Guardian* material also showed increased attention to the role of the US (48 per cent) and especially to that of Russia (51 per cent). It also led in commentary on the UN (36 per cent), Britain (26 per cent), the Arab League (20 per cent), and Israel (12 per cent). *The Globe and Mail* led all papers in opinion commentary on Iran and Canada (both at 30 per cent), Turkey (26 per cent), the UN Security Council and NATO (both at 22 per cent), and Hezbollah (11 per cent). Overall, increased attention to the role of Russia was by far the most important development—up by 32 per cent from the initial year of the conflict. From 2011 to 2012, overall attention paid to the US increased by 13 per cent; to Saudi Arabia, 11 per cent; and to Iran, 10 per cent.

Data in Table 5.2 show that in 2012, while opinion material overall remained strongly critical of the Syrian government (70 per cent), the percentage of negative material had decreased by 16 per cent from 2011. With respect to Assad's opponents, overall 20 per cent of content was negative—an increase of 17 per cent from 2011; at the same time, positive assessments of

Table 5.1 Salience of Domestic Combatants, Major Global and Regional Actors, 2012, by Newspaper (Per Cent of Opinion-Leading Items)

	Times N=52	Guardian N=61	Globe N=27	Total N=140
Domestic Combatants				
Syrian government*	88.5	78.7	66.7	80.0
Syrian opposition	48.1	75.4	29.6	56.4
Global Actors				
US*	61.5	47.5	33.3	50.0
Russia*	50.0	50.8	44.4	49.3
UN (General)	13.5	36.1	11.1	22.9
International community	32.7	3.3	29.6	19.3
NATO	11.5	14.8	22.2	15.0
Britain*	3.8	26.2	11.1	15.0
UN (Security Council)	9.6	14.8	22.2	14.3
Canada*	0	0	29.6	5.7
Regional Actors				
Iran	17.3	29.5	29.6	25.0
Saudi Arabia	9.6	37.7	14.8	22.9
Turkey	15.4	19.7	25.9	19.3
Arab League	13.5	19.7	3.7	14.3
Israel	3.8	11.5	7.4	7.9
Hezbollah	3.8	1.6	11.1	4.3

* Includes references to respective leaders: Presidents al-Assad, Obama, and Putin; Prime Ministers Cameron and Harper.

the opposition fell by 20 per cent (to 14 per cent). Particularly significant for *The Guardian*, positive commentary fell by 35 per cent while negative commentary increased by nearly an equal amount (34 per cent). Overall, this led to a dramatic reversal of the percentage difference for Syria's opposition: it had been plus 31 per cent in 2011—it was –6 per cent in 2012.

On the international side, material in *The Times* continued to be supportive of US actions, or lack thereof (31 per cent), while *The Guardian* criticized US policy in 34 per cent of its opinion content; it was also critical of British actions in 23 per cent of its items. *The Times* featured the most material critical of Russia (35 per cent), followed by *The Globe* (26 per cent) and *The Guardian* (20 per cent); overall, opinion material critical of Russia increased by 14 per cent from 2011 to 2012. Regionally, Saudi Arabia was on the receiving end of 30 per cent of *Guardian* negative commentary; and Turkey 15 per cent. In

Table 5.2 Evaluation of Domestic Combatants, Major Global and Regional Actors, 2012, by Newspaper (Per Cent of Opinion-Leading Items—Ambiguous Items Omitted)

	Times N=52		Guardian N=61		Globe N=27		Total N=140		Percentage Difference
	Pos	Neg	Pos	Neg	Pos	Neg	Pos	Neg	
Domestic Combatants									
Syrian government*	3.8	76.9	1.6	67.2	0	0.63	2.1	70.0	−67.9
Syrian opposition	13.5	7.7	16.4	39.3	11.1	0	14.3	20.0	−5.7
Global Actors									
US*	30.8	9.6	4.9	34.4	11.1	7.4	15.7	20.0	−4.3
Russia*	3.8	34.6	14.8	19.7	7.4	25.9	9.3	26.4	−17.1
UN (general reference)	3.8	3.8	27.9	3.3	3.7	3.7	14.3	3.6	+10.7
International community	9.6	3.8	1.6	1.6	0	11.1	4.3	4.3	0
NATO	7.7	0	4.9	9.8	7.4	7.4	6.4	5.7	+0.7
Britain*	1.9	0	1.6	23.0	7.4	3.7	2.9	10.7	−7.8
UN (Security Council)	1.9	1.9	1.6	11.5	0	7.4	1.4	7.1	−5.7
Canada*	0	0	0	0	7.4	3.7	1.4	0.7	+0.7
Regional Actors									
Iran	0	11.5	4.9	9.8	0	11.1	2.1	10.7	−8.6
Saudi Arabia	1.9	3.8	1.6	29.5	3.7	0	2.1	14.3	−12.2
Turkey	9.6	1.9	3.3	14.8	22.2	0	9.3	7.1	+2.2
Arab League	9.6	0	13.1	3.3	0	3.7	8.6	2.1	+6.5
Israel	1.9	0	3.3	4.9	0	0	2.1	2.1	0
Hezbollah	0	3.8	0	1.6	0	3.7	0	2.9	−2.9

*Includes references to respective leaders: Presidents al-Assad, Obama, and Putin; Prime Ministers Cameron and Harper.

contrast, material looked favourably on the actions of the UN (in general) in 28 per cent and on those of the Arab League in 13 per cent of material. *The Globe* led all papers in positive commentary on Turkey (22 per cent).

With the exception of opinion content in *The Times,* which reflected some hope for the success of a no-fly zone (14 per cent), data on conflict-ending strategies shown in Table 5.3 reveal greater pessimism than was shown in 2011. Especially notable is the shift in assessments on whether diplomacy might be successful—in 2011, 22 per cent of material was optimistic vs. 9 per cent pessimistic, while in 2012, 11 per cent was optimistic vs. 26 per cent pessimistic: overall the percentage difference flipped from plus 13 per cent in 2011 to −15

Table 5.3   Optimism vs. Pessimism toward Conflict-Ending Strategies, 2012, by Newspaper (Per Cent of Opinion-Leading Items—Ambiguous Items Omitted)

	Times N=52		Guardian N=61		Globe N=27		Total N=140		Percentage Difference
	Opt	Pess	Opt	Pess	Opt	Pess	Opt	Pess	
Strategies									
Diplomacy	11.5	11.5	9.6	36.1	14.8	33.3	11.4	26.4	–15.0
Arming the opposition	9.6	15.4	0	42.6	0	7.4	3.6	25.7	–22.1
Imposing a no-fly zone	13.5	5.8	1.6	6.6	7.4	11.1	7.1	7.1	0
Military action	0	13.5	1.6	41.0	0	18.5	0.7	26.4	-25.7

Table 5.4   Side Seen to Be Winning, 2012, by Newspaper (Per Cent of Opinion-Leading Items)

Times N=52			Guardian N=61			Globe N=27			Total N=140		
Gov't	Ambig	Oppos	Gov't	Ambig	Oppos	Gov't	Ambig	Oppos	Gov't	Ambig	Oppos
1.9	11.5	15.4	4.9	21.3	14.8	0	14.8	22.2	2.9	17.9	15.0

per cent in 2012. Arming the opposition and direct military action were seen as especially unhelpful in *Guardian* content (43 per cent and 41 per cent, respectively), while the idea of a no-fly zone was characterized as futile in 11 per cent of *Globe* material.

2012 was an optimistic year for the prospects of an opposition victory, as Table 5.4 shows that most material in both *The Globe* and *The Times* pointed to their likely victory over Assad's forces. *The Guardian* continued to reflect ambiguity, a position that overall enjoyed a 7 per cent advantage over an opposition win. As was the case in 2011, there was very little opinion anywhere that foresaw Assad and his government as emerging victorious.

Data in Table 5.5 point to contrasting trends. For *The Times* and *The Globe*, both pro- and anti-involvement framing increased from 2011. In *The Times*, opinion material favouring some sort of intervention increased by 14 per cent; and material opposed to involvement, by 13 per cent. Increases in *The Globe* were less substantial (6 per cent and 9 per cent, respectively). *The Guardian*, however, showed a slight decrease in material containing pro-international-involvement framing (5 per cent), combined with a robust 22 per cent increase in that counselling anti-involvement. Overall, from 2011 to 2012 there was

Table 5.5   The International Community "Should Do Something," 2012, by Newspaper (Per Cent of Opinion-Leading Items—Ambiguous Items Omitted)

Times N=52		Guardian N=61		Globe N=27		Total N=140		Percentage Difference
Pro	Anti	Pro	Anti	Pro	Anti	Pro	Anti	
17.3	23.1	3.3	39.3	11.1	18.5	10.0	29.3	–19.3

Table 5.6   Positive or Negative Outcomes for Democracy, 2012, by Newspaper (Per Cent of Opinion-Leading Items)

Times N=52			Guardian N=61			Globe N=27			Total N=140		
Pos	Ambig	Neg	Pos	Ambig	Neg	Pos	Ambig	Neg	Pos	Ambig	Neg
1.9	19.2	19.2	3.3	8.2	13.1	0	18.5	11.1	2.1	14.3	15.0

less media support for an international "will to intervene" than was initially the case: while pro-involvement framing increased by 4 per cent, that containing anti-involvement framing increased by 17 per cent. The percentage difference between pro- and anti-involvement framing stood at –19 per cent in 2012—it had been –7 per cent in 2011.

Data in Table 5.6 tell us that overall, while ambiguous assessments regarding Syria's future remained relatively constant from 2011 to 2012, there were changes in both positive and negative assessments. Positive assessments of outcomes fell in all newspapers by 11 per cent, while negative assessments rose by 1 per cent. In *Guardian* material, positive assessments fell by 14 per cent; in *Times* material, by 11 per cent; and in *Globe* material, by 5 per cent. Negative assessments increased by 2 per cent and 7 per cent for *The Times* and *The Guardian*, respectively, while they decreased by 3 per cent in *Globe* commentary. The net result was that in 2012 Syria's future looked bleaker, not brighter. In 2011 the overall percentage difference between positive and negative assessments had been –1 per cent—but in 2012 it stood at –13 per cent.

QUALITATIVE FINDINGS

The New York Times' Opinion Narrative

The New York Times began its 2012 opinion narrative by continuing to stress the same issues as were highlighted during the first nine months of the Syrian uprising. An editorial in mid-January argued that more needed to be done by the international community "to force Mr. Assad to stop the killing." While any compromise with the Syrian ruler was discouraged, neither were any easy solutions offered. However, "the international community needs to exert whatever diplomatic and economic pressure it can to make clear to Mr. Assad and his cronies that their time has run out" (*NYT*, 2012, Jan. 20, p. 26). A second editorial in early February continued to condemn Russia and China for blocking Security Council action on Syria, again pointing out that the cited reason for their vetoes (fears of a Libyan-type regime change mission) was specious. The editorial also repeated the argument that the key to ousting Assad was "to persuade army and business elites to abandon the government" (*NYT*, 2012, Feb. 2, p. 26).

University of Chicago Professor Robert Pape offered the first in-depth examination of "why the West does not intervene [in Syria] as it did in Libya last year" to *The Times* opinion narrative. The major difference centred on rebel control of territory. In Libya, "much of the coastal core of the population lived under rebel control." This allowed NATO to concentrate its operations effectively. In Syria, however, the opposition "has not achieved sustained control of any major population area." This negated the impact of Western air power, necessitating "a heavy ground campaign [that] would probably face stiff and bloody resistance." Pape acknowledged that "a mass-homicide campaign is under way [in Syria]. But a means to stop it without unacceptable loss of life is not yet available.... The main obstacle to intervention is the absence of a viable, low-casualty military solution" (Pape, 2012, Feb. 3, p. 25). Although the article focused on genocide and mass killing, international responses were analyzed in terms of *humanitarian intervention*, not specifically the *responsibility to protect* doctrine.

A series of editorial and opinion pieces focused on a possible shift in Russia's position on Syria. Thomas Friedman analyzed Vladimir Putin's relationship with Assad and found that there were good reasons for Putin to abandon Mr. Assad, who was described as "a dead man walking." For instance, the Syrian opposition might prove to be as good a customer for Russian arms as Assad had been. Nevertheless, Friedman remained skeptical that Putin would change course. He had reason to worry about creating precedents for international action to remove dictators, citing mission creep (seen in the application of the Libyan no-fly zone) as an example of what made him nervous (Friedman, 2012, Feb. 5, p. 11). An editorial two days later responded negatively to what was described as "growing talk in Washington ... of arming the Free Syrian Army." The editorial expressed fear that providing such arms would "make things worse. An all-out civil war would be even more damaging to civilians ... and increase the chances that the fight will spill over into the broader region or become a proxy war." The editorial went on to argue that Mr. Putin's image was being tarnished by "frequent public reminders of his responsibility for the killings" and that Russia needed to send the message to Damascus that "it is time for Mr. Assad to go" (*NYT*, 2012, Feb. 7, p. 30).

Efraim Halevy, former director of Israel's Mossad, discussed the role of Iran in the conflict, mainly in terms of Israeli security. His key argument was that regardless of the outcome, Iran's presence in Syria had to come to an end. On this point Halevy cited an interesting confluence of interests between the West and Russia—both had reasons to fear Iran. For Russia, "Iranian interventionism could wreak havoc in Muslim-majority areas to Russia's south," and the West (and of course Israel) had no reason to want Iran to have control of "long-range Syrian missiles with chemical warheads that can strike anywhere in Israel." Halevy suggested that the US should "offer Russia incentives to stop protecting the Assad regime" (Halevy, 2012, Feb. 8, p. 27). A mid-February editorial further pursued the idea of distancing Russia and China from Assad, also based on the need to contain the dangerous Iranian regime. For China, its need for oil could be used as leverage, and it was suggested that the statement by Saudi Arabia's King Abdullah that "'what happened at the United Nations ... [Russian and Chinese vetoes of a resolution calling for a peaceful transfer of power] ... is absolutely regrettable,'" seemed to have led to "China reconsidering its stance." The editorial suggested that "Beijing's shift could shame Moscow into reconsidering its support for Mr. Assad and approving United Nations action, including sanctions" (*NYT*, 2012, Feb. 15, p. 24).

Anne-Marie Slaughter, Princeton University professor and former director of policy planning at the US State Department, offered the first concrete plan for an international intervention in Syria that might involve military operations. She proposed the creation of "no-kill zones" close to the Turkish, Lebanese, and Jordanian borders, in order "to protect all Syrians regardless of creed, ethnicity or political allegiance." The "no-kill" (or "safe zones") would be set up by the Free Syrian Army, supported by "anti-tank, countersniper and portable antiaircraft weapons" supplied by Turkey, Lebanon, and Jordan, plus help from Special Forces from Turkey and Qatar and possibly "tactical and strategic advice" from Britain and France. Although the no-kill zone concept was focused on establishing a defensive capability, its ultimate goal was "to weaken and isolate government units charged with attacking particular towns; this would allow opposition forces to negotiate directly with army officers within each zone," a process seen as leading to "a regional, and ultimately national truce." Slaughter argued that "a lengthy civil war" was not in the best interest of the US and that, therefore, the US had "a major stake in helping Syria's neighbors stop the killing." However, she did not mention a specific US contribution in either establishing or maintaining the no-kill zones (Slaughter, 2012, Feb. 24, p. 27).

At the same time, Slaughter was opposed to "arming the opposition" because doing so would result in "the scenario the world should fear most: a proxy war that would spill into Lebanon, Turkey, Iraq and Jordan and fracture Syria along sectarian lines." She hoped that Russia and China could be persuaded "to abstain rather than exercise another massacre-enabling veto" in the Security Council (Slaughter, 2012, Feb. 24, p. 27). An editorial a day later called upon the US "to take a serious look at proposals by Turkey and others to create 'humanitarian corridors' linking besieged communities to neighboring countries or safe zones along those borders." The editorial pointed out, however, that "both would require air cover and would be risky." As for "arming the opposition," the editorial urged restraint: "At minimum, Washington and its allies should consider providing communications equipment, intelligence and military training" (*NYT*, 2012, Feb. 25, p. 18).

Toward the end of February, Thomas Friedman confirmed his earlier gloomy prognosis, not only regarding the outcome of the Syrian uprising but on the entire Arab Spring phenomenon. Comparing Eastern Europe to the Middle East, he argued that the former had a "recent liberal past ... [and a] ... compelling model ... for free-market democracy right next door." To the contrary, "most of the Arab world has neither, so when the iron rule of autocracy comes off, they fall back, not on liberalism, but Islamism, sectarianism, tribalism or military rule." Thus, Assad's strategy "was to push society to the brink ... confident that the threat of civil war would force citizens and outside players alike to agree on preserving the existing power structure as the only bulwark against collapse." He concluded with the hope that the Arab Spring would not end "with extremists going all the way and the moderates just going away" (Friedman, 2012, Feb. 29, p. 27).

On the cusp of the one-year anniversary of the uprising, a March editorial continued to emphasize past themes: the need for international pressure on Assad to leave, the need for Russia and China to stop supporting him, and the need for the US to use its "influence and coaching to help the opposition form a credible, multiethnic government, one that will respect all Syrians." At this point the US continued to be seen as "hav[ing] rightly ruled out military intervention" (*NYT*, 2012, Mar. 3, p. 18). *New York Times* columnist Bill Keller's mid-March opinion article offered a thoughtful examination of the perils of intervention. His analysis extended beyond Syria and he was clearly skeptical about the kind of neo-conservative thinking that had gotten the US involved in Iraq in 2003. As for a war Syria, it would be what Keller referred to as an "optional war"—one that was not vital to US national security. Beyond this, the first problem with a Syrian intervention was that there was no assurance that it would not make the situation worse. Second, Syria would be a far more difficult mission than the one recently concluded in Libya. Third, it would be "useful to have company ... [and] ... in Syria, no one is volunteering to join us yet." He also raised the troubling question regarding what sort of government would replace Assad's, pointing out the reality that no one seemed "up for another occupation of an Islamic country" (Keller, 2012, Mar. 19, p. 21).

Keller went on to raise a point critical to our analysis—the role of mass media in influencing responses to humanitarian crises—and he did so without reference to the R2P doctrine. He made the point that while public opinion should not be the determining factor in deciding to fight a war, it could not be overlooked. Keller argued that "public opinion puts a thumb on the scale," and he ventured that a critical difference behind the US's decision to intervene in Bosnia and not in Darfur was "that Americans (and American TV screens) were paying attention to the European slaughter, but not to the African atrocities." Overall, however, Keller's article was extremely cautionary with respect to calls for the US to intervene in order to halt "suffering and overthrow tyranny" (Keller, 2012, Mar. 19, p. 21).

An April editorial reiterated once again the consequences of Russian and Chinese obstructionism in the UN Security Council and called upon the US to "rally support for a strong resolution condemning Mr. Assad and imposing broader international sanctions." On the issue of "arming the opposition," the editorial noted without judgment that "Saudi Arabia, Qatar and other Arab states are supplying the opposition with weapons." For its part, the US "has offered nonlethal assistance, including communications equipment, night-vision goggles and intelligence" (*NYT*, 2012, Apr. 10, 22).

Law professors Asli Bali and Aziz Rana (at UCLA and Cornell, respectively) argued strongly against a range of international involvements in Syria, for a number of reasons. First, a "principal requirement of an intervention on humanitarian grounds is the prospect, on balance, that it will offer greater protection to vulnerable civilian populations." On this requirement, strategies of establishing "safe zones" and providing "nonlethal aid'" were seen to be "misguided at best, and counterproductive at worst." They further pointed out that Syrians were in fact split over the future of their president, with a significant number concerned about what type of government would replace him. In these circumstances the authors called "for a political transition that would include rather than explicitly threaten the Assad government." The authors criticized the Assad-must-go policy of the US government: "By relying exclusively on coercion through sanctions and threats, the practical effect of the current American approach has been to squeeze out all other diplomatic options and to make a proxy war (with local and international players on both sides) the only remaining possibility" (Bali & Rana, 2012, p. 23). A week and a half later, an editorial agreed with Bali and Rana that humanitarian corridors and safe zones were not a good idea as they "would require air patrols and possibly troops for protection; ... [plus] ... any outside intervention runs the risk of sparking a wider war." However, the editorial did agree with President Obama that "'the time has come for President Assad to step aside'" (*NYT*, 2012h, p. 20).

Thomas Friedman supported the idea of humanitarian corridors, arguing that if the plan put forward by former UN secretary-general Kofi Annan failed,

> the UN and the Arab League need to move swiftly to set up a no-fly zone or humanitarian corridor—on the Turkish-Syrian border—that can provide a safe haven for civilians ... and send a message to the exhausted Syrian Army ... that it is time for them to decapitate the regime and save themselves and the Syrian state. (2012c, Apr. 29, p. SR1)

Friedman believed that the conflict had evolved to the point where it was "a democratic struggle intertwined with a sectarian one" and that this entailed unfortunate consequences: "The bloodier and more sectarian the fight to depose Assad gets, the more deformed, violent and Islamic-dominated the post-Assad regime will likely be." He had "no illusions" that any democratic transition would be easily achieved or that there would be "a happy ending" (Friedman, 2012c, Apr. 29, p. SR1).

Syrian lawyer and opposition leader Haitham Maleh went a step beyond supporting the creation of humanitarian corridors, presenting a strong case for international intervention in the form of a "no-fly zone." The West had to "recognize that the regime has reached a point of no return, that resolutions are worthless and that the only future for Syria is without the Assad political dynasty." A military intervention along the lines of the one that deposed Libya's Colonel Qaddafi was in order: "to fail to do the same ... [in Syria] ... is hypocrisy."[1] Moreover, the West had good reason to act: "The longer the conflict drags on, the greater the chance there is for Syria to fall into chaotic war, with grave consequences for the international community. We do not want to see more failed states like Afghanistan" (Maleh, 2012, May 31, p. 29).

The first half of 2012 ended with the *New York Times* emphasizing the same set of issues that had occupied its prior editorial space; and little had changed in terms of the policies that it advocated. First, the paper believed that international military intervention was a bad idea; it "would be costly and could widen the war." Second, the paper continued to press for "comprehensive punishments" against the Assad regime on the part of the US, the EU, and others in the form of sanctions. And third, it stressed the need to get Russia and China "to stop enabling Mr. Assad's savagery." Also needed were "formal charges against Mr. Assad and his lieutenants for crimes against humanity" (*NYT*, 2012, June 9, p. 20).

An early July opinion piece by Ruslan Pukhov, director of the Russian Centre for Analysis of Strategies and Technologies, explained reasons why Russia supported the Assad regime and also countered some popular misconceptions regarding the factors contributing to that support. With respect to the latter, the chief misconception was that continued arms sales to Syria were especially important to Russia. Not so, maintained Pukhov, who pointed out that Syria accounted for "just 5 percent of Russia's global arms sales in 2011." Neither were Russian naval facilities at the Syrian port of Tartus of great strategic importance: "the facility in Tartus has more symbolic than practical significance." Interestingly, he argued that what was important was public opinion: "Many Russians believe that the collapse of the Assad government would be tantamount to the loss of Russia's last client and ally in the Middle East and the final elimination of former Soviet prowess there." This, coupled with a view of Assad as "not 'a bad dictator' but as a secular leader struggling with an uprising of Islamist barbarians" and a suspicion that the West was planning a regime change such as occurred in Libya, lay at the heart of the Russian position. In the final analysis Pukhov argued that Mr. Putin's support for Assad's government "is based on the firm conviction that an Islamist-led revolution in Syria, especially one that receives support through the intervention of Western and Arab states, will seriously harm Russia's long-term interests" (Pukhov, 2012, July 7, p. 17). An editorial appearing on July 19 reported that NATO "has shown no interest in becoming embroiled in Syria's bloody conflict" and reconfirmed thoughts that "doing so would be unwise." Interesting for future developments were reports that the "government is moving its stockpile of chemical weapons and might be preparing to use them"; these reports were described as "especially alarming" (*NYT*, 2012, July 19, p. 28).

Thomas Friedman's July 25 article was even more pessimistic regarding Syria's future than were his earlier contributions. He described Syria as "Iraq's twin—a multisectarian, minority-ruled dictatorship that was held together by an iron fist under Baathist ideology." The difference was that in Iraq the transition to democratic rule (flawed and bloody as it was) had the benefit of American midwifery—and this "is not likely to be repeated in Syria." On this point Friedman was emphatic: "I absolutely would not advocate US intervention on the ground in Syria or anywhere in the Arab world again … [noting as well that] … the US public would not support it." He claimed that "those who have been advocating a more activist US intervention in Syria—and excoriating President Obama for not leading that—are not being realistic about what it would take to create a decent outcome." He concluded that "without an external midwife or a Syrian Mandela, the fires of conflict could burn for a long time" (Friedman, 2012, July 25, p. 25).

Vali Nasr's second opinion piece on Syria dealt with the regional conse-quences of the conflict he described as having "all the markings of a grim and drawn-out civil war." And, because the conflict "threatens the stability of the whole Middle East,... the United States and its allies must enlist the coopera-tion of Mr. Assad's allies—Russia and, especially, Iran—to find a power-sharing agreement for a post-Assad Syria that all sides can support." Iran, in that it "has more influence with the Assad leadership than does Russia," was seen as key to a negotiated settlement. The problem was that the US was fixated on curbing Iran's nuclear program and was reluctant to have it involved in Syrian negotia-tions lest it gain some advantage on that issue. Yet, Nasr argued, Iran was "the single most important participant" in the peace process and was, moreover, at an impasse in its decision-making process vis-à-vis Syria; in Nasr's view, "it cannot abandon Mr. Assad, nor can it save him." Regardless of whether or not Iran would become part of the solution, he agreed with Thomas Friedman that no plan for a post-Assad Syria "will be credible without committing foreign troops to enforce the cease-fire and protect the defeated minority communities that have backed Mr. Assad" (Nasr, 2012, July 29, p. 22).

An editorial toward the beginning of August noted that "the opposition's chances of prevailing look better than they did six months ago." To achieve this, international pressure on Assad had to continue, but "the United States and its allies ... [also needed] ... to prepare the ground for a constructive future for Syria." This, however, would not involve military intervention: "The Obama administration and NATO have wisely resisted direct military involvement." However, it was noted that "this may change if, for example, Mr. Assad tries to use chemical weapons against his people." In any event, greater support for rebel forces through the provision of aid and intelligence (and perhaps weapons to screened groups) was encouraged to avoid what happened in Iraq, "where the government collapsed leaving chaos behind" (*NYT*, 2012, Aug.7, p. 22).

The summer of 2012 also saw Nicholas Kristof's second opinion piece on Syria; in it, he was critical of what he saw as President Obama's overly cautious approach, an approach that was described as "entirely reactive." Kristof agreed that while "the United States shouldn't invade Syria ... [it] ... should work with allies to supply weapons, training and intelligence to rebels who pass our vet-ting." To bolster his position he cited officials of prior administrations (William Perry and Madeleine Albright), who favoured increased American involvement, including creating a "no-fly zone in northern Syria." Kristof offered three rea-sons for supporting greater American action: first, "the longer the fighting goes on, the more it destabilizes the region; second, "Assad is believed to have many tons of sarin and VX nerve agents," which could cause significant problems if not controlled; and finally Kristof offered the "humanitarian imperative"—too

many people had been killed "and the toll is rising steeply." The article ended
with an R2P-type question: "Where is the United States?" (Kristof, 2012, Aug. 9,
p. 22).

In mid-August, journalist and author Bartle Breese Bull offered the strongest call yet for the US to become militarily involved in the civil war. President
Assad's rule was seen as "nearing its end," and the American policy of allowing
private assistance to the opposition, "while providing no weapons and limited nonlethal support … is not enough." Bull criticized American inaction
on two grounds: first, it "is turning the generally pro-American sentiment of
this important country to distrust"; and second, it "provides the extremists
with their only opening." What was needed was a policy that provided arms
(including Stinger missiles and anti-tank rockets) to the opposition and that
established a no-fly zone, thus "grounding Mr. Assad's air force, keeping his
tanks off the roads, and neutralizing his command-and-control [system]." Bull
predicted that such a policy would bring down Assad "within a couple of
months." If not, "covert, deniable drone and missile strikes would be both
effective and justified" (Bull, 2012, Aug. 15, p. 23).

An end-of-August editorial dealt with the "pressure on the United States
and its anti-Assad allies to establish a no-fly zone or humanitarian corridor
in Syria." On this issue, the paper's position remained cautious, pointing out
that such strategies "would require an international consensus to be credible
and effective." The use of chemical weapons, however, was an issue that might
necessitate direct US involvement. On this question the editorial cited President Obama's warning to Syria "that it would face American intervention
if there were signs its chemical weapons arsenal was being prepared for use"
(NYT, 2012, Aug. 29, p. 26).

A month later, the Brookings Institution's Michael Doran and the Council
on Foreign Relations' Max Boot weighed in strongly on the side of intervention. They began by praising what was termed "the Obama Doctrine." This
involved both getting in and getting out of foreign conflicts quickly, "without
ground wars or extended military occupation." Libya was cited as a successful
application of such an approach. The authors went on to argue that the Obama
Doctrine needed to be applied "where it would benefit the United States the
most—in Syria." They offered five reasons in support of their position: (1) it
"would diminish Iran's influence in the Arab world"; (2) it "could keep the conflict from spreading"; (3) it "could create a bulwark against extremist groups";
(4) it would "improve relations with key allies like Turkey and Qatar"; and
finally (5) it "could end a terrible human-rights disaster within Syria and stop
the exodus of refugees." American action was critical—the UN was dithering
and its friends would not "move until America does." The primary action called
for was "a country-wide no-fly zone, which would require taking apart Syrian

air defenses." Moreover, mission creep was built into the strategy: a no-fly zone "could then be extended to provide the kind of close air support that NATO warplanes provided to rebel fighters in Kosovo and Libya." Doran and Boot argued that the United States had "the weaponry needed to dismantle Syria's Russian-designed air defenses with little risk" (2012, Sept. 27, p. 29).

In October, writing from Aleppo, freelance journalist Benjamin Hall took the opposite position, casting doubt on the wisdom of any international intervention on the side of the opposition, which he characterized both as fragmented and suffering from "a general lack of leadership." As well, while there were also those among the opposition who "were fighting for a noble cause ... it is hard to pick them apart from those who seek to take advantage of the chaos to transform Syria into a Shariah-based fundamentalist state." A proposed no-fly zone might be an option, but Hall noted that such operations "are hugely expensive, and Syria is no Libya; its air defense system is far more sophisticated." In any event, Hill was not convinced that US action could make a difference (Hall, 2012, Oct. 19, p. 31).

In the midst of the 2012 presidential debates, Bill Keller offered some advice on Syria to the Republican candidate George Romney: "Don't rush in." He outlined the dilemma confronting American voters: a horrifying "humanitarian catastrophe" on the one hand, and war weariness on the other. In such circumstances "President Obama is right to be cautious about Syria." However, neither was it appropriate to sit "back while the situation deteriorates." Keller suggested that Mr. Romney opt for diplomacy and propose bringing NATO leaders, including the Turkish prime minister, to Camp David for "an urgent summit aimed at bringing the Syrian civil war, and the Assad regime, to an end" (Keller, 2012, Oct. 22, p. 23).

In mid-November, Thomas Friedman extended his earlier comparison of Syria and Iraq, this time focusing on the dual role the US played in "trigger[ing] the civil war in Iraq and contain[ing] it at the same time." According to Friedman, the problem in Syria was that "there is no outside power willing to fall on the ... grenade and midwife a new order." He feared that "toppling Assad without a neutral third party inside Syria to referee a transition, could lead not only to permanent civil war ... but one that spreads around the region." His solution was to work with Russia (admittedly "a real long-shot") "to see if together we can broker a power-sharing deal inside Syria and a United Nations-led multinational force to oversee it" (Friedman, 2012, Nov. 14, p. 29).

A day later, Nicholas Kristof provided another strong call for a no-fly zone. While accepting the legitimacy of arguments favouring Western inaction, he nonetheless claimed that it was time to "acknowledge that the existing hands-off approach has failed." Moreover, "Western passivity has backfired and accelerated all that Washington fears: chaos, regional instability, sectarianism and growing influence of Islamic militants." US direct military intervention continued to be deemed inappropriate, but for Kristof "a sensible menu included a NATO-backed no-fly zone over parts of northern Syria, transfers of weapons and ammunition (though not antiaircraft weapons) to the Free Syrian Army, training and intelligence support, and cooperation with rebels to secure chemical weapons" (Kristof, 2012, Nov. 15, p. 35).

Also in mid-November, Simon Adams, executive director of the Global Centre for the Responsibility to Protect, issued the first specific *genocide alert* in the Syrian conflict by citing the prediction of former American diplomat Peter W. Galbraith that "'the next genocide in the world ... will likely be against the Alawites in Syria'" (as quoted in Adams, 2012, Nov. 16, p. 35). Adams agreed: "A few months ago, talk of a possible massacre of Alawites ... seemed liked pro-regime propaganda. Now, it is a real possibility." In spite of this, Adams did not call for a military mission under the "responsibility to react" provisions of R2P. Rather, he asked all international actors to impress upon those they supported in the conflict to maintain "strict adherence to international humanitarian law ... [and to deny aid to] ... rebel groups who target Alawites and other minorities for reprisals or who commit other war crimes." As well, "all perpetrators of mass atrocities" needed to be held "accountable at the International Criminal Court" (Adams, 2012, Nov. 16, p. 35). Two days later, Kristof, again without bringing R2P into the discussion, repeated his call for NATO to "create a no-fly zone in Northern Syria and provide weapons (short of antiaircraft missiles) and intelligence and training for the rebels, to break the stalemate" (Kristof, 2012, Nov. 18, p. SR11). A December 1 editorial admitted that "it was necessary to look for ways to raise the pressure on Mr. Assad," but in that associated "hazards are substantial," did not go as far as endorsing a no-fly zone. The editorial did, however, propose a sort of compromise—the deployment of defensive surface-to-air Patriot missiles to Turkey for protection against a possible chemical weapons attack from Syria, as well as limiting "Syrian bombing of the northern border towns, where the rebels hold territory" (*NYT*, 2012, Dec. 1, p. 24).

In early December Thomas Friedman offered two background pieces on Syria, three days apart. The first dealt largely with domestic and regional issues: because of "the order he provided," many felt that President Assad would easily win if an election were held; increasingly, "Islamic fighters" were arriving in Syria, making a democratic outcome more difficult to achieve; and Saudi Arabia and Qatar (main suppliers of arms to the rebels) were only interested in seeing "Syria shift from being an Iranian-Shiite-dominated country to a Sunni-dominated one. Democracy per se is not their priority." He also repeated a previous argument that "Syria is the keystone of the Middle East. If and how it cracks apart could recast the entire region" (Friedman, 2012, Dec. 2, p. SR11).

Friedman's second article dealt with how minorities in the region are treated and began with a history lesson from the days of the Ottoman Empire, which he described as having had "a live-and-let-live mentality" toward minorities. The Ottoman period was followed by European colonialism, "which kept everyone in check." In turn, "the late 1960s and 1970s ... saw the emergence of a class of Arab dictators and monarchs who perfected Iron Fists (and multiple intelligence agencies) to decisively seize power for their sect or tribe—and they ruled over all other communities by force." What was now happening in Syria, and elsewhere as a result of the Arab Spring, was that people were rising up "against the iron-fisted dictators." The fallout was "ongoing contests for power—until and unless someone can forge a social contract for how communities can share power" (Friedman, 2012, Dec. 5, p. 31).

The final *Times* editorial of 2012 focused on issues pertaining to "the jihadi threat and end game in Syria." Chief among the worries cited was the presence of the al-Qaeda-connected al-Nusra Front. The editorial noted that while President Obama had "blacklisted the Nusra Front as a terrorist organization,... the designation by itself isn't sufficient." Pressure had to be applied to Qatar, Saudi Arabia, and Turkey to stop playing "a deadly game in empowering any affiliate of al-Qaeda." The piece discussed the idea of military intervention in the form of a no-fly zone but rejected that on the grounds that the Syrian situation was too complicated. It concluded that "President Obama's caution in resisting military intervention is the right approach," with Iraq and Afghanistan cited as examples of the failure of military power "to affect the course and outcome of armed conflict." Russian support was cited as crucial to the achievement of a peaceful outcome, but unfortunately there were no signs that "Moscow is prepared to abandon Mr. Assad" (*NYT*, 2012: Dec. 11, p. 30).

The final opinion article of 2012 picked up on the imperative to involve Russia in a positive way, and Dimitri Simes and Paul Saunders of the Center for the National Interest saw just such an opportunity as "Syria's rebels continue to gain ground and Russia loses faith in Mr. Assad." The key goal for the US was to avoid "an Iraqi-style security vacuum or an Afghan-style terrorist haven." To achieve such outcomes, the Obama administration faced a "stark choice. It can go for a knockout or opt for a brokered peace that brings stability." For the authors, the choice was clear. What was needed was a negotiated settlement to the conflict, a step "the Obama administration so far hasn't been prepared to take." Once a decision was made to negotiate, the next step would be "working together" with Russia, a process that had to go beyond "giving Russia the opportunity to adopt American positions and implement American policies without any meaningful input" (Simes & Saunders, 2012, Dec. 22, p. 25).

The Guardian's Opinion Narrative

The Guardian's 2012 narrative began with an opinion piece by the paper's former chief foreign correspondent Jonathan Steele, who criticized Western media for "biased coverage" of the Syrian conflict. Seen to be neglected by the media was a poll showing that "some 55% of Syrians want Assad to stay, motivated by fear of civil war." Also problematic were Western media criticisms of the Arab League observer mission, along with their suggestions that it should be replaced by a UN-led mission. Finally, media were ignoring the changed face of the conflict: "Armed violence is no longer confined to the regime's forces ... [and as a consequence] ... the image of peaceful protests brutally suppressed by the army and police is false." With the "danger of full-scale war" increasing, Steele was concerned about a Western, Libya-style international military intervention, when what was needed was "a dialogue between the regime and its critics" (Steele, 2012, Jan. 18, p. 32). An editorial about a week later claimed that "the civil war everyone feared has already started." The Assad regime was described as "crumb[ling]", while the numbers supporting a "pan-national ... [opposition] ... are growing." The editorial held out hope for the Arab League observer mission and suggested a "so-called Yemeni solution," whereby Assad would step down, leaving the "regime intact" (*Guardian,* 2012, Jan. 24, p. 30). An editorial on February 1 followed up on the idea of a continuation of the Assad regime without Assad: "The sooner Assad sees he has no future ... the sooner leading members of the regime will try to salvage something from the wreckage" (*Guardian,* 2012, Feb. 1, p. 30).

Academic and media commentator Rami Khouri compared foreign- and domestic-initiated regime change in the Arab world in terms of four factors: "the power and limits of domestic civil disobedience, the role of foreign armies, the impact of Arab League action, and the nature and consequences of Islamist politics." Foreign intervention was not seen as "a good idea"; rather "domestic mass dissent ... [was presented as] ... the preferred route to regime change." In that they represented a step toward regional responsibility, efforts of the Arab League to press for protection of Syrians were applauded—albeit Khouri saw such actions as "strange" coming from countries "that are mostly non-democratic and non-representative of their peoples." Written well before the Egyptian coup that ousted President Morsi in the summer of 2013, Khouri saw popularly elected Islamist governments "as likely to lead to stable governance systems" (Khouri, 2013, Jan. 26, p. 34).

Former al-Jazeera TV network executive Wadah Khanfar explained the "hesitancy" of the international community to intervene in Syria in terms of the regional balance of power and the lack of a domestic alternative to Assad. On the first, he argued that the overthrow of Assad would break the Tehran-Baghdad-Damascus-Beirut "strategic axis,... [thus] ... Iran has a strong strategic interest in defending the Syrian regime until the bitter end." As for Israel, it "would face a new situation with unpredictable consequences." On the domestic side, Khanfar placed a lot of faith in the astuteness of "the Syrian street" to avoid the pitfalls of sectarianism and claimed that the Free Syrian Army had "a huge capacity to organize and instill discipline" (Khanfar, 2012, Feb. 7, p. 30).

An editorial in early February dealing with Russian and Chinese vetoes of a UN Security Council Resolution on Syria asked whether "Russia really want[s] to be the global protector of tyrants who turn their guns on their own people simply in order to get one back against the west after the overthrow of a worthless leader like Gaddafi?" It was time for Russia to decide "whether it is part of the problem or the solution" (*Guardian*, 2012, Feb. 7, p. 32). Based on the view that "externally imposed regime change, which is what the resolution entailed," would not work, Seumas Milne took a different view of the Russian/ Chinese vetoes. Bringing a regional dimension to his analysis, Milne claimed that "Western intervention in Syria—and Russia and Chinese opposition to it—can only be understood … as a part of a proxy war against Iran, which disastrously threatens to become a direct one." He also argued that the West was "busy setting up a new coalition of the willing" for intervention in Syria, and that the strategy of Assad's armed opposition was "based on creating the conditions of a Libyan-style no-fly zone" (Milne, 2012, Feb. 8, p. 29).

Guardian executive editor Jonathan Freedland's February 11 article took aim at the British peace organization Stop the War Coalition, whose efforts were seen to be focused not on stopping the civil war but, rather, on stopping the US from getting involved in it. At the root of the problem was the 2003 invasion of Iraq, which had "tainted for a generation the idea once known as "'liberal interventionism.'" This was unfortunate, as in Freedland's view, "the post-Iraq blanket rejection of intervention makes no moral sense." What was needed was a case-by-case judgment on the use of force, which "should always be a last resort," but neither should it be dismissed a priori (Freedland, 2012, Feb. 11, p. 45). Kevin Ovenden of the Stop the War Coalition, on the other hand, defended the organization's position, arguing that increasing calls for intervention in Syria were really an effort to confront Iran, "wrapped in the rhetoric of humanitarian intervention." Nor would Syria be the first example of the misuse of humanitarian motivation: international military actions in Kosovo, Afghanistan, Iraq, and Libya were all cited as examples of human-itarianism gone astray. The idea of "humanitarian corridors" for Syria was specifically criticized because "it would mean troops on the ground." Ovenden concluded that the main problem in Syria was the West's insistence on "rul[ing] out any political settlement between the government and the armed opposi-tion." While he claimed that his organization did not "defend Assad's actions," he maintained that the solution to the crisis was not more intervention in the Middle East (Ovenden, 2012, Feb. 17, p. 32).

Abdel Bari Atwan, editor of the London-based newspaper *Al-Quds Al-Arabi*, pointed to the "accumulated risks associated with each option of intervention" as key to explaining international reluctance to become involved. Among those risks was the reality that there was "no single, identifiable, unified opposition to negotiate with, let alone arm." Atwan believed that key to a solution was the removal of the Syrian president, and for this the UN needed to insist on "real constitutional change … [combined with] … a face-saving exit plan [for Assad]." Foreign intervention was not the answer because "any military intervention … would be taken as a declaration of war with the potential for rapid regional escalation pitting the Sunni states, led by Saudi Arabia, against the mighty Shia bloc headed by Iran" (Atwan, 2012, Feb. 29, p. 32).

A *Guardian* editorial in March outlined gloomy prospects for Syria's future. Even if the international community (including the West and Russia) could come to an agreement, given the military and organizational weakness of the opposition, why, it asked, would Assad want to negotiate his departure? Moreover, sectarian warfare was growing in intensity, spurred on by Saudi Arabia, which was "playing a double game … simultaneously posing as the protectors of the Sunnis against a minority Shia regime; and … telling their people that Syria is what happens when people turn on their rulers" (*Guardian*, 2012, Mar. 10, p. 38).

A mid-March meeting in Washington between David Cameron and Barack Obama occasioned an important opinion article by *Guardian* associate editor Martin Kettle. Kettle described the meeting as "mark[ing] the close of the phase of US-UK foreign policy that began after 9/11 with the coming together of American imperial power and British support for the active promoting of democracy and liberal institutions, particularly in the Muslim world." In addition, he noted that "the two leaders do not march in lockstep"—the US had a special relationship with Israel to consider, while Cameron was seen to be "keener on intervention in Syria than Obama." Beyond these considerations, Kettle saw the meeting as marking "the end of an era" and signalling gradual American withdrawal from the Middle East. The American president explained that "'people get weary'" and that, consequently, it was necessary for whatever intervention that occurred in Syria to be "at a distance, with strict limits." In Kettle's view, most of the world had probably welcomed Obama's caution in substitution for George Bush's greater military adventurism, but a critical problem remained: "The era of Mullah Omar, Ayatollah Khamenei and Bashar al-Assad goes on, posing questions that will one day have to be answered" (Kettle, 2012, Mar. 15, p. 35).

Kofi Annan's peace plan (a mutual secession of hostilities followed by a negotiated transition to a democratic government with or without Assad) was the subject of numerous opinion pieces and *Guardian* editorials, with none expressing much hope for a breakthrough. In Steele's opinion, it was problematic that the opposition was holding out for "a Libyan-style NATO intervention," in spite of Western governments' apparent abandonment of military options. That Russia had managed to get the Syrian government to agree to international mediation, while the West was still insisting on Assad's departure prior to the beginning of talks, was another significant problem. In addition, there was no assurance that Assad was "ready for a genuine shift from minority rule to pluralistic democracy" (Steele, 2012, Mar. 20, p. 34). An editorial a week later was even more pessimistic, suggesting that "the success of the plan ... depends on persuading both sides that it will allow them to set a trap for the other." The most optimistic result, even if the plan succeeded, would be to "extend the conflict in a new form, but one which might reduce its human costs" (*Guardian*, 2012, Mar. 28, p. 32). A second editorial in mid-April noted that "with Assad talking the talk while ordering his snipers to keep on shooting ... [it would be] ... tempting to dismiss this ceasefire plan as another attempt by Assad to buy time." Regardless, Assad's options were not good: by accepting the plan he would give up the use of force to suppress the rebellion, while "without it he is more vulnerable to a Yemeni-style deal" (*Guardian*, 2012, Apr. 13, p. 36).

Rami Khouri assessed the fate of the Annan plan in terms of three factors: "the capacity of the security council to intervene in a sovereign state's affairs; the Syrian government's sense of its own durability; and the capacity of the opposition groups to form a more coherent movement." Khouri identified the last as the most crucial factor as the first two were seen to more or less balance each other out (Khouri, 2012, Apr. 10, p. 30). Patrick Seale, as had others, saw the Annan plan as "the only alternative to the horrors of an international civil war," but he warned that it would likely be undermined by "US hawks and their Israeli allies ... [who wanted Assad gone] ... in order to weaken and isolate Iran." The key was how Assad would "rise to the challenge created by the ceasefire." Seale added two pertinent observations: (1) that "the motor of the Syrian uprising ... [as in other countries experiencing the Arab Spring] ... has been the government's inability to satisfy the basic aspirations of a rapidly growing population"; and (2) that "a new Syrian political system, in which power and perks are more equally distributed, will not be built in a weekend" (Seale, 2012, Apr. 14, p. 40). In another article toward the end of May, Seale claimed that the ceasefire was "in tatters." For this he saw the opposition as being at fault, as its strategy was "to seek to trigger a foreign armed intervention by staging lethal clashes and blaming the resulting carnage on the regime." And, while the US was not likely to get involved in the war directly, it was "said to be co-ordinating the flow of weapons and intelligence to the rebels" (Seale, 2012, May 28, p. 27). Abdel Bari Atwan judged that opposition forces were "unlikely to prevail ... [and therefore] ... were, understandably, gambling on foreign intervention." He also noted the arrival in Syria of the al-Qaeda-connected al-Nusra Front, a group that claimed "that Sunni Muslims need 'protection' from the ruling Alawites, who will be made to 'pay the price'" (Atwan, 2012, May 14, p. 24).

An end-of-May editorial claimed that Assad was "undermining the Annan plan" and that a senior Iranian general had admitted that their forces were active in Syria. For *The Guardian* editorial board, the future looked clear: "If the conflict carries on Syria will disintegrate into a Lebanese-style civil war, with shockwaves throughout the region" (*Guardian*, 2012, May 29, p. 32). Another editorial in early June confirmed that Annan's peace plan was in trouble and that "the Lebanese-style civil war everyone has been predicting may already have started." The problem was that Syria's popular uprising was "not a universal one. One third of Syrian society support an insurrection, one third are pro-government and the remainder do not like either but fear the alternative" (*Guardian*, 2012, June 8, p. 36). Haytham Manna, president of the National Coordination Body for Democratic Change Abroad, agreed that the Annan plan had failed and blamed both domestic participants: "The armed opposition saw it as an opportunity for the regime to gain time so did not deal with it seriously, while the Syrian authorities used any breach of the ceasefire to launch yet more military action" (Manna, 2012, June 23, p. 38).

In an early-June opinion article, Seumas Milne responded to what he described as "pressure for another western military intervention" being voiced by Obama administration officials Susan Rice and Hillary Clinton. Milne maintained "that intervention in Syria by the US and its allies has already begun.... [and that] ... the US and its gulf allies are sponsoring regime change through civil war." And, as he had argued earlier, their motivation was the weakening of Iran: "US intervention in Syria would be a 'risk worth taking' because Iran 'would no longer have a Mediterranean foothold from which to threaten Israel and destabilize the region'" (former assistant secretary of state James Rubin, as quoted in Milne, 2012, June 6, p. 30). Milne was incredulous: "Why the states that brought blood and destruction to Iraq and Afghanistan should be thought suitable vehicles of humanitarian deliverance to Syria is a mystery." He again called for "an internationally guaranteed negotiated settlement" (Milne, 2012, June 6, p. 30).

Former British foreign secretary Lord David Owen called upon the Arab League to bring forward a UN Security Council Chapter VII resolution to stop the fighting in Syria (as it had done for Libya), on the grounds that it constituted "a threat to world peace and security."[2] Lord Owen believed strongly that "the days of going it alone, without UN authority are over." He proposed the NATO no-fly zone in Bosnia-Herzegovina in 1995 as a possible model for a response, with Turkey taking the lead, supported by Russia (Owen, 2012, June 9, p. 43).

An editorial in early July identified the problem in implementing the Annan peace plan as "the destructive competition between rival members" of the UN Security Council. On the one side, the editorial cited demands from Secretary of State Hillary Clinton that "Russia and China pay a price for sabotaging western and Arab attempts to strong-arm Bashar al-Assad out of the way." On the other, because the Syrian revolt was about "a people rising up against a deeply entrenched tyranny," the editorial pointed out that this was precisely what President Putin had feared. Thus, the situation did not appear about to improve. With the UN deadlocked, two options remained for Syria: "the gradual implosion of the regime or a long, hard, bloody grind." Implosion was unlikely due to "a lack of genuine political alternatives … [with the] … fear of the future" providing the glue that held "the security state" together. It ended with a pessimistic conclusion—that what Syria faced was "a long, hard slog" (*Guardian*, 2012, July 7, p. 38). Jonathan Steele agreed that the Security Council would be unable to come to an agreement on action on Syria, and, with the government thinking it could win and the opposition "bank[ing] on a Libyan-style NATO onslaught of massive air strikes once the US presidential election has passed," the future of Syria as "a place of religious tolerance and communal good-neighbourliness" looked grim. Steele's answer was an arms embargo combined with a Yemeni-type solution, which would have to include amnesty for Assad (Steele, 2012, July 10, p. 28).

Toward the end of July an editorial explored the reasons for the failure of the Annan peace plan and laid blame squarely at the feet of President Obama. The initial mistake, the editorial claimed, was a premature call for the end of the Assad regime "in an irrevocably public way." This resulted in a situation where neither of the combatants had any incentive to negotiate; it also undermined any possibility of cooperation between Russia and the US. With diplomacy dead, particularly troubling was "the possibility that extremists, al-Qaida and others, will try to move in." In fact, the editorial predicted the strategy followed by ISIS in 2014: "the grim news from Iraq … suggests that Sunni extremists may now envisage a common front aimed at restoring Sunni dominance in both countries." Furthermore, the piece argued that a reset of Russian–US diplomacy "cries out for consideration" (*Guardian*, 2012, July 28, p. 40). Jonathan Steele's position was that Western action in the UN Security Council (adding punishments, threats of sanctions, and "veiled hints of eventual military force") had provoked a late June Russian and Chinese veto of the resolution containing Annan's recommendations. In that "Brazil, India and South Africa all objected,... [he suggested that] ... it's time to take notice." Steele also repeated a continuing thread in *The Guardian*'s narrative—that "under Saudi, Qatari and US leadership, and with British, French and Israeli approval ... [the civil war] ... has turned into an anti-Iranian proxy war" (Steele, 2012, Aug. 6, p. 20).

Simon Jenkins reacted to what he saw as a 25-year craving for "action" on the part of the West—a post-Somalia "'duty to protect' the victims of author-itarian rule ... [had become] ... an assumed duty to take up arms against any dictator, in favour of any insurgency that could muster an international lobby." He was relieved over an apparent turn toward non-intervention but claimed there was "no point in politicians frothing at the mouth over every misdeed of a foreign power if they have no intention of doing anything about it." What was needed was "a way of reacting to the horrors that take place in foreign countries with an engagement that has meaning short of war" (Jenkins, 2012, July 20, p. 39).

Events over the summer pointed to a victory by opposition forces, and this produced significant opinion commentary regarding what lay ahead. Jon-athan Freedland, for example, was less than certain that Assad was finished; he claimed that the regime "could cling on, fighting a sectarian civil war that could last months or even ... years." And if that happened, the stakes were high: "Syria won't implode; it will explode. Put simply, the battle for Syria is a battle for the entire Middle East." Freedland further argued that "the fall of Assad will do more than diminish Iran. It will mark the passing of an entire political culture in the region ... [because Assad was] ... the last representative of a form that dominated the Middle East for half a century ... the secular strongman, the dictator backed by a merciless intelligence apparatus." What "a post-dictatorship Middle East" would look like was not clear but what was clear was that "Syria is on the brink ... [and] ... on the fate of Syria hangs the fate of the earth's most combustible region" (Freedland, 2012, July 21, p. 43). Syrian Democratic Forum member Samir Aita further explored what would follow the downfall of the Assad regime, which he fully expected. On this, the key question was "whether the US wants a stable and united Syria ... and does it have the means to influence such an outcome through the emerging regional powers of Qatar, Saudi Arabia and Turkey?" The answers to both questions were unclear (Aita, July 23, p. 22). For London School of Economics professor Fawaz Gerges, the question was "not how long Assad can cling to power, but will the authoritarian structure survive him?" While "Assad is bleeding, besieged internally and externally, it may be too early to write his obituary or that of the authoritarian state." Because "the durability of the Assad rule had depended not only on coercion and hegemony but also on co-optation and the balancing of various interests and communal groups," it had considerable staying power. Another factor was that "international diplomacy ... [had] ... mainly focused on forcing Assad out while keeping the system in place." The net result was that following the fall of Assad, "the structure of the authoritarian state" would likely remain in place. In turn, Gerges saw this as "exacerbate[ing] and prolong[ing] transition from political authoritarianism to pluralism" (Gerges, 2012: July 26, p. 30).

Syria's Muslim Brotherhood political deputy chairman Ali al-Bayanouni repeated the argument that fears of future chaos "only serve the interests of the rapists and child killers of Bashar al-Assad's regime." In addition, he felt that "negative stereotyping of Islamic society" was unfair in light of the rich history of Islamic civilization. He claimed that

the future that Syrians aspire to is an extension of the earlier era ... [and that] ... the Muslim Brotherhood is committed to a Syria in which citizenship is the basis of rights and duties, and Syrians can reconstruct their unified civil society where the concept of majority and minority rights gradually disappears. (Al-Bayanouni, 2012, Aug. 7, p. 24)

Seumas Milne continued to oppose international intervention into what he described as "an all-out civil war fuelled by regional and global powers." While President Obama had held out against "a direct military assault,... [he had] ... authorized more traditional forms of CIA covert military backing, Nicaragua-style, for the Syrian rebels." This of course raised the risks of "turning groups dependent on it into instruments of their sponsors." Milne repeated the charge that the "Syrian struggle ... [had turned] ... into a proxy war against Iran and a global conflict." In addition, he criticized Western media for neglecting "unavoidable evidence of rebel torture and prisoner executions" (Milne, 2012, Aug. 8, p. 27). Similarly, *Guardian* foreign affairs editor Peter Beaumont agreed that "human rights abuses by the Free Syrian Army ... have not attracted the same levels of opprobrium as those committed by the Assad regime." Citing announced increases in support for the rebels by the UK, he noted that "there is little evidence that abuses by rebel fighters have appeared on the radar of the foreign secretary" (Beaumont, 2012, Aug. 11, p. 33).

The perception of a likely rebel win also prompted assessments about the implications of such an outcome on Syria's neighbours. Itamar Rabinovich, a former Israeli chief negotiator with Syria, pointed to a change in Israeli attitudes toward the war. He claimed that Israel's earlier "passive stance" was over and that its "leaders and security establishment are now looking at the potential ramifications of the regime's collapse." Chief among these were what might

happen to Syria's weapons of mass destruction, specifically "the danger that Syria's stockpiles of WMD's [might] fall into the wrong hands." Rabinovich called
upon the US "to try to persuade Moscow to abandon its sweeping support for
Assad's regime and to co-operate at least in this issue, if not in guaranteeing a
smoother transition to a new political order in Syria" (Rabinovich, 2012, Aug. 2,
p. 30).

The impact of the war on Lebanon was the subject of an opinion piece by
author David Hirst. He judged that "the primary struggle for democracy has
been supplanted and penetrated by others … [with the result that the war] …
threatens … to spill over into its Arab neighbours"—with Lebanon in the
crosshairs. Lebanon's earlier Muslim/Christian fault line was now seen to mirror
"that of the region at large, Sunni versus Shia Islam," with the Shia-Hezbollah
militia supporting the Assad regime to the discomfort of Lebanese Sunnis.
Since Assad was seen to be on his way out, this placed Hezbollah in a difficult
spot, as its Iranian patron was on record as saying that it would support Assad
"by any means." Lurking in the background was a possible "Israeli attack on
Iran's nuclear installations," opening up the possibility of "another war between
Israel and Hezbollah" (Hirst, 2012, Aug. 16, p. 34). Wadah Khanfar concluded
that "it is just a matter of time before the Assad regime falls" and examined the
implications of this for Iran. His assessment was that "it is imperative that Iran
recognizes this is the last opportunity to correct its strategic error of supporting
a regime that is about to fall" (Khanfar, 2012, Aug. 31, p. 34).

An August editorial noted that in the battle for the city of Aleppo, the
local population did not see the Free Syrian Army as a liberating force "but as
harbingers of terrible suffering to come." The editorial also described the situation in Syria as one where "the possibilities of exporting chaos are legion" and
assessed the impact of the war on Turkey. On this, a significant development
was Assad's "withdraw[al] of his forces from Kurdish parts of Syria." The piece
claimed that this was done in order "to provoke a Turkish incursion" (*Guardian*, 2012, Aug. 22, p. 30). In October, Michigan State professor Mohammed
Ayoob further assessed the situation vis-à-vis Turkey, noting that Turkey was
rethinking its commitment to Syria's opposition forces. This was prompted by
its dependence on Iran for energy but also because "its active support for the
anti-Assad rebels has widened its own sectarian divide between the majority
Sunnis … and the minority Alevis, who are sympathetic to the Alawite-dom-
inated Assad regime." In addition, "Turkey's perennial Kurdish problem also
risks being exacerbated." Given the demographic realities of Kurds living on
both sides of the border, Ayoob observed that very easily "the Syrian mess could
become a Turkish mess" (Ayoob, 2012, Oct. 5, p. 38).

In September, seasoned negotiator Lakhdar Brahimi took over the UN/
Arab League file on Syria, and former British ambassador to Libya Oliver Miles

described him as "by far the best man for the job." Brahimi likened the situation he faced to "a brick wall" with no cracks. While Miles did not foresee an early end to the conflict, he did note that "even civil wars come to an end" and that if there were a chance for peace, Brahimi would be the one "to spot it" (Miles, 2012, Sept. 4, p. 30).

Jonathan Freedland returned to a topic that he first addressed in February—the lack of popular outrage over the ongoing killings in Syria. While he did not necessarily believe that public protests could influence the British government to intervene, or that such intervention would necessarily be beneficial, what he couldn't comprehend was "the lack of public pressure on those doing the actual killing—starting with the Assad regime. Instead, public opinion seems utterly disengaged, unbothered by the slaughter under way in Aleppo, Homs and Damascus." By way of contrast, he noted that there had been no such reluctance to become engaged over Israeli actions in Gaza in 2009, which had caused a fraction of the casualties seen thus far in Syria—1,400 vs. 30,000. British peace groups were criticized for appearing to endorse the idea that "a Muslim death matters less when the killer is a fellow Muslim" (Freedland, 2012, Oct. 20, p. 45).

Peter Hain, former Labour government minister for the Middle East, characterized the West's policy toward Syria as no less than "catastrophic." At the centre of this catastrophe was the demand for "regime change," when one-third of the Syrian population backed Assad. This reality, along with the growing regionalization of the war, prompted Hain's belief that a political settlement was needed before the Assad regime fell: "If the regime was somehow toppled without a settlement being in place, the country would descend into even greater chaos." Any such settlement would require Russian co-operation and, most likely, some form of immunity for Assad "to get him to sign up and stop his barbarity" (Hain, 2012, Oct. 22, p. 24). An editorial a few days later presented a similar case, stating that the Western position demanding regime change, combined with Russian refusal to pressure Assad to step aside, left both powers "paralyzed." The editorial suggested that "an anti-Assad Alawite coup" might result in new leaders "who would then be able to talk, with relatively clean hands, to some on the other side" (*Guardian*, 2012, Oct. 25, p. 34). Jonathan Steele added his opinion that "diplomatic intervention [was] the only solution" and that in order for diplomacy to succeed, "Washington needs to change policy. One-sided support for the opposition condemns Syrians to months, perhaps years, of bloodshed." He added that "a Libya-style intervention would be a worse escalation" (Steele, 2012, Oct. 29, p. 28).

Journalist James Harkin advanced the idea that "ever since ... [Hafez al-Assad] ... made Syria a cornerstone of regional stability, America and the west have had their uses for the Ba'athist regime," including what was termed the post 9/11 "vigorous interrogation" of suspected members of al-Qaeda. He further argued that "the lack of hi-tech weaponry" among that supplied to Assad's opposition indicated that

> their cheerleaders in the Gulf are merely toying with their indigenous revolt.... The Sunni Gulf states are keen to give Syria's secular institutions a kicking, but their main concern is control and the avoidance of contagion.... Their primary goal isn't to topple the Assad regime but to jockey for regional position—and keep a lid on the Arab spring. (Harkin, 2012, Nov. 21, p. 32)

In December, Simon Jenkins took on the issue of what he saw as the propensity of British politicians to lecture the world on how to solve their problems, when their own track record was less than stellar. With respect to Syria, Prime Minister David Cameron was seen to be "constantly asserting that 'doing nothing is not an option,'" while Foreign Secretary William Hague was on record as being "'appalled at the widespread and systematic human rights violations committed by the regime and its militia' which 'deserve the strongest condemnation.'" Such language, which Jenkins described as a "frenzy of rhetorical intervention," was seen as "a mildly embarrassing post-imperial itch." The real problem occurred when military actions followed such rhetoric: "They sometimes succeed in toppling regimes at huge cost in foreign lives and British taxes, but rarely lead to peace and democracy" (Jenkins, 2012, Dec. 7, p. 44).

The comment by Russia's deputy foreign minister, also in December, that "it was entirely conceivable that the rebels would win," prompted yet another round of speculation regarding the approaching fall of Assad and what might lie ahead. *The Guardian's* final 2012 editorial noted that Assad had been "written off casually before," but it speculated that this time the end "may be closer than we think." On the issue of a possible escalation of repression by Assad to include the use of chemical weapons, the piece cited the regime's self-imposed red line that it claimed it would not cross (*Guardian*, 2012, Dec. 14, p. 44). Haytham Manna addressed the worrisome problem of growing "Islamization" among the opposition, particularly the growing strength of al-Nusra and the marginalization of "secular democrats." Manna framed the support for "Islamization" by the Gulf States in terms of "protection against genuine democracy in Syria, which would pose a threat to them." He also predicted that "the fight for Syria will last a long time, and will not end with the fall of the regime" (Manna, 2012, Dec. 18, p. 28).

Not convinced that Assad was finished, Seumas Milne again claimed that "the west is preparing to escalate military intervention in the Arab and Muslim world.... Direct intervention, US and British officials are reported to insist, is 'now inevitable.'" In light of a deteriorating situation, with atrocities committed by both sides, David Cameron cited "a 'strategic imperative' to act because the Syrian war … is 'empowering al-Qaida-linked extremists.'" Not so, according to Milne: the true "aim is intervention for influence, both before and after the expected fall of the Assad regime—dressed up, as in Libya, in the language of 'protecting civilians.'" He claimed, as he had earlier, that "the only way out of an increasingly grim conflict is a negotiated settlement" (Milne, 2012, Dec. 19, p. 27).

The Globe and Mail's Opinion Narrative

The new year of 2012 had barely begun when it became apparent that *The Globe*'s editorial board had become disillusioned with its earlier idea that the Arab League could play a useful role in resolving the Syrian conflict. Calling the League's observer mission to Syria a failure, an editorial in January claimed that the mission showcased "the League's impotence and irrelevancy and dashed any hope that League observers might help stem the bloodshed." Seen as particularly egregious was the League's selection of Sudanese general Mohamed Mustafa al-Dabi (wanted by the ICC on charges of genocide stemming from his role in Darfur) to lead the mission (*Globe*, 2012, Jan. 3, p. 12). Also significant in *The Globe and Mail* at this time was the transition in language in early 2012 from describing anti-Assad activists as "demonstrators," "dissidents," and "civilian protesters" to accepting that Syria was involved in a "nascent civil war … [waged by] … armed insurgents." The editorial also addressed regional geopolitics (chiefly the roles of Turkey and Qatar), as well as the fragile support claimed to be enjoyed by President Assad, whose views on the conflict were described as delusional (*Globe*, 2012, Jan.12, p. 12; italics added).

Michael Bell changed his earlier forecast for the survival of the Assad regime and explained the national and regional consequences of what he now saw as its likely downfall. At the national level, there would initially be "Sunni domination … [yielding to] … Muslim Brotherhood rule." The latter, in turn, would have dire implications for Israel, Hezbollah, Lebanon, and Iran. Regionally, because Syria was a key player in its bid for Shia dominance in the region, Iran was identified as "a major loser should the Assad regime fall." Bell acknowledged that the West's belief that pluralism would emerge from the Arab Spring appeared "naïve," and he predicted that "tumult and chaos will be the region's leitmotif for the foreseeable future" (Bell, 2012, Feb. 3, p. 19).

In late February, retired Canadian general Lewis MacKenzie added a new dimension to distance framing by calling into question the "Western proclivity for anointing a 'good' side and vilifying a 'bad' side … [that had as usual] … been hasty." He noted that "extremist fighters" had become part of the opposition and that "55 per cent of Syrians support Mr. Assad." He cautioned the

West to think carefully about "who we are dealing with in the opposition" (MacKenzie, 2012, Feb. 22, p. 17). According to MacKenzie, what was needed was a Russian diplomatic initiative. It was Russian diplomacy that convinced Serbian President Slobodan Milosevic to withdraw from Kosovo in 1999, and MacKenzie argued that in fact Russian influence had been more important than the NATO bombing campaign in determining that outcome. He concluded that *"the only solution to the Syrian conflict goes through Moscow"* and urged Canada to "convince Vladimir Putin to visit Damascus" (MacKenzie, 2012, Feb. 22, p. 17; italics added). Then University of Toronto professor Michael Ignatieff agreed that pressure had to be placed on Mr. Putin, whom he described as Assad's "last remaining friend on earth." Putin should be told that if "you want respect … you can't gain it by backing a tyrant whose rule destabilized a region." He reiterated the point that Assad was gambling on Syrians' deciding "that his tyranny is a better guarantee of regional stability than civil war" (Ignatieff, 2012, Mar. 20, p. 13).

In early April, as background to a possible Turkish role in resolving the Syrian crisis, Oxford University professor Timothy Garton Ash offered another history lesson on the final years of the Ottoman Empire. Premised on the lack of a Western response ("don't expect any Libya- or Kosovo-type intervention anytime soon"), he looked to regional powers "to determine the fate of the Syrian people," seeing Turkey, Iran, Saudi Arabia, and Russia as more important than Britain, Germany, France, and the US (Garton Ash, 2012, Apr, 12, p. 15). A *Globe* editorial supported the regional argument advanced by its opinion contributors by endorsing Russia as "more likely than any country" to be able to end the killing and calling upon Moscow "to live up to its responsibility" (*Globe*, 2012, May 29, p. 14).

In another opinion piece, Garton Ash followed up his earlier regional analysis with an examination of the possibility that the international community would mount an R2P-type intervention along the lines of Kosovo and Libya; however, he saw the chances of this happening as slim. First, a necessary condition of military intervention was to make things better, not worse, and "one step … [such as a no-fly zone] … could morph into a messy, long drawn-out partial occupation, or even a kind of war by proxy." While Garton Ash described Russia's role in the conflict to date as "shocking, mendacious and indefensible," he agreed with MacKenzie that "the road to Damascus goes through Moscow" and urged the international community to pressure Vladimir Putin to aid in resolving the conflict (Garton Ash, 2012, June 14, p. 19).

Michael Bell concluded that the UN had failed to rein in the conflict, and, as a result, hard-nosed *realpolitik* prevailed—a situation "where different and committed actors, inside and outside Syria, are playing by standards that liberal internationalists abhor." Bell feared that even "a severe sanctions regime" imposed by the international community "might have less impact than thought … [while] … NATO boots on the ground would be a disaster." Russia and Iran were seen to be key players, protecting their national interests by supporting Assad, while "Washington is acting covertly with hard-core regional allies like Saudi Arabia and Qatar to support the Free Syrian Army on the ground." Bell described the Syrian regime as being in trouble—"tottering hopelessly…. Rats increasingly abandoning the ship … a sure sign of panic." Although at this point Bell felt that the international community had little influence in determining the conflict's ultimate outcome, he argued it "should be developing plans for a wobbly and highly uncertain [post-Assad] era" (Bell, 2012, July 23, p. 11).

Breaking the strong trend toward anti-intervention framing, Canadian senator Hugh Segal argued the case for Western intervention. Invoking the pre-WWII analogy of the loss of Czechoslovakia to Hitler, he argued "that the price we pay for not acting is often far greater than the actual price of deciding to act in the name of humanity." The situation in Syria, with its military "deeply involved in the killing of thousands," was an obvious case for the application of R2P. The international response to date, however, had been feeble—"the world stands idly by." Segal proposed a Libya-type, no-fly zone intervention: "The Syrian military will have little to fear until NATO and the Arab League declare and enforce a no-fly zone to keep Syrian helicopters from attacking their own civilian population." He acknowledged that such an "intervention will be hard, complex and messy … [but that] … standing by and watching is … simply criminal" (Segal, 2012, June 22, p. 13).

Former UN high commissioner for human rights, ICC chief prosecutor, and International Crisis Group president and CEO Louise Arbour offered a theoretical critique of R2P, pointing to the uneasy relationship between its stated objectives (protection of civilians and prosecution of criminals) and what she called the wider "objective of peace." She argued that while R2P addressed the protection, and the ICC the justice components, neither dealt with the "ultimate resolution" of a conflict. R2P's shortcoming was that in focusing on the inability or unwillingness of states to protect their citizens, it failed to address situations such as Syria, where the state "has embarked on a deliberate rampage against part of its population." In such circumstances, Arbour argued that "regime change" had to become an explicit goal of R2P: "After all how else could it credibly purport to protect Syria's population?" While this addition would make R2P logically consistent, she acknowledged that adding the unambiguous goal of regime change to an R2P mandate "would make an already elusive Security Council consensus to support intervention completely unattainable" (Arbour, 2012, June 27, p. 13). The resulting dilemma was left unresolved.

Doug Saunders revisited one of the first themes identified in *The Globe's* 2011 opinion narrative: the negative impact of the application of R2P to the insurrection in Libya. He first outlined R2P's quick rise to prominence to become "part of UN policy," culminating in its use in Libya. He then explained how its over-extension there, resulting in regime change, had alienated not only Russia and China but former colonies as well, to the point of their rethinking the wisdom of the entire doctrine, proposing instead a return to the idea of "'sovereign equality'—that is making national borders sacred again." Saunders concluded that this reassertion of state sovereignty in response to Libya could possibly mark "the end of the era when 'we' [the West] can easily invade a country to protect its people" (Saunders, 2012, Sept. 22, p. F9).

University of Toronto professor Wesley Wark shifted focus to an analysis of international intervention in Syria based on conventional Western national interests. And, although there would be obvious costs, along with the potential for "political setbacks," he argued that "the reasons for sitting on our hands while Syria burns are gone." He presented two options: (1) the "covert war model," whereby the rebels would be supported clandestinely by the West; and (2) the overt "Libya-style solution." Wark preferred the latter on the grounds that it would give the West greater influence in a post-Assad Syria. As well, he claimed that NATO had the ability to "mount the forces for a no-fly zone mission against Syria … [and that such a mission] … would decisively tip the military balance." Whatever the choice, he argued that "we have to accept that diplomacy has failed and military force has presented itself as the last resort, as it always should" (Wark, 2012, July 19, p. 13). On the same day, however, *The Globe's* editorial board had not given up on diplomacy. Disagreeing with its opinion contributor, it argued that diplomacy was not yet dead and that "faced with an otherwise inevitable bloody end … [the Syrian government] … may yet be induced to negotiate some sort of transition for itself and the country." Moreover, Russia was again put forward as the most likely candidate to facilitate such a transition (*Globe*, 2012, July 19, p. 12).

US and Canadian foreign policies were addressed in two opinion pieces. In one, *Globe* columnist Jeffrey Simpson praised US president Barack Obama for understanding "that his country was powerful but not all-powerful … [and that] … he wisely kept the United States out of direct intervention in Syria" (Simpson, 2012, Oct. 24, p. 15). In the other article, retired diplomats Mike Molloy and Michael Bell were more cautionary in their assessment of Canadian prime minister Stephen Harper's response to the crisis. They acknowledged that much in the way of positives had been accomplished—the imposition of sanctions, travel and investment bans—but there was still too much "belligerent rhetoric." This was problematic because "belligerent rhetoric risks inflaming the situation by implying that armed force is a realistic alternative" whereas in reality the application of such force "is not feasible." Reasons for the lack of a military response were identified as a Security Council in deadlock and a US seen as "rightly leery of stepping into the quicksand that overwhelmed it in Iran and Afghanistan." Given Canada's limited power and influence to "oust the Syrian regime," the authors believed its efforts would best be directed at aiding the conflict's refugees (Molloy and Bell, 2012, Oct. 29, p. 11).

DISCUSSION

For *The New York Times*, initial opinion commentary in 2012 focused on strategies to force Mr. Assad from power. In spite of the recognition of a worsening situation on the ground, however, international military intervention was not among those favoured strategies. Instead, the paper called on Russia to use its influence to persuade Assad to step down. Then, later in the spring, the wisdom of the "Assad must go" strategy was questioned. The feasibility of creating "safe zones" along the Turkish border was also discussed, but there was no consensus on whether they could be easily established or whether they would work. Also, the negative impact of the long wars in Afghanistan and Iraq on US public opinion was first raised as a factor possibly limiting any forceful US response.

As the year progressed, the discussion of possible Western responses to the Syrian crisis continued and included calls for a Libya-style, US-led, and NATO-enforced no-fly zone in Syria. Both proponents and skeptics of the proposal argued their respective cases, with columnist Nicholas Kristof at the forefront of those pushing for such a robust intervention. In its editorials, however, the newspaper never went as far as endorsing the move; instead, the paper continued to express support for President Obama's cautious approach to the application of American military muscle. Importantly, no one called for an intervention that entailed Western troops on the ground; to the contrary, questions were raised whether Obama had in fact gone too far in his insistence that Assad must go.

Due largely to the many opinion articles by columnist Thomas Friedman, the dominant message conveyed in *The Times'* 2012 opinion narrative was that Syria specifically (and the Arab Spring generally) would not end well. Articles presented the Syrian situation as extraordinarily complex, both domestically and regionally. Bright spots were few and pitfalls were many, particularly the growing influence of Islamic extremists affiliated with al-Qaeda and the troubling presence of Syria's chemical weapons. The former was seen as complicating the provision of any military aid to the rebels as well as making some compromise with Assad a more acceptable outcome. Possible Russian (and Iranian) support for a solution remained a wild card—one worth playing but not one that offered a high probability of success. However, Syria's troublesome stockpile of chemical weapons was seen as possibly forcing the West into some type of military response.

In 2012, commentary in *The Guardian* focused on the conflict's transition from a revolt into a fragmented secular civil war that stressed the dynamic of Saudi–Iranian competition for regional supremacy. Assad's opponents, widely praised for their noble motives and bravery in 2011, were increasingly criticized in 2012 for encouraging a Libyan-style, NATO military intervention. Seumas Milne in particular advanced the idea that the West was interested in the Syrian conflict mainly as an opportunity to weaken Iran. Also mentioned prominently was the idea of a "Yemini solution," whereby Assad would give up power but the existing state structure would remain largely intact. There was a good deal of argument that the US, in particular, had irrevocably poisoned the possibility of a diplomatic solution by insisting on the departure of Assad as a precondition for any negotiations. Kofi Annan's peace plan received considerable attention, with virtually everyone involved in the conflict assessed blame for its failure.

Martin Kettle's article proclaimed the end of the Bush era of international interventions aimed at regime change, to be followed by one characterized by "disengagement" brought on by war weariness. Kettle did not, however, offer any new strategy for dealing with the problems of the world, which, he noted, unfortunately remained. He assessed the impact of the conflict on regional neighbours, such as Turkey, Lebanon, Iraq, Iran, and Israel, with the judgment that continuing conflict would almost undoubtedly destabilize the entire region.

Above all else, *The Guardian* believed that Western intervention, in all its shapes and forms, was a terrible idea—the result would be more people killed, as, the newspaper pointed out, happened with the UN-NATO no-fly zone in Libya. Unique to *Guardian* commentary was criticism of the focus of British peace groups on keeping the US from intervening in the conflict, rather than on ending the war. The paper also acknowledged growing Islamization, largely associated with Gulf states' support for radical fighters, although this was seen less as an effort to depose Assad than one to discredit the Arab Spring, which the Gulf states feared might spread to them. *The Guardian* discussed Syria's chemical weapons largely in the context of their possible use against Israel, should they fall into the wrong hands. While it was widely predicted that Assad was on his way out, especially during the final six months of 2012, there was some skepticism about this, as well as the view that the Syrian conflict would very likely carry on without him in any case. Along with the insistence on no international intervention, a dominant theme in *The Guardian*'s 2012 narrative was that a negotiated settlement was the only solution to the conflict.

Throughout the course of 2012 a number of new themes emerged in *The Globe*'s opinion narrative, with most discouraging the international community's direct involvement in Syria. First, it was widely acknowledged that the conflict had reached the stage of civil war and that the survival of the Assad regime was highly unlikely. Adding to the problem was that a victory by the opposition was increasingly portrayed as possibly a worse outcome than the survival of the incumbent. The Arab League observer mission, for which *The Globe* had expressed great hope in 2011, was now seen as a failure. There was also a strong suggestion that, given the high degree of ethnic and religious fragmentation in Syria, the political situation there was likely to be chaotic regardless of the outcome of the war.

It was also now clear that a military intervention in the form of a Libya-style, no-fly zone (a strategy advocated by some opinion contributors, such as Senator Hugh Segal and Wesley Wark)[3] was simply not going to happen: the UN Security Council was not going to approve an enabling resolution, and due to war weariness, the US was unlikely to lead a "coalition of the willing." This left diplomacy as the default strategy, according to *The Globe*, and whether it held out a solution was unclear. But if there were any chance of its being successful, regional players, including Turkey and Iran but chiefly Russia, would have to step up to the plate. And, while Russia was at best seen as a long shot to act as conciliator, the dominant theme of 2012 *Globe* commentary was that the West needed to exercise influence to get Mr. Putin to step up and assume the role of statesman.

CHAPTER 6

Conflict Framing in 2013: January 1 through August 21

INTRODUCTION

In light of the extraordinary volume of opinion material occasioned by the use of chemical weapons against Syrian civilians during the third week of August, we have opted to present the analysis of respective newspapers' 2013 framing of the conflict in two chapters. Tables and opinion narratives based on material appearing up to and including August 21 will be presented in this chapter, while those for material covering the period between August 22 and September 30 (focused largely on British and American responses to the attack) will follow in Chapter 7.

The first seven and a half months of 2013 included the second anniversary of the start of the Syrian conflict, and opinion-leading material in all newspapers focused attention on the following themes:

- An early and/or easy resolution to the civil war was unlikely.
- The growing number of refugees fleeing the fighting was increasingly cited with concern and dismay.
- The changing composition of Syria's opposition forces from primarily supporters of democratic reform to an unknown mixture, including various brands of radical Islam, was identified as a significant factor in discouraging Western support.
- There was a continued focus on the regionalization of the war, in part prompted by Israeli air strikes targeting Syrian weapons shipments to the Hezbollah militia.

In addition, it was during the spring of 2013 that the use of Syria's chemical weapons first emerged as an issue when it was reported that Assad's forces appeared to have used them "in small amounts," in direct defiance of President Obama's "red line," declared in the previous August. Disagreements also continued over whether greater Western support for anti-Assad forces would improve or hinder chances for a negotiated settlement. *The New York Times* focused a good deal of its commentary on US policy and favoured continued relative non-involvement in the conflict, while *The Guardian* focused on British policy that favoured ending the EU ban on the export of weapons to Syria (thereby allowing arms to be sent to the rebels). *The Globe and Mail* canvassed a wide range of issues but cannot be said to have pursued a particular focus.

QUANTITATIVE FINDINGS

Data in Table 6.1 indicate a continuation of the trend established in 2012 toward a reduced focus on the actions of the Syrian government—down an additional 26 per cent from 2012. In contrast, the actions of leading global and regional actors (with the exception of Russia) attracted greater attention in the newspapers' opinion pages. Significantly, for the first time the number of opinion pieces commenting on the role of the US in the conflict exceeded

Table 6.1   Salience of Domestic Combatants, Major Global and Regional Actors, Jan. 1 to Aug. 21, 2013, by Newspaper (Per Cent of Opinion-Leading Items)

	Times N=34	Guardian N=33	Globe N=18	Total N=85
Domestic Combatants				
Syrian government*	52.9	48.5	66.7	54.1
Syrian opposition	50.0	57.6	50.0	52.9
Global Actors				
US*	79.4	72.7	61.1	72.9
Russia*	32.4	45.5	44.4	40.0
Britain*	17.4	61.0	27.8	36.2
International community	14.7	36.4	50.0	30.6
Canada*	0	0	44.4	9.4
Saudi Arabia	5.9	18.2	0	9.4
UN (General)	5.9	9.1	11.1	8.2
NATO	5.9	0	27.8	8.2
UN (Security Council)	2.9	3.0	11.1	4.7
Regional Actors				
Iran	17.6	51.5	33.3	34.1
Israel	11.8	24.2	27.8	20.0
Hezbollah	5.9	27.3	22.2	17.6
Saudi Arabia	5.9	18.2	0	9.4
Arab League	0	6.1	5.8	3.5
Turkey	0	3.0	0	1.2

*Includes references to respective leaders: Presidents al-Assad, Obama, and Putin; Prime Ministers Cameron and Harper.

those commenting on the Syrian government in both *The Times* (up by 27 per cent) and *The Guardian* (up by 24 per cent). The opposite was true for *The Globe*, however. From the initial year of the conflict, attention to the Syrian government had decreased by 40 per cent, attention paid to the opposition remained relatively constant, while that garnered by the US, Britain, Russia, and Iran increased by 36, 32, 23, and 19 per cent, respectively.

Table 6.2 tells us that opinion commentators writing in all three newspapers had little good to say about either side contesting the civil war and much to say that was critical. Global and regional actors fared little better, as persistent negativism dominated editorial and opinion pages. With respect to

Table 6.2   Evaluation of Domestic Combatants, Major Global and Regional Actors, Jan. 1 to Aug. 21, 2013, by Newspaper (Per Cent of Opinion-Leading Items—Ambiguous Items Omitted)

	Times N=34		Guardian N=33		Globe N=18		Total N=85		Percentage Difference
	Pos	Neg	Pos	Neg	Pos	Neg	Pos	Neg	
Domestic Combatants									
Syrian government*	0	47.1	3.0	24.2	0	61.1	1.2	41.2	−40.0
Syrian opposition	0	26.5	3.0	39.4	0	33.3	1.2	32.9	−31.7
Global Actors									
US*	17.6	17.6	9.1	45.5	11.1	16.7	12.9	28.2	−15.3
Russia*	2.9	17.6	3.0	36.4	0	33.3	2.4	28.2	−25.8
Britain	0	0	3.0	45.5	11.1	5.6	3.5	18.8	−15.3
International Community	0	0	0	30.3	5.6	16.7	1.2	15.3	−14.1
Canada*	0	0	0	0	11.1	11.1	2.4	2.4	0
UN (General)	5.9	0	0	3.0	5.6	5.6	3.5	2.4	+1.1
NATO	2.9	0	0	0	0	22.2	1.2	4.7	−3.5
UN (Security Council)	0	0	0	3.0	0	3.0	0	1.2	−1.2
Regional Actors									
Iran	0	8.8	3.0	42.4	0	33.3	1.2	27.1	−25.9
Israel	0	0	6.1	9.1	5.6	0	3.5	3.5	0
Hezbollah	0	2.9	0	21.2	0	22.2	0	14.1	−14.1
Saudi Arabia	0	2.9	3.0	12.1	0	0	1.2	5.9	−4.7
Arab League	0	0	0	6.1	0	5.6	0	3.5	−3.5
Turkey	0	0	0	3.0	0	0	0	1.2	−1.2

*Includes references to respective leaders: Presidents al-Assad, Obama, and Putin; Prime Ministers Cameron and Harper.

the US, only in *The Times* was there an equal amount of positive and negative content, and interestingly the paper was no more negative about Russia than about the US. *The Guardian* registered the highest level of negativity toward most global and regional actors: the US, Britain, Iran, Russia, the international community, and Saudi Arabia. *The Globe* was especially critical of the Syrian, Russian, and Iranian governments.

Data in Table 6.3 indicate that with respect to possible strategies available to the international community to deal with the Syrian crisis, *The Times* in particular evaluated both diplomacy and military action more positively than a year earlier, although overall the latter remained on the negative side of the ledger. Overall, creating a no-fly zone and, especially, arming the opposition had clearly fallen out of favour. With the exception of military action, which climbed from a percentage difference of –15 per cent to –7 per cent, all other strategies were viewed more pessimistically in 2013 than in 2011.

Data in Table 6.4 tell us that in 2013 the tide had turned dramatically toward assessments that President Assad would emerge victorious—overall, an 11 per cent increase over 2012 and fully 19 per cent in *The Guardian*. At the same time, the fortunes of the opposition were seen to have taken a sharp

Table 6.3   Optimism vs. Pessimism toward Conflict-Ending Strategies, Jan. 1 to Aug. 21, 2013, by Newspaper (Per Cent of Opinion-Leading Items—Ambiguous Items Omitted)

Strategies	Times N=34		Guardian N=33		Globe N=18		Total N=85		Percentage Difference
	Opt	Pess	Opt	Pess	Opt	Pess	Opt	Pess	
Diplomacy	11.8	8.8	15.2	18.2	11.1	11.1	12.9	12.9	0
Arming the opposition	5.9	32.4	6.1	54.5	5.6	27.8	5.9	40.0	–34.1
Imposing a no-fly zone	0	8.8	0	18.2	11.1	16.7	2.4	14.1	–11.7
Military action	5.9	2.9	0	12.1	5.6	22.2	3.5	10.6	–7.1

Table 6.4   Side Seen to Be Winning, Jan. 1 to Aug. 21, 2013, by Newspaper (Per Cent of Opinion-Leading Items)

Times N=34			Guardian N=33			Globe N=18			Total N=85		
Gov't	Ambig	Oppos	Gov't	Ambig	Oppos	Govt	Ambig	Oppos	Govt	Ambig	Oppos
8.8	14.9	0	24.2	21.2	0	5.6	16.7	5.6	14.1	17.6	1.2

turn for the worse—a drop of 14 per cent from the previous year. Nonetheless, uncertainty regarding who was winning still predominated.

Data in Table 6.5 indicate that in 2013 international involvement in the Syrian civil war was greeted with the lowest level of enthusiasm seen at any time in our study; in all three newspapers, negative percentages approached or exceeded 40 per cent of opinion commentary. Overall, anti-involvement content in 2013 had increased by 27 per cent from 2011. While opinion content favouring involvement also increased from 2011, but only by 10 per cent, only in *The Globe* did pro-involvement content come within 10 per cent of negative totals. Compared to 2011, while greater percentages of content both favoured and opposed international involvement, the percentage difference was greatest in 2013—(–25 per cent, as opposed to –7 per cent in 2011 and –19 per cent in 2012). In short, as the Syrian civil war entered its third year, a smaller percentage of opinion content took the position that the international community should become more involved.

Table 6.6 tells us that during the first seven-plus months of 2013 not a single opinion-leading item foresaw a positive outcome emerging from Syria's civil war—a further decrease of 14 per cent from 2012. Additionally, for the first time negative predictions regarding the future exceeded ambiguous ones— overall, by 11 per cent. While ambiguous assessments also increased by 4 per cent, negative assessments topped out at 29 per cent of content, a 15 per cent increase over such pessimistic predictions in 2011.

Table 6.5   The International Community "Should Do Something," Jan. 1 to Aug. 21, 2013, by Newspaper (Per Cent of Opinion-Leading Items—Ambiguous Items Omitted)

Times N=34		Guardian N=33		Globe N=18		Total N=85		Percentage Difference
Pro	Anti	Pro	Anti	Pro	Anti	Pro	Anti	
11.8	38.2	12.1	42.4	27.8	38.9	15.3	40.0	–24.7

Table 6.6   Positive or Negative Outcomes for Democracy, Jan. 1 to Aug. 21, 2013, by Newspaper (Per Cent of Opinion-Leading Items)

Times N=34			Guardian N=33			Globe N=18			Total N=85		
Pos	Amb	Neg	Pos	Amb	Neg	Pos	Amb	Neg	Pos	Amb	Neg
0	17.6	23.5	0	24.2	30.3	0	11.1	38.9	0	18.8	29.4

QUALITATIVE FINDINGS

The New York Times' Opinion Narrative

The Times began its 2013 editorial commentary on Syria with a focus on the refugees produced by the conflict. Their numbers were seen to be "creating a disaster that is threatening to destabilize the region." The editorial emphasized that the international community had "an obligation to do more to ease the suffering" because efforts in that direction so far had been unimpressive. In particular, "wealthy Persian Gulf states" were criticized for not doing more, as were Russia and China, who were cited for having "enabled Mr. Assad in his brutal war" (*NYT*, 2013, Jan. 21, p. 20).

Problems associated with Syria's opposition were the topic of Jamestown Foundation's Middle East analyst Ramzy Mardini's early February opinion article. In it, he claimed that Assad's "political opposition is showing signs of failure." A new leadership group had replaced the Syrian National Council, but it "isn't willing to negotiate with the Syrian government, nor is it remotely prepared to assume power." In addition, Mardini noted that among opposition groups, "Islamists are overpowering secularists; exiles are eclipsing insiders; and very few members seem to have credibility on the ground back home." He saw the solution to the crisis in the form of "a political settlement," which would require "a truly representative opposition ... [combined with] ... a new approach, especially from America" (Mardini, 2013, Feb. 4, p. 19).

In mid-February, freelance journalist J. Malcolm Garcia confirmed this bleak appraisal of Syria's opposition, maintaining that following Assad's overthrow, the Free Syrian Army had "no idea of what will happen ... Democracy? An Islamic republic? An Islamic dictatorship?" Disquieting as well was Garcia's assessment that only the "Islamic militants ... [had] ... a firm sense of direction"—to impose "an Islamic state in place of Mr. Assad." Garcia also criticized Western inaction: "If the West and moderate Arab states want to prevent a Taliban-style dictatorship from replacing the current Baathist regime, it's time for them to offer Syrians more than hope." Exactly what "more than hope" entailed was not specified, but Garcia made it clear that talk was not enough (Garcia, 2013, Feb. 15, p. 27).

Thomas Friedman's first column in 2013 continued in the pessimistic vein seen in previous years. He maintained that the historical interaction of peoples in the Middle East going back to the days of "old civilizations ... [had established] ... long-set patterns of behavior" that were not easily changed. Cited as especially problematic was "the long-running Sunni-Shiite civil war." The implication for Syria was that any direct international intervention would have to entail far more than just the removal of President Assad: "The only way you'll get a multisectarian transition is with a U.N. resolution backed by Russia and backed by a well-armed referee on the ground to cajole, hammer and induce the parties to live together." The US was not seen as a likely contributor to such a venture as President Obama's approach to Syria was described as "'you-touch-it-you-own-it-so-don't-even-touch-it'" (Friedman, 2013, Feb. 10, p. SR11).

In its continuing commentary on US policy with respect to the crisis, *The Times* maintained its support for what it termed Obama's "wise approach." It acknowledged, however, that "al-Qaeda-linked foreign jihadists are gaining ground" and, therefore, questioned whether it was possible "to vet rebel groups so that aid goes to those who are most effective and likely to pursue a democratic course." Russia remained key to a solution to the overall problem, and it "could still have a positive effect if it withdrew its unconscionable support for Mr. Assad and stopped sending him weapons" (*NYT*, 2013, Mar. 1, p. 22). An editorial toward the end of April continued to distance the US from the conflict, again noting that "the president has wisely resisted calls to supply American weapons and to intervene directly" (*NYT*, 2013, Apr. 23, p. 30). Friedman's column on March 27 also expressed skepticism regarding what he saw as likely deeper US involvement in Syria following from increased support for the rebels. Two key questions demanded satisfactory answers: "Why has [Assad] been able to hang on so long? … [and] … What are Qatar's and Saudi Arabia's goals?" Friedman reiterated his previous argument that "some global coalition" was needed "to invade Syria,… sit on the parties and forge the kind of Syria we want." Cited as problematic for this strategy was that it hadn't worked in Iraq and had "zero support" among the American people. Friedman was not convinced that "just arming 'nice' rebels will produce the Syria we want; it could though, drag us in in ways we might not want" (Friedman, 2013, Mar. 27, p. 23).

In a mid-April opinion article, David Pollock, a Senior Fellow at the Washington Institute for Near East Studies, explored the impact of the Syrian crisis on neighbouring Israel. He saw the real possibility that Israel would invade Syria to set up "a buffer zone." To avoid this, he suggested that the US "should broker a tacit agreement between Israel and moderate elements of the Syrian opposition." Citing the adverse consequences of Israel's earlier invasion of Lebanon, Pollock claimed that "establish[ing] proxy forces in a buffer zone along the border … would almost certainly backfire" (Pollock, 2013, Apr. 16, p. 2).

An April 24 article by US Senator Bob Corker, ranking Republican on the Senate Foreign Relations Committee, marked the first instance of what Piers Robinson termed "elite dissensus" appearing in *Times* opinion material. Corker's article followed closely on widely reported suspicions that Syria had used chemical weapons in small amounts, which, if confirmed, he argued "will force the White House and Congress to decide about expanding our involvement there." He claimed that until then the president had been "indecisive, neither

fully 'in' nor 'out' … [and that] … the time for 'leading from behind' is over."
Corker did not support the deployment of American forces to topple Assad but
maintained that "American leadership, including providing arms and training
to moderate rebels, are likely to be the only things that can tip the balance,
help end the bloodshed and halt brewing threats to us and our allies." Corker
counselled the president "to work closely with Congress in devising his strategy
and not deploy any military forces without Congressional consent" (Corker,
2013, Apr. 24, p. 23).

An editorial appearing a day later took up the issue of Assad's possible use
of chemical weapons. It acknowledged that Assad "may be capable of using
weapons of mass destruction … [but] … there is no proof that he has done
so." In fact, the case against Assad was described as "thin." As such, in light
of the failure to find alleged weapons of mass destruction in Iraq in 2003,
the editorial argued that an American military response "might be justified,
but only if there is incontrovertible proof of the use of chemical weapons and
only if other countries join in the response—if it comes to that" (*NYT*, 2013,
Apr. 25, p. 30). Less than a week later, another editorial responded directly to
senators John McCain and Lindsey Graham's claims that "the US should be
doing more, directly arming the rebels … and establishing a no-fly zone." The
editorial argued that

> what the senators and like-minded critics have not offered is a coherent
> argument for how a more muscular approach might be accomplished
> without dragging the United States into another extended and costly
> war and how it would yield the kind of influence and good will for this
> country that the interventions in Iraq and Afghanistan have not. (*NYT*,
> 2013, Apr. 30, p. 18)

The piece also acknowledged that "there have never been easy options for the
United States in Syria" but pressed the president to "soon provide a clearer
picture of how he plans to use American influence in dealing with the jihadi
threat and the endgame in Syria" (*NYT*, 2013, Apr. 30, p. 18).

Opinion pieces in May continued to probe the alleged use of chemical
weapons by Assad's military forces. Georgetown University professor Daniel Byman questioned the utility of issuing so-called red lines "that won't be
enforced," claiming that "in the Syrian case, the red line on chemical weapons
appears to have been issued without a decision as to how to respond to a Syrian
breach or even whether to escalate the situation." Byman discussed both the
positives and the negatives of enforcing declared red lines and, in this case,
did not urge the president to respond with greater US involvement (Byman,
2013, May 5, p. 4).

Times columnist Bill Keller did, however. Acknowledging that he had earlier supported the president's cautious approach, Keller now "fear[ed] prudence has become fatalism, and our caution has been the father of missed opportunities, diminished credibility and enlarged tragedy." He offered a range of reasons for greater American involvement, including national interest (that Syria could become "a haven for terrorists"), that a sectarian war (feared if the US became involved) was "already under way," that the US had options other than "putting American troops on the ground," and that "we have allies waiting for us to step up and lead." Keller went well beyond advocating a no-fly zone, stating that Mr. Assad needed to be put on notice to stop killing and start negotiating; and, if he didn't, there should be consequences: "We send missiles against his military installations until he, or more likely those around him, calculate that they should sue for peace" (Keller, 2013, May 6, p. 27).

An editorial on May 9 did not deal with the implications of the alleged breach of the red line in terms of an increased military response but, rather, supported a proposed Russian–US plan for an international conference on Syria. The editorial claimed that there were reasons to hope that a change in Russian policy was forthcoming—such as the avoidance of prolonged conflict in the region and the fear of seeing "Syria devolve into a state dominated by terrorist groups." The piece noted speculation that "increasing talk in Washington that the United States could become involved militarily in the conflict" might also have contributed to "Moscow's new interest in diplomacy" (*NYT*, 2013, May 9, p. 28). However, an editorial two weeks later conceded that hopes that the conference would even be held, much less lead to progress, were all but dead—and that "Russia is a big reason" (*NYT*, 2013, May 21: 24).

University of Illinois professor Feisal Mohamed introduced the concept "tyrannicide" as a way of dealing with the Syrian president. Although Mohamed fell short of actually advocating Assad's assassination, he did not dismiss a strategy that took "aim at the tyrant rather than the victims" instead of a military intervention that would result in many victims (Mohamed, 2013, May 12, p. 3). Another academic, Christopher Hill, dean of the University of Denver's School of International Studies, argued that "the real shortcoming of the administration's policy on Syria has not been an unwillingness to engage militarily … but the ill-advised decision, in August 2011, to preclude the possibility of a diplomatic resolution involving all sides." While not exonerating Assad, "who should face prosecution for war crimes," Hill counselled diplomatic re-engagement with Russian assistance, claiming "that the only realistic outcome is negotiated settlement" (Hill, 2013, May 16, p. 27).

Thomas Friedman's May 22 column was even more negative than his earlier ones as he speculated that Syria (as well as other countries of the Arab Spring) might prove to be "ungovernable by any group or ideology." The missing ingredient was *trust*—"that intangible thing that says you can rule over me even though you come from a different tribe, sect or political party"—without which he didn't see how any of the Arab "awakenings" could succeed. Friedman restated the need for an international force to referee what was likely to be a period of post-Assad chaos and cautioned against arming opposition groups: "Before we start sending guns to more people, let's ask ourselves for what exact ends we want those guns used and what else would be required of them and us to realize those ends" (Friedman, 2013, May 22, p. 27).

Ray Takeyh, an Iranian expert at the Council on Foreign Relations, addressed whether a US intervention in Syria might deter Iran's quest for nuclear weapons. On this issue he argued that only "an overwhelming show of military force" might accomplish that end. In that he saw any move by the Obama administration as "likely to be tentative and halting," such intervention would neither dislodge Assad nor impress Iran's rulers. To do both would require

> more than no-fly zones and arms. It would mean disabling Mr. Assad's air power and putting boots on the ground. America would have to take the lead in organizing a regional military force blessed by the Arab League and supported by its own intelligence assets and Special Forces. (Takeyh, 2013, May 28, p. 19)

Opinion commentary in June began with an editorial commenting on President Obama's selections of Susan Rice for national security advisor and Samantha Power as ambassador to the United Nations. Both were described as "liberal interventionists who favor using American power on behalf of humanitarian causes overseas." The editorial concluded, however, that "it is unlikely they will push Mr. Obama into an unwise intervention in Syria" (*NYT*, 2013, June 7, p. 26).

However, US policy appeared to change quickly as an editorial a week later criticized the president's decision "to begin supplying the rebels with small arms and ammunition" in response to the reported small-scale use of chemical weapons by Assad's forces. Such a move was seen as "open[ing] the door to an even larger American role." The editorial also criticized former president Bill Clinton and Senator John McCain for "fault[ing] Mr. Obama without explaining how the United States can change the course of that brutal war without being dragged into it" (*NYT*, 2013, June 15, p. 20). These positions were reiterated a day later in an article by Ramzy Mardini, now an adjunct fellow at the Institute for Strategic Studies based in Lebanon. Mardini claimed that the president's choice to "adopt the doctrine of intervention and provide arms to the rebels" was wrong. He argued that Assad continued to have "strong support from many Syrians …

[and, moreover that] … the rebels don't have the support or trust of a clear majority of the population, and the political opposition is neither credible nor representative." He saw a rebel victory as "likely to destabilize Iraq and Lebanon … [and] … the inevitable disorder as a greater threat to Israel than the status quo." Mardini also argued that the US had mishandled diplomacy early in the conflict; "once it called for Mr. Assad to step down in August 2011, the United States fully abdicated the role of credible arbiter." As a result, he called for rescinding the position that Assad must go, as it was unrealistic to attempt to negotiate "a political settlement if the outcome is already predetermined." Finally, former president Clinton was wrong in invoking the Kosovo analogy: "dropping a few bombs" would not end the war—"intervention in Syria won't end as Kosovo did for Mr. Clinton" (Mardini, 2013, June 16, p. SR5).

Elite dissensus continued as Maureen Dowd devoted a column to the criticism levelled against President Obama by Bill Clinton, and, although taking some jabs at the former president, she largely agreed with his assessment. She claimed that Clinton correctly took Obama to "the leadership woodshed" for not being more "forceful on Syria" and for his tendency to base decisions on opinion polls in particular. In the latter connection she approvingly quoted Clinton's comment that "if you blamed a poll for lack of action, 'you'd look like a total wuss.'" Dowd added her own criticism of the president, claiming that he "has turned out to be a leaden salesman in the Oval Office…. He seems incapable of getting in front of issues and shaping public and Congressional opinion with a strong selling job" (Dowd, 2013, June 16, p. SR11). She also thought that former national security advisor Zbigniew Brzezinski's charge that the president's decision to arm the rebels was "sporadic, chaotic, unstructured, undirected" had merit as did his claim that there needed to be "a serious policy review with the top people involved" (as quoted in Dowd, 2013, June 16, p. SR11).

Wesley Clark, former NATO Supreme Allied Commander for Europe, on the other hand, supported the decision to arm the rebels. He claimed that an increased military commitment on the part of the US was needed as a "catalyst" in reopening diplomatic talks leading to a negotiated settlement. For Clark there was a clear path forward that involved "a cease-fire agreement; a United Nations presence; departure of foreign fighters; disarmament of Syrian fighters; international supervision of Syria's military; a peaceful exit for Mr. Assad and his family and key supporters; a transitional government; and plans for a new Syria" (Clark, 2013, June 18, p. 25).

Thomas Friedman was unclear as to "where the president is going on Syria" and discussed "three possible strategies: the realist, the idealist and the God-I-hope-we-are-lucky approaches." Realism dictated arming the rebels in order to weaken "two of America's main regional foes—Hezbollah and Iran," although how far this might go toward ending the conflict was uncertain; idealism focused on creating a "unified, multisectarian, democratic Syria." Freidman restated his earlier assessment of what would be needed to accomplish this—on the ground involvement—pointing out that in Iraq, "this is something we did not do well, and which very few Americans would vote to repeat." The "God-I-hope-we-are-lucky" approach was in fact used in Libya, and he noted that "so far, we've not been very lucky."[1] Freidman's best outcome involved a negotiated settlement that included Assad's departure. However, for this to work "we would still need an international peacekeeping force to referee a post-Assad power-sharing deal" (Freidman, 2013, June 23, p. 11).

July's opinion pieces shifted the focus away from direct US involvement. Leslie Gelb of the Council on Foreign Relations and Dimitri Simes of the Center for the National Interest explored reasons why Russia and China were so uncompromising in their support for the Assad government. They concluded that both countries sought additional "diplomatic clout" and believed that this could best be achieved by "constraining the United States." They counselled the president to "see China and Russia as neither enemies nor friends, but as significant powers with their own interests." In any case, dealing with them was essential because "most security threats around the world ... [including Syria] ... can't be managed without Russia's and China's cooperation" (Gelb and Simes, 2013, July 7, p. 5).

Edward Luttwak of the Washington-based Center for Strategic and International Studies believed that the United States would neither benefit from an Assad victory nor a rebel victory and proposed what might be termed an ultra-realist strategy. In an article most likely written prior to the situation-changing chemical weapons attack, he argued that the best outcome for the US was "an indefinite draw,... [and that] ... a stalemate should be America's objective." To accomplish this, the US needed "to arm the rebels when it seems that Mr. Assad's forces are ascendant and to stop supplying the rebels if they actually seem to be winning." He asserted that "this strategy actually approximates the Obama administration's policy so far" (Luttwak, 2013, Aug. 25, p. 4).

The Guardian's Opinion Narrative

The Guardian's 2013 opinion narrative began with an article by University of London's University College law professor Philippe Sands. He noted that Switzerland had called upon the UN Security Council "to refer the situation in Syria to the International Criminal Court." However, since Russia saw the request as "'untimely' and 'counterproductive,'" he acknowledged that the request might not go far. Sands reviewed past referrals to the ICC (Sudan in 2005 and Libya in 2011) and argued that the 2011 referral had "pav[ed] the way to UN resolution 1973, that authorized 'all necessary measures' to protect Libyan civilians."

In Syria's case, referral to the ICC was not presented as a means of bringing an end to the conflict but, rather, as "chang[ing] the balance of factors that come into play in defining the nature and direction of the conflict" (Sands, 2013, Jan. 17, p. 32).

At the beginning of February an Israeli air strike against Hezbollah targets in Syria prompted journalist Jonathan Steele to push for talks between the opposition and Assad's government. Describing the situation as "urgent," he argued that "Syria's turmoil is having dangerously unpredictable consequences across the region." He analyzed the complicated relationship among opposition groups within and outside of Syria and concluded that the precondition that Assad step down prior to negotiations was unrealistic and that the West needed to back away from this demand. Western support for the opposition, even the so-called "non-lethal equipment" supplied by Britain, was seen as unhelpful in resolving the crisis; in Steele's opinion, "Britain has blood on its hands" (Steele, 2013, Feb. 1, p. 34).

Some weeks later, Steele followed up with an article on the contentious relationship between the Syrian National Coalition (SNC) and the US, detailing the rebel organization's rejection of a meeting with the newly appointed US Secretary of State John Kerry—the SNC had "accus[ed] the US and its allies of being complicit in the destruction of Syria by not intervening militarily." Steele speculated that the SNC might well be taking its orders from "the folks in the Pentagon, the CIA and the neocon thinktanks who want to deepen the militarization of the conflict." For Steele, this was a wrong-headed idea as "arming the rebels is not going to change the military situation, which is stalemated." The state of affairs was portrayed as bleak: "Little can save Syria now…. The country will probably be condemned to bloodshed on the pattern of Iraq, where car bombs and suicide bombs kill hundreds every month" (Steele, 2013, Feb. 26, p. 28).

Human Rights Watch executive director Kenneth Roth focused on the need for any post-Assad government in Syria to respect basic human rights, especially those related to the rights of women and free speech. In reference to what were seen to be some less than helpful developments unfolding during the Arab Spring (especially in Egypt), he argued "that the uncertainties of freedom are no reason to revert to the enforced predictability of authoritarian rule." He added as well that "it is wrong to contend that the prognosis for elected government under an Islamic party is so bleak that a return to the dark days of the past is warranted" (Roth, 2013, Feb. 4, p. 26).

In early March an opinion piece by former ABC News chief Middle East correspondent Charles Glass focused on the role that arms from outside Syria played in sustaining the conflict. Pointing out that "the gap between … [Assad and his opponents] … was narrowing sufficiently for deft diplomacy to bridge it," he criticized efforts by Britain to get "the EU to lift its embargo on arms sales to the opposition." What was needed was movement in the opposite direction: "Rather than lift the US-European arms embargo on lethal aid,... why not ask the Russians and Iranians to join it?" (Glass, 2013, Mar. 5, p. 32). Likewise, opposition MP Douglas Alexander was unimpressed with British efforts to arm rebel groups, arguing that "the pressing task remains not to arm the rebels but to unify them." He described the war as having reached the stage of "a destructive stalemate ... [and, that] ... if Europe were to decide to arm the rebel forces, the Russians would simply increase their supply of arms to the Assad regime" (Alexander, 2013, Mar. 13, p. 30).

In mid-March former al-Jazeera executive Wadah Khanfar offered an article that, in light of the crisis that developed in Iraq in 2014, turned out to be prophetic. He argued that Western strategy had aimed for a stalemate in the conflict when what was needed was the overthrow of Assad: "If the Assad government does not fall soon, the conflict will spread to the entire region, from Basra on the Gulf to Beirut on the Mediterranean Sea." In Iraq, the government of Nouri al-Maliki was described as unresponsive to demands of Sunni protesters, which had led to "another round of bloody violence, to which the Syrian conflict will be a natural extension." Such a spillover of the conflict into Iraq was seen as "tak[ing] the sectarian conflict in the area to unprecedented levels." Khanfar criticized the international community for its hesitation in deposing Assad: "So far the efforts of the international community have strengthened Assad's hand, sown confusion, and driven the revolutionaries toward extremism" (Khanfar, 2013, Mar. 16, p. 42).

Chatham House's Claire Spencer put a different spin on international involvement—namely, that the efforts by "the US, EU, Turkey, Saudi Arabia and Quatar ... [to aid the opposition, and by] ... Russia, China, Iran and sundry others [to support Assad]" had cancelled each other out. Western options, including a no-fly zone and humanitarian corridors, were assessed and found to be nowhere "close to being legally viable or practical on the ground." With respect to R2P, Spencer described NATO's military operation in Libya as possibly "one of the last actions of a consensus-based 'international community'" (Spencer, 2013, Mar. 27, p. 38).

The first *Guardian* editorial of 2013 regarding Syria appeared toward the end of March, two years into the conflict, and offered a sobering appraisal of the situation. President Assad appeared firmly in control, with his army "intact ... [and with] ... plenty of force in reserve." As well, Russia and Iran remained "steadfast in their support for Assad." In addition, things were not going well for the opposition, which was described as "in crisis mode ... [and] ... back to square one in trying to unite its disparate groups." In that the opposition refused to talk to the government (such talks were presented as "the least worst option") unless Assad agreed to step down, there were in fact, "no good options in Syria" (*Guardian*, 2013, Mar. 26, p. 34).

Opposition leader Haytham Manna assessed the situation in Syria as "the gravest it has been since peaceful protests began in March 2011." He described democratic forces as "scattered and fragmented." The Free Syrian Army was losing strength and had "no ideology, no common vision and no real independence," while jihadist groups were gaining strength. Mr. Assad appeared "confident that the opposition's political forces no longer represent any real power ... [and thus were] ... not serious in calling for a negotiated political solution." To achieve one, what was needed, according to Manna, was "reconciliation between the two strongest powers, Russia and the US" (Manna, 2013, Apr. 19, p. 30).

A *Guardian* editorial toward the end of April compared the suspected "small-scale" use of sarin gas by the Syrian army to the supposed discovery of "weapons of mass destruction" in Iraq, which had been used to justify the invasion of Iraq in 2003. While the editorial acknowledged that "the use of chemical weapons is a war crime," it emphasized that the mistakes of Iraq should not be repeated: "the evidence is there to be examined ... [and] ... the US appears ready to allow the UN to do its job." It was suggested that Russia and China adopt the same stance, arguing that "surely even President Putin cannot object to that" (*Guardian*, 2013, Apr. 27, p. 40).

Former British foreign secretary Lord David Owen called for a political settlement to the conflict and saw a solution in the form of "a regional settlement that is owned by the region." In order to achieve this, with UN and US assistance and with no preconditions, all Middle Eastern countries "including Iraq, Turkey, Iran, Israel, Lebanon, Egypt and Palestine," as well as representatives from the West Bank and Gaza, should attend a regional security conference. Adding more armaments to the conflict would be counterproductive. The UN was called upon to step up and get the job done: "The UN security council permanent five should stop the blame game and get on with their real responsibility—bringing the conflict to an end and hammering out a regional security [framework] involving far more than just Syria" (Owen, 2013, May 4, p. 42).

An editorial on May 5 confirmed what had long been suspected—that "Hezbollah fighters were helping Bashar al-Assad." This, along with Israeli air strikes and Iran's being "ready to train Assad's army," meant that the feared regionalization of the civil war was in fact a reality. Moreover, Israeli air strikes pointed to "the yawning lack of direction from Barack Obama." In that it looked increasingly like "Assad could be here in a year's time,... nothing America is doing, or not doing, is preparing for that possibility" (*Guardian*, 2013, May 5).

Two days later, another opinion piece by Wadah Khanfar also focused on the regional dynamics of the conflict. He advanced the idea that "the entire region is now undergoing the most important geopolitical shift since the political map of the Middle East was redrawn after the first world war," establishing boundaries that were "illogical and impractical ... [and never] ... enjoyed any legitimacy in the minds of Arab people." Khanfar argued that "since ancient times—Arabs, Kurds, Turks and Iranians ... [had lived in the region] ... in an open social and economic environment." What was needed now was "unity and integration," to be brought about through a "Middle Eastern economic zone that embraces Iraq, Syria, Lebanon and Jordan, and opens up to Turkey and Iran." In that sectarian conflicts tend to "know no borders," the alternative was that "all will be losers" (Khanfar, 2013, May 7, p. 26). Citing increased tensions in neighbouriing Iraq, a *Guardian* editorial three days later re-emphasized the importance of curbing arms supplies to the rebels: "It is not difficult to wargame a conflict that freewheels over three countries—Iraq, Syria and Lebanon." The suggested alternative to arming the rebels was "de-escalation," and key to the success of this strategy was "pressuring the Gulf states to starve rival militias of arms. Without this happening, there is no political solution" (*Guardian*, 2013, May 11, p. 44).

Seumas Milne's May 8 opinion piece was highly critical of "Israel's string of aerial attacks on Syrian military installations near Damascus." These were described as "unprovoked and illegal" as well as an indication that "Israel is clearly intervening in the war." For Milne, it was "Syria's role as the pivot of Iranian influence across the Middle East that has turned the Syrian civil war into a potential regional conflagration." He concluded that Israeli air strikes indicated that "it regards the prospect of Islamic and jihadist groups taking over from the Assad regime as less threatening than the existing 'Syria-Iran-Hezbollah axis.'" Israel was not the only international actor criticized. For example, "among those pushing for more intervention is David Cameron—anxious to ingratiate himself with the Gulf dictators." Efforts by Cameron and others in the West to increase arms supplies to the rebels were characterized as "reckless and cynical." Milne claimed that the fate awaiting Syria was "a Yugoslavian-style fragmentation" should the war continue to drag on, and he argued that "an internationally and regionally backed deal now looks the only way to bring the war to an end" (Milne, 2013, May 8, p. 26). An opinion article published on the same day by retired Israeli general Michael Herzog refuted the charge that Israel was in fact intervening in the civil war; he argued that "Israel has no interest is getting drawn into the quagmire." Instead, he identified Iran as "Israel's most dangerous foe," followed by Hezbollah, and he claimed that the air strikes were aimed at the latter, which had been "armed to the teeth by its patrons in Tehran" (Herzog, 2013, May 8, p. 26).

Jeremy Greenstock, former UK special envoy for Iraq, described the situation in Syria as "a destructive stalemate, which intensified military action and offers no real prospect of breaking." Moreover, even the fall of the Assad government would not bring an end to the civil war. There was "no obvious successor ... in sight, which means a vacuum.... [As a result] ... the chances of disorder are very high." Diplomacy was favoured over outside intervention, and Greenstock proposed "a conference-in-continuity," which, even if ignored for some time, would "eventually create the framework for a solution inside Syria" (Greenstock, 2013, May 16, p. 38).

Jonathan Steele's May 21 opinion article repeated Owen's and Greenstock's idea for an ongoing conference in a somewhat different form. Specifically, a system of "working committees" was needed to deal with issues such as "constitutional reform, humanitarian access, detainee release, local ceasefires and the introduction of UN observers." Steele also suggested the formation of "a coalition government of national unity," including representation from the current government and the opposition. However, even if these changes came about, Steele cautioned that no miracles should be expected: "Syria is probably doomed to face a long-term armed insurgency in parts of the country for years to come" (Steele, 2013, May 21, p. 30). The latter pessimistic theme was developed further in an editorial that appeared on the same day, which argued that what had been a "proxy war" on the part of Iran and Hezbollah was now one in which pro-government "foreign fighters openly engaged in combat,... signaling that Assad's fate has become a matter of existential survival for them too." This meant that Syria "is no longer master of its own territory or fate," making any reconciliation among strictly Syrian factions, "already a faint hope,... virtually impossible." As well, the editorial criticized the West for insisting that peace talks could not include the Assad government (*Guardian*, 2013, May 21, p. 32).

The British policy initiative seeking to end the EU embargo on arms to Syria was criticized by former Liberal Democratic leader Menzies Campbell, who argued that "outrage and frustration are not enough to provide an efficient justification or sound basis for such a material policy change." The character and motivation of the opposition were called into question: at least some among them "most certainly do not share our values of democracy and human rights ... [and] ... have proved themselves to be as brutal as Assad." Campbell also cited "a risk of weapons falling into the wrong hands" (Campbell, 2013, May 24, p. 52).

Simon Jenkins argued much the same point—that there was "no more dreadful idea than to pour armaments into the sectarian war now consuming Syria." He then added a theme not seen in any previous commentary, criticizing Britain (along with the West) for having abandoned the region's "secularist dictators." While "they had faults in abundance ... they succeeded in suppressing religious discord, instilling rudimentary tolerance and keeping the region mostly in order.... Turning turtle and abetting their downfall may yet prove the most disastrous miscalculation of western diplomacy since the rise of fascism." Applying this argument to the situation in Syria, Jenkins maintained that intervening against Assad was the wrong course and concluded with the distancing observation that the liberal interventionist argument that "'we cannot allow this to happen' assumes potency over other people's affairs that 'we' do not possess" (Jenkins, 2013, May 29, p. 26).

An early-June editorial confirmed fears that "the end result [of the civil war] would not be a liberated Syria, but a divided one ... with years of warfare to come." Moreover, the sectarian nature of the conflict indicated that "when it finishes, there will be new enclaves and new borders." Yet again the editorial condemned British moves toward sending arms to the rebels: "Forcing the end of the EU arms embargo makes little strategic sense. It is unlikely to change the balance of power between different rebel groups ... but is certain to ensure that Assad's supplies of heavy weapons continue" (*Guardian*, 2013, June 6, p. 34).

Charles Glass shifted the opinion commentary to US policy, which fared no better than Britain's. Secretary of State Hillary Clinton's policy (she had "demanded [Assad's] overthrow, making it a precondition for negotiation") had clearly failed. Further, although the Syrian National Council was described as "a creation of American diplomacy," the US had not been able to get it to take part in peace talks. And, without the SNC in attendance, "there can be no conference. No conference, no peace" (Glass, 2013, June 7, p. 42).

An editorial on June 15 responded to President Obama's "decision to authorize military aid to the Syria rebels," a decision that, it was noted, was quickly welcomed by Senator John McCain and Prime Minister David Cameron. The decision, however, was not welcomed by *The Guardian*'s editorial board, as it was seen to diminish the chances of holding a second Geneva peace conference: rebels would be encouraged to not attend, and, in any event, Russia and Iran would simply increase their supplies of weapons to the Syrian army to offset any advantage gained by the rebels from the arrival of arms from the West. As for Mr. Assad, he "will not be deterred by the fresh inflow of arms as long as the military battlefield favours him" (*Guardian*, 2013, June 15, p. 52). Two days later, US policy was clarified in an opinion piece by Alastair Crooke, the director of Conflicts Forum: "The US deputy national security advisor has said there will be no escalation in the weapons supplied to the insurgents and there will be no no-fly zones. Supplies already are at the limit of what can be safely given—and if advanced items ever were to reach al-Qaida this would be a 9/11 'hot button' event for the US." Britain and France favoured arming the insurgents, but in doing so Crooke suggested that they "risk being lured into finding themselves ever more closely allied with Sunni proxies of al-Qaida" (Crooke, 2013, June 17, p. 26).

History professor Marko Attila Hoare offered a rare *Guardian* pro-intervention piece, in which he criticized "western inaction" as undermining the only viable alternative to a brutal dictatorship. Specifically, in that Russia and Iran were already "intervening in Syria with weapons and troops ... it is the west's failure to support the [Free Syrian Army] that strengthens al-Qaida's hand." Anti-interventionists in Britain came in for special criticism. In their eyes, according to Hoare, "anyone resisting Assad automatically becomes an Islamic extremist." As well, he charged anti-interventionists with being blind to what was described as "the far-greater Islamist menace facing Syria: the Shia extremism promoted by Iran and embodied in its proxy, Hezbollah." Hoare also noted that "arms supplied to the FSA and a no-fly zone—would enjoy broad support in the region, including from Turkey and the Arab League" (Hoare, 2013, June 19, p. 30).

An editorial that appeared after the G8 Meeting in Northern Ireland focused primarily on President Vladimir Putin, who was portrayed as seeing jihadists, especially Sunni Islamists, as "the common enemies that the civilized world is facing." The editorial explained that such a view "precludes the legitimacy of popular uprisings against tyrannies, least of all in the Arab world." In that Mr. Putin "takes all threats of regime change personally ... [his] ... sympathy is with the despots, not their people." The editorial expressed "no surprise that the G8 leaders had difficulty in arriving at even the blandest of statements on Syria," and it repeated earlier arguments that Western decisions to increase armaments to the opposition at a time when the conflict was taking on an international character would lead to its "deepening and continuation ... [with the end game looking like] ... a permanently divided country" (*Guardian*, 2013, June 19, p. 32).

Toward the end of June, writer and journalist Malise Ruthven decried "the spectre of modern sectarian barbarism" that had been unleashed in the Middle East, noting that in the history of Islam, it "stands in stark contrast to an older narrative of tolerance and pluralism." He pointed out that theological questions surrounding "beliefs about 'God'" were not the issue. At fault was "the way in which group identities are formed by centuries of cultural programming underpinned by religious practices." Syria's current problems were rooted in the Alawi, described as "a Shia sectarian group from the margins," which was able to seize control of the Ba'th party in 1970. The result was "clannism—rooted in authoritarian patriarchal structures ... [not in] ... the public good" (Ruthven, 2013, June 28, p. 46).

Guardian editorials in July continued to focus on the intractable nature of the Syrian civil war but emphasized its impact on refugees and, in turn, their impact on the stability of the surrounding region. Pessimism and distance framing continued to predominate in the editorials. For example, a mid-July piece described the Middle East as "grim terrain for intervention, diplomacy or mediation of any kind." Recent advocacy for military action was seen as "never quite real," and it was noted that it "has died down, thank goodness, on both sides of the Atlantic." In terms of what might have been, the United States was criticized for "com[ing] out so plainly and unequivocally for regime change, a decision which has undermined every subsequent effort to mediate, and which has probably irretrievably alienated Russia." The editorial also pointed to a paradox: just as the region desperately needed international help, "the governments and the peoples of the regions are making their own decisions, good or bad, with less and less reference to what outsiders, including the United States desire." In that "the record of the outsiders … has plainly been littered with dismal mistakes," there was no clear judgment regarding whether this development would turn out to be helpful or not (*Guardian*, 2013, July 19, p. 34).

In late July, *The Guardian* ran a number of stories that described the war as having "generated the world's gravest refugee crisis in a generation." In the introduction to the series, the human costs of the conflict were stressed, as was the considerable "potential for destabilization" in the region at large. Apathy on the part of the international community was noted and deplored:

> Refugee stories are hard to project. There is an air of inevitability about the narrative, the wretched predicament of the victims, the horrible things that have been done to them. Even the word "refugee" tends to engender fatigue. We've heard it all before. Yet Syria has its own story of "unimaginable brutality, the senseless destruction of what was, until recently, a relatively comfortable place to live, work and raise a family…. [And] no one knows when it will end. (Mahmood, Letsch, Smith, Kingsley, & Chulov, 2013, July 25, p. 19)

The editorial that accompanied the focus on refugees also dealt with the potential of the refugee crisis to destabilize neighbouring countries, noting that "refugees rarely turn their backs on the conflict that displaced them." It pointed out that the humanitarian crisis in Syria was "now worse than that in the former Yugoslavia in the '90s." Moreover, the editorial reprimanded the international community for not "honouring the pledges of assistance they have made to the UNHCR [United Nations High Commissioner for Refugees]." The only solution to the refugee crisis was "a political settlement," and on that issue the editorial noted that "we need a plan and we haven't got one" (*Guardian*, 2013, July 25, p. 30).[2]

The Guardian's last editorial before the August sarin gas attack carried the title "Syria: There is worse to come." It claimed that the fighting in Syria had created "the biggest refugee crisis since Rwanda" and pointed out that its impact on neighbouring Iraq, Lebanon, and Jordan was "no longer a matter of conjecture but of fact." In spite of this, it observed that "the civil war is slipping down the international agenda." Specifically, the editorial criticized President Obama for cancelling a meeting with Vladimir Putin "in full knowledge that one casualty of the slight ... would be the declared aim of the resumption of the peace talks in Geneva." However, this was perhaps of little consequence as the Syrian opposition was portrayed as so disorganized that it was unlikely to be able "to agree on whom should represent them." The efforts of Iran and Hezbollah on behalf of Assad and those of Saudi Arabia, Qatar, and Turkey on behalf of the opposition meant that the war "has become first and foremost a struggle for regional ambitions." The editorial ended with the observation that "without the international will to stop this, this conflict has fuel enough to burn for a long time indeed" (*Guardian*, 2013, Aug. 9, p. 30).

The Globe and Mail's Opinion Narrative

The first *Globe and Mail* editorial of 2013 conveyed a sense of urgency not seen previously: "The Syrian civil war has reached a point at which the international community—that is to say the world's responsible powers—need to take *a more active hand*, still with caution, favouring carefully selected insurgent groups that are not Salafist, and have no affinities to al-Qaeda." Moreover, such an "active hand" included arming the anti-government forces by "supplying equipment, *such as surface-to-air missiles*, to certain opposition groups." The motivation for such a policy was that the Assad regime would likely fall and that, in the resulting chaos, "a group such as Jabhat al-Nusra, a Syrian group affiliated to the Iraqi factions that are in turn aligned with al-Qaeda, could well find and keep a foothold." Even more critical was the judgment that if Assad resorted to the use of chemical weapons, "*foreign intervention would become almost inevitable and indeed morally desirable*" (*Globe*, 2013, Jan. 2, p. 12; italics added). While a mid-March opinion article by Paul Heinbecker also endorsed the use of military force in Syria, it did so circumspectly. The article focused on a possible US attack on Iran, which Heinbecker strongly opposed based on "the lessons of Iraq," a war that he claimed had "so damaged America's reputation that it will take generations to recover." Syria, however, was a different matter, which he described as "the most pressing current case for military intercession, despite the fear of making things worse." Heinbecker argued that an intervention in Syria could be accomplished by establishing "safe havens and no-fly zones," which were described as "limited but viable alternatives." At the same time, keeping "Western boots" out of Syria was a priority because Heinbecker claimed that "intervention fatigue ... [was widespread in] ... financially strapped and politically distracted Washington and Europe." In such circumstances Canada was urged "to accept a greater share of the lead" (Heinbecker, 2013, Mar. 15, p. 15).

Timothy Garton Ash's end-of-April opinion piece began with the premise that "no one knows what to do about [Syria]" and from there reviewed a number of military and diplomatic strategies to end the violence—all of which came up short. R2P should apply to Syria, according to Garton Ash, but it suffered from "a kind of subconscious racism" that might help explain the asymmetric international responses to the Balkans as opposed to the Middle East as well as Africa. Involvement of multiple regional powers in Syria, all with a stake in the outcome, reduced the chances of defusing the proxy component of the war, while al-Qaeda influence among rebel forces complicated a domestic solution. Predicting a future "no-polar world," Garton Ash foresaw a bloody twenty-first century "unless we develop new ways of conflict resolution, strong enough to constrain this new world disorder" (Garton Ash, 2013, Apr, 25, p. 15).

A *Globe* editorial a few days later opened commentary on the issue of Syria's chemical weapons in the context of the Obama-declared "red line" against their use. It cited US evidence that "Syria is probably using nerve gas on a small scale," a finding that it claimed had been confirmed by British and French intelligence agencies. The editorial switched focus to the implications of Syria's chemical weapons for Israel, and these were not positive, regardless of which side won. The focus then returned to Mr. Obama, who was advised to give "some practical substance to his words, in such a way as to protect Syrian citizens while not putting Islamic extremists in power" (*Globe*, 2013, Apr. 28, p. 14).

Barry Rubin, director of the Israel-based Global Research in International Affairs Center (now called the Rubin Center for Research in International Affairs), examined Israel's own "red line," which had been invoked against "the transport of advanced weapons" to Hezbollah. Rubin argued that Israel had no interest in becoming involved in Syria's civil war beyond ensuring that advanced weapons did not end up in the hands of Hezbollah. With respect to the war itself, he maintained that Israel had "no side to root for." The Assad regime was described as having been "unremittingly hostile [to Israel] and allied with Iran,... [while] ... a rebel victory could bring risk-taking extremists to power who might attack across the Syria-Israel border." He concluded with the sad reminder "that in the Middle East, there are often no purely good solutions" (Rubin, 2013, May 7, p. 15).

Globe foreign affairs reporter Campbell Clark assessed the Canadian House of Commons emergency debate on Syria held in May and concluded that there wasn't much to show for it: "no vote on what steps to take, no call to back military intervention or a no-fly zone or to arm rebels." While Ottawa's reluctance to back the rebels stemmed from the presence of "extremists in their midst," he pointed out that in fact "there is no prospective military mission to join." For Clark, Canada was left with a policy that called for "Mr. al-Assad to go, but is so wary of jihadists among rebels it does not want to help tip the balance in their favour." He suggested that a similar calculation was in play in US decision-making (Clark, 2013, May 9, p. 8).

In an opinion article toward the end of May, Princeton University professor Anne-Marie Slaughter criticized President Obama for timidity in not pursuing a military option (his "strategy in Syria seems to be 'speak loudly and throw away your stick'") and argued the case for intervention. For Slaughter, the issue was that at least a credible threat of military force on the part of US was required to get Assad to negotiate a settlement. She argued that the war needed to come to an end: "Killing always begets more killing … [as people involved] … carry vengeance in their hearts from generation to generation." As a consequence, "in Syria, the moral, strategic and political arguments all converge in favour of decisive action to stop the killing, at least for now, to create space for peace" (Slaughter, 2013, May 29, p. 15).[3]

In early June, citing the failures of intervention in Iraq, Afghanistan, and Libya, prominent *Globe* columnists Lysiane Gagnon (2013, June 5) and Jeffrey Simpson (2013, June 7) counselled Canada to avoid becoming involved in any military action in Syria. However, while conceding that "reasons for not intervening militarily are not trivial," Paul Heinbecker pointed out that "not acting in Syria is far from cost-free." Chief among these costs were the "strengthening" of Iran and Hezbollah and the weakening of the United States. He supported the creation of no-fly zones, a solution that would not stop the killing and was not without risks but was one that "would diminish Mr. al-Assad's capability to visit vast destruction on his citizens by air." It was noted that "Canada has the capability to contribute … [and] … if it doesn't want to do so, it should not impede others who do" (Heinbecker, 2013, June 18, p. 15).

Former Diplomat Derek Burney and academic Fen Osler Hampson took the opposite view, advancing "five reasons to stay out of Syria:" an untrustworthy opposition, a possibility of conflict escalation, a worsening of relations with Russia, that the removal of Assad would not end the conflict and that "Western democracies simply do not have the stomach for protracted, inconclusive military gambits." They claimed that Canada did not "have a dog in this fight … [and] … should not be stoking its fires or trying to pick winners" (Burney and Hampson, 2013, June 19: 15).

Retired general Lewis MacKenzie offered a history of no-fly zones and was not impressed. The concept had its origins following the first Gulf War, with this simple warning to Iraqi pilots: "Don't fly or you're going to die." By 1999, in the Serbia-Kosovo conflict, no-fly zones had become more all-encompassing. Although the international use of force had not been authorized by the Security Council, NATO used the no-fly zone concept to launch "an all-out bombing campaign against the infrastructure of the former Yugoslavia." In Libya, a no-fly zone had been authorized by the Security Council, and MacKenzie argued that Russia and China had been "truly duped" into thinking they were approving something along the lines of the limited application seen in Iraq. Instead, NATO was just as aggressive as it had been in Kosovo, commencing "all-out attacks on Libya's aircraft on the ground, airfields, command-and-control centres, supply depots, military units and so on." As for Syria, MacKenzie saw no way that Russia and China would be fooled again. And, while NATO might be able to mount a successful no-fly zone, he counselled that it "would not be wise" for Canada to sign on (MacKenzie, 2013, June 25, p. 13).

DISCUSSION

For *The New York Times*, framing that distanced the US from the conflict still prevailed early on in 2013. Commentary called attention to a shift in the makeup of the Syrian opposition toward Islamic fundamentalism, which complicated any Western efforts to provide arms to rebel forces. Spring, however, brought criticism of the president's cautionary policies from both key Republicans and some influential Democrats. As well, suspected incidents of the minor use of chemical weapons by Mr. Assad prompted a discussion of the wisdom of Mr. Obama's declaration of a "red line" against their use, and there were increasing calls to arm the moderate opposition, with some suggestions that the time for military intervention had arrived. Thomas Friedman repeatedly pointed out that there was no way that Syria could undergo a democratic transition without a major commitment on the part of the international community, which would have to include somebody's "boots on the ground," thus serving as a midwife and/or referee for a long time to come—and even this would provide no guarantee for success. At the time of the chemical attack in August, there was much discussion but little consensus among policy commentators regarding what direction US policy toward Syria should take, but in the mix the president's cautionary approach came under increasing scrutiny.

During the early months of 2013 opinion-leading material in *The Guardian* began with dire assessments that the deteriorating situation in Syria might bring about the feared regionalization of the war. The paper also viewed as problematic the effort of Britain to repeal the EU ban on the export of weapons to Syria and continued to see arming the opposition as a very bad idea. At that point, the situation on the battlefield was interpreted to be clearly favouring Assad, and talks without preconditions were presented as the only solution to the conflict. As well, the sectarian nature of the war suggested the likelihood of permanent divisions in a postwar Syria. In July commentary shifted to consider the plight of refugees; in dealing with this issue, fatigue on the part of the international community meant that this problem had not been adequately addressed.

The Globe's 2013 opinion narrative up to the chemical weapons attack can be characterized by two themes. First, the paper's editorial position took an early hard line, calling for arming the opposition. The push for international action continued over that summer with support for a no-fly zone and, ultimately, as we shall see in the following chapter, support for air strikes against the Assad regime. Second, as was the case previously, opinion articles in The Globe offered arguments both in favour of and opposed to greater international involvement, including the use of military force; in that many of these articles counselled restraint, they argued against the paper's editorial position.

The August 2013 Chemical Weapons Attack: Framing of a Possible Military Response

INTRODUCTION

On August 21, 2013, with the devastating civil war two and a half years old, a nerve gas attack on a civilian suburb of Damascus, almost certainly launched by Assad's forces, killed an estimated 1,400 people. This time, few doubted that the Obama "red line" of a year earlier had been crossed or that the 1925 treaty banning the use of chemical weapons had been contravened; a war crime had been committed. At this point, for opinion writers, the issues were reduced to two:

- The possible "use of force" as a response to Assad's atrocity
- Whether the agreement to collect and destroy Syria's stockpile of chemical weapons (which removed Western military action from consideration) was an adequate response

Given the seriousness of the situation, the world could scarcely avoid consideration of decisive action against the Syrian regime. In the weeks that followed, the governments of both the United States and the United Kingdom scheduled votes in their respective legislatures seeking approval for a military response. But shortly after the British Parliament rejected participation in a military operation, and before the same issue came to a vote in the US Congress, an agreement to remove and destroy Syria's stock of chemical weapons was proposed. At the time, the idea for such an agreement as a substitute for air strikes against Assad was attributed to Russia's President Vladimir Putin, but we now know that it was in fact proposed by President Obama and negotiated between Russian and US officials (Goldberg, 2016, April). We end the data-based chapters of the book with an account of these two interrelated issues as opinion-leading material in our selected newspapers assessed the policy adjustments necessitated by quickly changing events.

QUANTITATIVE FINDINGS

During the final 40 days of our study, the critical actors in the Syrian conflict were effectively reduced to three: (1) Great Britain, where Prime Minister David Cameron strongly favoured an international military response and scheduled an early Parliamentary vote to approve British participation in one; (2) the United States, where initially President Barack Obama reluctantly decided that a military response of an indeterminate size was unavoidable; and (3) Russia, where President Vladimir Putin continued to oppose any forceful military involvement and, to avoid American air strikes, managed to get President Assad to agree to relinquish his stock of chemical weapons to international inspectors.

Mr. Cameron's plan of action was the first to derail, brought to a halt by a failed vote in Parliament. Mr. Obama had at first contemplated personally ordering military strikes, as he had the power as president to do, but, in the face of continuing division of opinion concerning the wisdom of such a move, he reconsidered and called instead for a Congressional vote of approval on the matter. Just prior to the scheduled vote, however, the chemical weapons deal was announced, and Mr. Obama postponed the Congressional vote. By the end of September, the UN Security Council had finalized the chemical weapons deal in a resolution, and an international military response no longer appeared imminent.

As we look at data in Table 7.1, we see that actions by the US were the primary focus of opinion-leading commentary in all three newspapers—overall, in close to 90 per cent of content. Russian actions (largely the chemical weapons deal) followed, commented on in just over 40 per cent of items—especially salient in *The Globe and Mail* opinion material (56 per cent of items). No doubt due to Britain's early exit as a possible player, its actions were the focus of only 36 per cent of items overall, although commented on in 61 per cent of *Guardian* material. By way of contrast, only 17 per cent of *Times'* material commented on British actions, 10 per cent lower than that seen in *The Globe*.

What is most interesting in an overview of data in Table 7.2 is that none of the opinion material in any of the papers evaluated the action of any of the

Table 7.1   Salience of American, Russian, and British Actions, Aug. 22 to Sept. 30, 2013, by Newspaper (Per Cent of Opinion-Leading Items)

	Times N=46	*Guardian* N=41	*Globe* N=18	Total N=105
US	93.5	80.5	88.9	87.6
Russia	39.1	39.0	55.6	41.9
Britain	17.4	61.0	27.8	36.2

Table 7.2 Evaluation of American, Russian, and British Actions, Aug. 22 to Sept. 30, 2013, by Newspaper (Per Cent of Opinion-Leading Items—Ambiguous Items Omitted)

	Times N=46		Guardian N=41		Globe N=18		Total N=105		Percentage Difference
	Pos	Neg	Pos	Neg	Pos	Neg	Pos	Neg	
US	19.6	26.1	4.9	34.1	11.1	27.8	12.4	29.5	−17.1
Russia	10.9	13.0	0	24.4	11.1	22.2	6.7	19.0	−12.3
Britain	2.2	4.3	12.2	17.1	0	5.6	5.7	9.5	−3.8

Table 7.3 Evaluation of Direct Military Action, Aug. 22 to Sept. 30, 2013, by Newspaper (Per Cent of Opinion-Leading Items—Ambiguous Items Omitted)

Times N=46		Guardian N=41		Globe N=18		Total N=105		Percentage Difference
Pos	Neg	Pos	Neg	Pos	Neg	Pos	Neg	
21.7	19.6	4.9	43.9	27.8	33.3	16.2	31.4	−15.2

three critical actors positively. Material in *The Guardian* was most negative toward actions of the US (34 per cent), of Russia (24 per cent), and of its home country (17 per cent). *The Guardian* also featured material that was most favourable toward British actions (12 per cent), approving in particular the vote that blocked any British participation in a military response. Notably, *The Guardian* had nothing at all positive to say about Russia's actions, while *The Globe* was most favourable toward Russia, by a fraction over *The Times*. Material in *The Times* was most favourable toward US actions (20 per cent) as well as least critical (26 per cent).

As reported in Table 7.3, the issue of direct military action as a response to the chemical weapons attack drew a good deal of attention, but only in *The Times* did positive judgments outweigh negative ones, and even then by only a small margin (22 per cent to 20 per cent). In contrast, *Guardian* commentary rejected military force by a margin of close to 40 per cent, while in *The Globe* negative assessments prevailed by a margin of 6 per cent. Overall, when actual decisions on military action were being made, the percentage difference on the use of force stood at −15 per cent, an increase in negativity of 8 per cent from that recorded for the first eight and a half months of the year.

Table 7.4   Evaluation of the Chemical Weapons Agreement, Sept. 10 to Sept. 30, 2013, by Newspaper (Actual Number of Items)

Times			Guardian			Globe			Total		
Fav	Amb	Unfav	Fav	Amb	Unfav	Fav	Amb	Unfav	Fav	Amb	Unfav
6	4	2	3	2	1	0	5	1	9	11	4

In Table 7.4 we are looking at very small subset of data—24 editorials and opinion articles that were published between the announcement on September 10 of a possible deal to remove and destroy Syria's chemical weapons and the end of the month. In that numbers are not sufficient to calculate percentages, the table shows the actual number of opinion pieces that were coded Favourable, Ambiguous, or Unfavourable with respect to the agreement.

Evaluations can best be described as more positive than negative but, at the same time, clearly less than wholeheartedly committed to the agreement; indeed, ambiguous assessments outnumbered positive ones by two items. Only in *The Times* was there a relatively strong number of favourable pieces (6), with somewhat fewer ambiguous ones (4), and only two that were unfavourable to the agreement. Opinion material in *The Guardian* covered all options: favourable (3), ambiguous (2), and unfavourable (1). Opinion in *The Globe* was the least enthusiastic: favourable (0), ambiguous (5), and unfavourable (1). We must stress that some of these evaluations appeared in the very early stages of the process of putting together an agreement that was only approved by the UN Security Council late in September. Along with commentary on possible military action, arguments pro and con and in between on the agreement will be examined more fully in the following opinion narratives.

QUALITATIVE FINDINGS

The New York Times' Opinion Narrative

The chemical weapons attack against civilians late in August, widely attributed to President Assad's forces, not only changed the parameters of the debate but for the first time prompted *The Times* to rethink its previous editorial position, largely supporting President Obama's cautious approach to the Syrian disaster. While maintaining that proof was still needed that the Syrian government was indeed responsible for the atrocity, an editorial on August 23 suggested that if the allegation proved to be true, "the United States and other major powers will almost certainly have to respond much more aggressively than they have so far." It described the situation as "a moment of reckoning" and noted that in view of his previous statement that "'there will be consequences,' … President Obama's credibility is also on the line." The editorial argued that "at some point, those words have to mean something," although at this point that "something" was left vague (*NYT*, 2013, Aug. 23, p. 26).

What "something" might mean was clarified in a second editorial a day later—it should come in the form of a military response, although the paper continued to vacillate between appearing to accept that Assad was responsible for the attack and warning that the evidence had not clearly established this. In any case, since Security Council approval of a military response was extremely unlikely, the 1999 NATO-led bombing campaign against Serbia was cited as an appropriate model. However, even as it was advocating a strong military response, *The Times* cautioned against US involvement in the war itself: "The aim is to punish Mr. Assad for slaughtering his people with chemical arms, not to be drawn into another civil war." The editorial's final sentence reiterated this position: "Though Mr. Assad's use of chemical weapons surely requires a response of some kind, the argument against deep American involvement remains as compelling as ever" (*NYT*, 2013, Aug. 27, p. 20). Two days later, a third editorial appeared to be even less supportive of military action, pointing out that the president "has failed to lay out any legal basis for it and has not won support from key organizations—namely the Arab League and NATO—that could provide legitimacy." It further called upon the president to make "public immediately" whatever evidence he had that Assad's forces were in fact responsible for the attack. The editorial argued as well that although it would be unlikely to survive Russian-Chinese vetoes, a resolution calling for a military strike needed to be brought before the UN Security Council "since chemical weapons use is a war crime and banned under international treaties" (*NYT*, 2013, Aug. 29, p. 26). A fourth editorial appearing on August 31 moved yet further away from support of a military strike. It noted that neither the US Congress nor the UN Security Council had approved of military action and, beyond that, that the British Parliament had voted against "involvement in a military operation," leaving only France supporting a military strike. It also noted President Obama's 2007 position that "'the president does not have the power under the Constitution to unilaterally authorize a military attack in a situation that does not involve stopping an actual or imminent threat to the nation'" (as quoted in *NYT*, 2013, Aug. 31, p. 18). The editorial ended on a cautionary note: "Even in the best of circumstances, military action could go wrong in so many ways; the lack of strong domestic and international support will make it even more difficult" (*NYT*, 2013, Aug. 31, p. 18).

Opinion pieces on the issue of a military response ranged widely in terms of issues covered and positions advocated. Northwestern University political science professor Ian Hurd agreed that a US military response to Assad's use of chemical weapons was appropriate; however, he argued that in terms of international law, the case for intervention was weak at best. To deal with this problem,

Hurd proposed "adding humanitarian intervention as a third category of lawful war under the concept of the 'responsibility to protect,' [which he noted was] widely accepted ... [but] lacks the force of law." He claimed that there were two legitimizing strategies for an intervention that bypassed the UN Security Council, both based on what he termed "constructive noncompliance." The first was the "illegal but legitimate" argument emerging from the case of Kosovo, while the second was the argument that following the UN's approval of R2P, "international law has changed." Of the two, Hurd favoured the latter, "urging Mr. Obama and allied leaders ... [to pursue a new legal strategy and] ... declare that international law has evolved and that they don't need Security Council approval to intervene in Syria" (Hurd, 2013, Aug. 28, p. 27).

In a period of seven days, five *New York Times* columnists weighed in on the issues of the wisdom and appropriateness of a US military response, with no clear consensus emerging. Nicholas Kristof supported a military response, although somewhat reluctantly. He concluded that the president's "policy toward Syria has failed, and it's time the try a tougher approach." He acknowledged that "critics are raising legitimate concerns" regarding what an escalation of American involvement might bring in its wake. However, without specifically invoking the R2P doctrine, he argued that "in conjunction with diplomacy, military force can save lives." He maintained that Mr. Obama "can't just whimper and back down ... it's better to stand up inconsistently to some atrocities than to acquiesce consistently in them all" (Kristof, 2013, Aug. 29, p. 27).

David Brooks assessed the implications of the impact of the Syrian civil war on the wider Middle East as well as on Syria and was pessimistic with respect to the US's ability to influence outcomes in either. For Syria, the options increasingly looked like "anarchy" or "atrocity," while for the region, "the forces ripping people into polarized groups seem stronger than the forces bringing them together." While a planned military strike might "establish American credibility ... it's not clear whether American and other outside interference would help quash hatreds or inflame them." Brooks concluded that "the policy options for dealing with the Syria situation ... are all terrible or too late" (Brooks, 2013, Aug. 30, p. 19).

Charles Blow addressed the issue of where the American people stood on the issue of enforcement of international norms, and, on the basis of polling, which showed only 21 per cent agreeing that military action was "in our national interest," he concluded that "America seems war weary." He characterized the rejection of British participation in a military strike by Parliament as "a shocking move by one of America's staunchest allies" that certainly did not help matters. Mr. Obama summed up the situation: "'A lot of people think something should be done, but nobody wants to do it'" (as quoted in Blow, 2013,

Aug. 31, p. 19). The article ended on a note of uncertainty: "The president is out on a most precarious limb on this issue. It is an unenviable position, where the right moral move could be the wrong political one, where the to-what-end question has a lack-of-clarity answer" (Blow, 2013, Aug. 31, p. 19).

Ross Douthat offered strong support for a military response in the form of a hypothetical speech that the president might have given to the American people on air strikes against Syria had he not "changed course and decided to seek Congressional approval first." While not minimizing the dangers inherent in military engagement, Douthat argued for "a mix of realism and liberal internationalism, in which military force would be used more sparingly, and American power would be placed in the service of a stable, rule-based, multilateral world order." In the case of Syria this meant that "it's the Pax Americana or nothing. There's nobody else prepared to act to limit the ambitions of bad actors and keep them successfully boxed in…. There has to be a price for crossing lines" (Douthat, 2013, Sept. 1, p. 11).

Thomas Friedman agreed that some response was necessary but that Mr. Obama had made the wrong choice in selecting "a one-time 'shock and awe' missile attack on Syrian military targets." Fearing that such an attack would "risk changing the subject from Assad's behavior to ours,… [he claimed that] … the right strategy is 'arm and shame.'" Specifically, the Free Syrian Army should be trained and armed, while the Syrian president, his wife, his brother "and every member of his cabinet or military whom we can identify as being involved in this gas attack" should be shamed. He acknowledged that his strategy wasn't perfect, "but perfect is not on the menu in Syria" (Friedman, 2013, Sept. 4, p. 23).

Yale law professors Oona Hathaway and Scott Shapiro presented a strong case that the US would be wrong to launch an armed attack against Syria based either on the Kosovo "illegal but legitimate" interpretation or on the "responsibility to protect" doctrine. Invoking Kosovo risked the possibility of others justifying "a similar use of force down the line." As for R2P, it had been interpreted by Ban Ki-moon as reinforcing "the legal obligations of Member States to refrain except in conformity with the Charter." Thus, the authors maintained, authorization by the UN Security Council was an absolute necessity for the use of force. Their argument rested on the need to preserve the rules of the UN Charter, which, although seen as flawed in giving veto powers to the P5, had "made for a more peaceful world than the one that had preceded it." Mr. Obama was asked to consider "whether employing force to punish Mr. Assad's use of chemical weapons is worth endangering the fragile international order that is World War II's most significant legacy" (Hathaway and Shapiro, 2013, Sept. 4, p. 23).

In early September President Obama decided "to seek Congressional authorization for his announced plan to order unilateral strikes against Syria," and this too provided a fertile topic for editorial and opinion commentary. Citing the need for "a vigorous and honest public debate," *The Times* editorial board thought that Mr. Obama "had made the right decision" in going to Congress, although the board was not pleased that by initially proclaiming a red line, he had "created a political situation in which his credibility could be challenged." It argued that the president "should have long ago put in place, with our allies and partners, a plan for international action ... if Mr. Assad used chemical weapons." The UN Security Council, the international community, Russia, China, and the Arab League were all on the receiving end of editorial criticism for not taking stronger stands against Syria's use of chemical weapons (*NYT*, 2013, Sept. 3, p. 24).

A day later, an editorial sought to explain the reasons for the British Parliament's rejection of the use of force. It was pointed out that not only did Prime Minister Cameron head a minority government but he had mistimed and carelessly prepared for the vote. The legacy of British involvement in "the costly quagmire of Iraq" and the "tentative evidence" the prime minister had presented that the gas attack had actually been ordered by the Syrian president were also contributing factors. In spite of the rejection, the editorial argued that "Britain has been America's most reliable European ally, and it remains so today" (*NYT*, 2013, Sept. 4, p. 22).

It was now up to the US to act, and a third editorial published on the following day noted that "there is no strong consensus yet" in Congress whether to support air strikes. Cited as problematic was an early sense of "mission creep." The president had first characterized the air strikes as "a 'shot across the bow,'" but in Senate hearings, the aim of military action had been expanded "'to deter and degrade' Mr. Assad's ability to use [chemical] weapons." Also, while Mr. Obama claimed that he was "not asking America to go to war," the key unanswered question was what would "the United States do if Mr. Assad uses chemical weapons again?" And, on this issue, "the public deserves fuller explanation" (*NYT*, 2013, Sept. 5, p. 24).

Maureen Dowd insisted that "it should not be hard to reach consensus on trying to prevent Bashar al-Assad from killing tens of thousands and making refugees of millions more, with chemical weapons and traditional ones." Why this had not happened was attributed to former president George W. Bush and the legacy of Iraq. In 2003, Bush had both "mischaracterized and miscalculated ... [to the point where] ... he ended up driving America into a grey haze, where we are unsure of our old role as John Wayne taking on the global bad guys is even right." President Obama was given credit for understanding "the difference between Sunnis and Shiites,... [however] ... our previous gigantic misreading of the Middle East, and the treacherous job of fathoming which sides to support in the Arab uprisings ... have left us literally gun shy." Dowd called upon the president to step up and "unlike his predecessor ... show Americans that he knows what he is doing" (Dowd, 2013, Sept. 4, p. 23).

Alex De Waal, president of the World Peace Foundation, and research director Bridget Conley-Zilkic sidestepped the question of the legality of air strikes and instead presented the case that they were an ineffective tool to protect civilians. They maintained that successful military operations "depend on whether they reinforce a political plan; ... effective interventions support diplomacy, they don't replace it." They argued that any punishment of Assad must be linked to the protection of civilians and, ultimately, to ending the war. Moreover, they pointed out that the problem with Syria was not the lack of international involvement but, rather, "too much external intervention.... The result is a conflict with a seemingly infinite capacity to metastasize." They characterized the pending American attack on Syria as "an act of desperation with incalculable consequences" (De Waal & Conley-Zilkic, 2013, Sept. 5, p. 25).

Two *Times* columnists, Nicholas Kristof and Charles Blow, took opposite positions on the use of force in pursuit of humanitarian objectives. Kristof continued to support military action, although, as previously, he acknowledged that critics of the use of force "are right to point out all the risks and uncertainties of missile strikes, and they have American public opinion on their side." Again, without invoking R2P, Kristof focused on the protection of Syrian civilians, now being killed "at a rate of 5,000 every month." To deal with this ongoing slaughter, critics were asked what they proposed to do "other than that we wave our fingers as a government uses chemical weapons on its own people." With respect to the risks involved, Kristof suggested that the appropriate question to ask was "Are the risks greater if we launch missiles, or if we continue to sit on our hands?" His answer was that "in this case, the humanitarian and strategic risks of inaction are greater" (Kristof, 2013, Sept. 5, p. 25).

Charles Blow directly addressed the humanitarian argument that children had been killed by Assad's sarin attack: "What message will we send if a dictator can gas hundreds of children to death in plain sight and pay no price?" He claimed, however, that "the bombs-or-nothing argument ... rings hollow ... [arguing] ... there is a mile of distance between grieving for dead children and avenging those deaths through military force." Beyond that, he argued that a military response "is no longer about punishing al-Assad for chemical weapons ... it's now about sending a signal and shoring up American credibility at the risk of war spreading throughout the region. So creeps the mission." While not discounting the death toll among Syrian children, he refocused his argument by pointing out that "there are millions of other children who die each year on the planet with little notice." Specifically, malnutrition was cited as contributing "to 3.1 million under-5 deaths annually," while in 2010 the number of children and teens in the US killed by guns "was nearly five times the number of US soldiers killed in action that year in Iraq and Afghanistan." Blow did not go so far as to advocate no response to the atrocities in Syria, but he did point out that "every death of a child is a tragedy, and that the humanitarian impulse to help should also apply to the children of the world who die out of view of cameras and out of range of wars" (Blow, 2013, Sept. 7, p. 23).

A September 7 editorial restated fears that air strikes would lead the US to "inevitably become involved in another costly Middle East war." It claimed that "the administration may already be engaging in mission creep by asking the Pentagon to expand the list of potential targets beyond the 50 or so previously identified." It noted that Congressional approval for air strikes was far from assured and that "the public deserves to understand more fully what 'limited' military action actually means" (*NYT*, 2013, Sept. 7, p. 22). House Intelligence Committee member Alan Grayson was clearly unhappy with the way the Obama administration was handling the intelligence file surrounding the sarin attack. Citing the run-up to the 2003 invasion of Iraq as an example of what not to do, Grayson charged that not much had changed over the past decade: "By refusing to disclose the underlying data even to members of Congress, the administration is making it impossible for anyone to judge, independently, whether that statement is correct. Perhaps the edict of an earlier administration applies: 'Trust, but verify'" (Grayson, 2013, Sept. 7, p. 23).

Nicholas Kristof offered yet another argument on behalf of a military response based on the spirit of the responsibility to protect but again without specifically mentioning the doctrine. Syria was characterized as a special case; "the scale of the slaughter" had exceeded 100,000, with another 5,000 being killed per month. He noted that he had covered humanitarian catastrophes "from Darfur to eastern Congo" and concluded that "Syria is today the world capital of human suffering." He further acknowledged that "while neither intervention nor paralysis is appealing, that's pretty much the menu." And, quoting the earlier words of President Assad that "'there is no substitute for the United States,'" he asked whether "when history looks back on this moment, will it view those who opposed intervening as champions of peace ... or will our descendants puzzle that we took pride in retreating to passivity during this slaughter?" Kristof clearly was not among those who favoured sitting on the fence while the "dead piled up" (Kristof, 2013, Sept. 8, p. 1).

Ross Douthat remained committed to a military strike but was disappointed with the American president on a number of grounds: he shouldn't have "staked his credibility on a vote whose outcome he failed to game out in advance"; he hadn't seemed "to have figured out what kind of intervention [his administration] was proposing or why"; and, that if the "intervention is actually about making Syria safe for democracy, the strike being contemplated is wildly insufficient to that end." In spite of these misgivings, Douthat counselled members of Congress to weigh carefully the consequences of a no vote: "It would be a remarkable institutional rebuke of [Obama's] presidency, with unknowable consequences for the credibility of American foreign policy, not only in Syria but around the world" (Douthat, 2013, Sept. 8, p. 12).

Maureen Dowd likewise was not pleased with the president's performance in mustering support for military action against Syria, both abroad and at home. At a G20 meeting in St. Petersburg, "the man elected because of his magical powers of persuasion had failed to persuade other world leaders … about a strike on Syria." In dealing with Congress, he was seen to be "mixing high principles with low motives": the high principle being that "it is proper to get Congressional approval and let the people chime in," while the low motive was that "he also wanted to make life difficult for Congressional Republicans who like to 'snipe' … from the sidelines with no accountability." The impact of a no vote on the president's credibility was also assessed, especially in the context of American support for Israel: "If Congress ratifies that there is no appetite among Americans to police the Middle East, does it doom any chance of a US pre-emptive strike on Iran and indicate that the US won't be there for Israel?" Mr. Obama was presented as knowing that he had to "punish Bashar al-Assad; … [if not] … his presidency will forever be reduced." Given the stakes, a more inspired presidential selling job was clearly in order (Dowd, 2013, Sept. 8, p. 11).

Columnist Bill Keller assessed the impact of growing isolationism in the US, not only for action on Syria but for involvement in the Middle East more generally. For Keller,

> isolationism is not just an aversion to war.… It is a broader reluctance to engage, to assert responsibility, to commit. Isolationism tends to be pessimistic (we will get it wrong, we will make it worse) and amoral (it is none of our business unless it threatens us directly) and inward-looking (foreign aid is a waste of money better spent at home). (Keller, 2013, Sept. 9, p. 21)

He presented the situation as analogous to the late 1930s, even with respect to anti-Semitic undertones: "'So how many Americans will die for Israel this time around?'" In spite of these problems, Keller still favoured a "calibrated intervention to shift the balance" in the civil war and hoped "the president can persuade Congress that the US still has an important role to play in the world, and that sometimes you have to put some spine in your diplomacy" (Keller, 2013, Sept. 9, p. 21).

In an article that began with a stinging attack on the Assad government, long-time Syrian political activist Yassin al-Haj Saleh presented the case for international (although not necessarily American) intervention. Interestingly, he did not characterize the conflict as a civil war: "When a government murders its own citizens and they resist, this can hardly be called a civil war. It is a barbaric campaign of the first degree." In the face of this barbarism, inaction on the part of the international community was described as "catastrophic." The spectre of jihadism was portrayed as but a new excuse for international inaction: "Justice and humanity demand that the Assad regime be punished for its crimes. Even though the Russians and the Chinese have managed to impair the Security Council, it is still possible for an international and regional coalition to carry out this task" (Al-Haj Saleh, 2013, Sept. 10, p. 23).

A *Times* editorial on September 10 was the first to address the arrangement to remove Syria's chemical weapons and destroy them under international supervision. The announcement of a possible agreement came just as the president was planning to address the nation on the need for air strikes, and it again shifted the focus of opinion material. While there was some skepticism regarding the agreement, *The Times* editorial board presented it as worth pursuing as it "would ensure greater safety for the Syrian people … and it would have longer lasting deterrent effects than the limited strikes Mr. Obama wants to deliver, without the likelihood of more civilian casualties." Moreover, the editorial noted that the president "has won little support for his plan [for air strikes] internationally, in Congress or with the American public," and, with this in mind, the agreement "could mean that the United States would not have to go it alone in standing firm against the Syrian regime" (*NYT*, 2013, Sept. 10, p. 22). A day later, Thomas Friedman followed with an article that while somewhat more skeptical about the agreement's chances for success, nevertheless argued that "it now makes sense to take a time out." He presented the chemical weapons deal as "a good end to this near-term crisis,… [because] … no one, hawk or dove, wants to see American boots on the ground in Syria, under any conditions." As well, "the global taboo on poison gas would be upheld." More, however, was needed. Friedman continued to maintain that some external force would be required "to put boots on the ground" in order to oversee a transition to democracy in "a multitribal and multisectarian" society such as Syria: "The United Nations Security Council will eventually have to address this reality, otherwise Syria will become Afghanistan on the Mediterranean" (Friedman, 2013, Sept. 11, p. 27).

Another editorial on September 12 focused on Mr. Obama's speech to the nation regarding Syria, with the president getting mixed reviews. The editorial acknowledged that "after a muddled start on his lurch toward military action,… he offered a forceful moral argument for a limited strike." It also described "his decision to give in to the diplomatic reality of the moment and ask Congress to postpone a vote on military action … [as] … wise." At the same time, the editorial claimed that "the speech lacked any real sense of what Mr. Obama's long-term or even medium-term strategy might be, other than his promise not to drag a nation fed up with wars into a 'boots-on-the-ground' fight." In addition, the chemical weapons agreement was seen as "the first real sign of life on the diplomatic side of the conflict." Even though there were no guarantees that it would work, it was argued that "diplomacy could provide more of an immediate deterrent against further chemical attacks than the threat of an attack." The editorial, moreover, counselled prudence: "Congress and Mr. Obama should be careful about setting hard deadlines or drawing any more red lines" (*NYT*, 2013, Sept. 12, p. 30).

With four days to reflect on the situation, *The Times* editorial board confirmed its initial appraisal of the chemical weapons agreement as "offering a better chance of deterring this threat than the limited military strikes that President Obama was considering." The editorial conceded that President Putin had "undoubtedly elevated his stature in the Middle East," but at the same time he was now on the record as "draw[ing] the line at poison gas." As for Mr. Obama, he "deserves credit for putting a focus on upholding an international ban on chemical weapons and for setting aside military action at this time in favor of a diplomatic deal" (*NYT*, 2013, Sept. 16, p. 22).

Maureen Dowd equivocated. She characterized the agreement as a Vladimir Putin–thrown "lifeline" to Mr. Obama. Moreover, given his lackluster job in "explain[ing] the stakes there … [and doing] … the necessary work to line up support," the agreement was one that the president should firmly grasp. Dowd also noted that Americans had "had it with Shiites vs. Sunnis, with Alawites and all the ancient hatreds…. [And] … with Joe Sixpack … now a peacenik," a military response looked like a hard sell. For this, according to Dowd, George W. Bush, Dick Cheney, and Donald Rumsfeld clearly shared the blame; not only had their ideas about democracy failed in the Middle East, they had changed "the mindset … [at home] … in the opposite way than they intended" (Dowd, 2013, Sept. 11, p. 27).

On September 12, *The Times* published an opinion article by Russian president Vladimir Putin, who argued that "we must stop using the language of force and return to the path of civilized diplomatic and political settlement." Putin underscored the importance of the UN, particularly the need to get Security Council approval for any use of force.[1] In that the military strikes proposed by the US against Syria would lack such approval, he argued that they were not only illegal but posed grave threats to the international system far beyond Syria and the region; they "could throw the entire system of international law and order out of balance." He presented the case that Russia had acted responsibly in Syria, "advocat[ing] peaceful dialog enabling Syrians to develop a compromise plan for their own future." Pointing to the US military venture into Iraq, he questioned why the US "would want to repeat recent mistakes." He was also critical of what he described as a tendency toward US "military intervention in internal conflicts in foreign countries," as well as President Obama's invocation of American exceptionalism, claiming that "it is extremely dangerous to encourage people to see themselves as exceptional, whatever the motivation." Mr. Putin framed the chemical weapons agreement as "*a new opportunity to avoid military action* that has emerged in the past few days" and judged that by his response Mr. Obama also saw it "*as an alternative to military action*" (Putin, 2013, Sept. 12, p. 31; italics added).

On the same day, Nicholas Kristof put a very different spin on the agreement—that it was the threat of the use of force by the US that was responsible for the breakthrough on chemical weapons: "The mere flexing of military power worked—initially and tentatively." However, it would be "critical to keep the military option alive in the coming weeks or Russia and Syria will play us like a yo-yo." For Kristof, the use military force was not always the answer to responding to humanitarian crises (he had opposed the war in Iraq and the "surge" in Afghanistan), but in a number of cases (Sierra Leone, Mali, Ivory Coast, Bosnia, and Kosovo) he argued that "an outside military force intervened at minimal cost and saved large numbers of lives." In any event, the use of force had to be decided "on a case-by-case basis," and, with respect to Syria, even the threat of its use seemed to have managed to rein in the most egregious abuses of the Syrian government (Kristof, 2013, Sept. 12, p. 31). In another opinion piece three days later, Kristof addressed various objections to the use of force that had been brought up by his readers: high costs; possible civilian casualties; an opposition just as distasteful as the government it sought to replace; the legacy of Iraq; failures in Afghanistan and Vietnam; the question "what's so different about death by chemical weapons?"; and the belief that a response should have come earlier. For all of these he offered counter-arguments, on the last arguing that while "we should have stood up to the butchery in Syria earlier," upon Assad's use of poison gas, military strikes were clearly appropriate: "There's a crucial principle at stake about the need to stand up to genocide or mass atrocities where it is feasible." Kristof admitted that Syria was

> a hard case, with uncertain consequences. But if we are broadly retreating from the principle of *humanitarian intervention* to avert mass atrocities because of compassion fatigue in a tumultuous and ungrateful world, then we're landing on the wrong side of history, and some day we will look back in shame. (Kristof, 2013, Sept. 15, p. 11; italics added)

Times columnist Roger Cohen dealt with the problems associated with what he described as "a post-American world." He argued that in "clutch[ing] at this Syrian straw and defer[ring] to Russian mediation," the United States had in fact backed away from its leadership role in the world—"and that means chaos." He described the Obama administration as "careening" with respect to its policy toward Syria and quoted a former US ambassador's claim that "'if these guys were building cars, you would not buy one.'" Cohen argued that the president's "hesitancy since the chemical weapons attack has highlighted a lack of US leadership throughout the Syrian crisis." He explained this as a case of the president's "deferr[ing] to a growing isolationism. His wavering has looked like acquiescence to a global power shift." Clearly, Cohen was not impressed with the implications of these developments, and he ended his article with a guilt-laden quote from a leading German news magazine: "'We will be asked by our children what we did against this mass murder, as we asked our parents about Nazism. We will then lower our eyes and have to remain silent'" (Cohen, 2013, Sept. 13, p. 25).

Michael Ignatieff, who had been a member of the International Commission on Intervention and State Sovereignty (ICISS) and later served as leader of the Canadian Liberal Party, dealt directly with the troubles facing R2P from the vantage point of his Harvard professorship. He acknowledged that it was "obvious that our idea is facing a crisis of democratic legitimacy." While citing the impact of factors such as compassion fatigue, isolationism, high costs, and war weariness, Ignatieff maintained

> that the core problem is public anger at the manipulation of consent: disillusion with the way in which leaders and policy elites have used moral and humanitarian arguments to extract popular support for the use of force in Iraq and Libya, and then conducted those interventions in ways that betrayed their lack of true commitment to those principles. (2013, Sept. 14, p. 19)

For Ignatieff, R2P meant "protection," not "regime change" or other manifestations of "mission creep." He saw the need for "rebuild[ing] popular democratic support for the idea of our duty to protect civilians, when no one else can or will … [to be] … a critical challenge in the years ahead." With respect to the use of force he took the position that "democratic legitimacy" (going to the "people for permission to save civilians") could in fact be used to authorize the use of force in circumstances where the Security Council was deadlocked. Accordingly, both Mr. Obama and Mr. Cameron were correct in seeking legislative approval for the use of force. "Although it hasn't turned out the way they wanted," Ignatieff expressed hope that in the future people would "say yes" to missions to "fight genocide, ethnic cleansing and chemical weapons attacks" (Ignatieff, 2013, Sept. 14, p. 19).

In one of the very few articles that dealt directly with the role of media in the framing of the conflict, *New York Times* public editor Margaret Sullivan addressed the impact of emotion-laden photos in coverage of the Syrian civil war. She argued that photos showing the bodies of young children who were victims of the August sarin attack, as well as those showing rebels executing Syrian soldiers, were "capable of changing the narrative, possibly the course of history." Sullivan noted that President Obama had in fact invoked the images of death by nerve gas in his speech to the nation to build "support for a possible American strike against Syria" (Sullivan, 2013, Sept. 15, p. 12).

With military action on the shelf, at least for the moment, *Times* columnist Frank Bruni outlined the human costs of war that were not picked up by the omnipresent phrase "boots on the ground." He argued that "we're not good at discussing this and confronting head-on what the toll of our best intentions and tortured interventions can be." Employing strong distance framing, he assessed the administration's possible missile strike on Syria as "confused and confusing." He likened it to "lighting a fuse…. You can't predict the moment or shape of the explosion, and you can't guess the size of the temptation to follow it up with just one more maneuver, one additional push." He then reviewed the costs of Iraq and Afghanistan on the two million–plus troops sent to fight in those wars: "More than 6,500 of them are dead. Tens of thousands were physically injured, including some 1,500 amputees." Bruni suggested that those contemplating a new war needed to "keep in mind … the ravages of the last one" (2013, Sept. 15, p. 3).

Thomas Freidman analyzed some of the factors underlying the recent shift from military action to diplomacy: the American president had been "blindsided" by the lack of support from the American people; plus, he had received unexpected support from Vladimir Putin, who "felt the only way he could save his client, the Syrian president, was by also saving the American president." As for the agreement itself, Friedman was skeptical, but he deemed it "worth a try." He agreed with Mr. Obama that "no matter how we got here, we're in a potentially better place." While not a major focus of his article, he made the interesting point that the issue of "intervening in Syria was driven by elites and debated by elites; the mass population, beyond being confused, was basically not involved" (Friedman, 2013, Sept. 18, p. 23).[2]

Writing from Jordan, Nicholas Kristof offered two empathy-framed columns. The first was premised on the reality that the "agreement brokered by the world's powers,… limited to chemical weapons—while useful—seems a bit irrelevant to the atrocities that define the lives of most Syrians." He characterized "talk in Washington … [on] … whether the Syrian crisis had been resolved … [as] … bizarre and narcissistic…. Maybe the politicians' crisis there has been eased, but the human catastrophe here just gets worse." While Kristof conceded that military strikes had little support in the US, he argued that even if there was no agreement on protecting civilians, at least there should be agreement about helping victims: "We should find common ground in insisting that international negotiations address not only chemical stockpiles but also humanitarian access." And, while it might not be possible "to solve Syria's problems,… we can try, and a starting point would be a big push for humanitarian access" (Kristof, 2013, Sept. 19, p. 31). Kristof's second article recounted the story of an eleven-year-old boy who defied Syrian authorities and was tortured and badly injured by security forces. The story was offered in the hope that an account of "children's courage can help build spine in world leaders, who for two and a half years have largely averted their eyes from the human catastrophe that is Syria." His assessment of the chemical weapons agreement was again restrained: it "may be a genuine step forward, but it does not seem particularly relevant to Syrians suffering from the more banal methods of mass murder." While Kristof still favoured "missile strikes on President Bashar al-Assad's air force to reduce his capacity to bomb civilians," he now recognized that this would not happen. He suggested, however, that it was still possible to "bolster moderate rebel groups with weapons, training and intelligence … [and to] … push harder for humanitarian access to aid needy Syrians" (Kristof, 2013, Sept. 22, p. 11).

The final editorial published by *The Times* during our study period appeared on September 27 and focused on the UN Security Council resolution's setting conditions for the removal and destruction of Syria's chemical weapons. In that it "would legally obligate Syria to give up its stockpile of poison gas," it was applauded. In that it did not bring automatic action under Chapter VII for non-compliance (thus giving Russia a veto over a possible military response), it was criticized. The editorial acknowledged, however, that "the two-step enforcement process … appears to be the best that … [the US and France] … could get." In addition, "huge challenges" were seen in the future, not only in operationalizing the removal and destruction of the chemical weapons but in "trying to reach a broader deal that could end the fighting and put a transitional government in place." The editorial noted that the chemical weapons agreement was a step in that direction but that "it will take unity among the major powers to push it forward" (*NYT*, 2013, Sept. 27, p. 22).

Robin Wright, who held joint appointments at the US Institute of Peace and the Woodrow Wilson International Center for Scholars, offered *The Times'* final opinion piece. In it, she analyzed the combined impact of the Syrian civil war and the Arab Spring on the map of the Middle East that had been "defined by European colonial powers a century ago and defended by Arab autocrats ever since." The result was likely to be fragmentation and localism. Syria, "the strategic center of the Middle East," was described as having "crumbled into three identifiable regions," one dominated by Alawi, one by Kurds, and the largest by Sunni. According to Wright, Iraq, with its own Sunni-Shia split as well as a Kurdish population, would also be affected by events in Syria, with perhaps cross-border connections emerging. Beyond Syria, she saw the Arab Spring as leading to a decentralization of power, "reflect[ing] local identity or rights to resources." With the Arab Spring as the "kindling" and the Syrian civil war as the "match," Wright described a process whereby in countries such as Libya, Yemen, and Saudi Arabia, "new borders may be drawn in disparate, and potentially chaotic, ways. Countries could unravel through phases of federation, soft partition or autonomy, ending in geographic divorce." While Wright did not examine the role of the West in this process, she did predict that "the longer Syria's war rages on, the greater the instability and dangers for the whole region" (Wright, 2013, Sept. 29, p. 7).

The Guardian's Opinion Narrative

The August 21 chemical weapons attack on a Damascus suburb was the subject of an immediate *Guardian* editorial and opinion article, both of which sought to explain why the attack might have been launched, who launched it, and how the West was likely to or should respond.

On the first question, the editorial reviewed four possible reasons: (1) an order from a rogue commander; (2) an order from Mr. Assad, "in the knowledge that Mr. Obama would not respond"; (3) a military decision "to up the firepower against the rebels who ... still control half the country"; or (4) "an attack that went wrong, killing many more than intended." Whatever the explanation, the attack was seen as "an unmistakable challenge to the vow Barack Obama made a year ago that, if proved, the use of chemical or biological weapons would 'change my calculus.'" The editorial noted that while "France and Turkey were pushing for military action and Britain would not rule it out," force was not a good option. Russia and China would veto any Security Council proposal authorizing its use; and, besides this, it was "doubtful" that air strikes would serve as a deterrent to future use of chemical weapons (*Guardian*, 2013, Aug. 23, p. 38).

In an opinion article on the same day, London School of Economics professor Fawaz Gerges claimed that Assad's "alleged use of [chemical] weapons defies logic," and thus the most likely answer to the question of why they were used was a "reckless and irrational" Syrian president. Nevertheless, the result was domestic pressure on Mr. Obama "to intervene more decisively in the Syrian conflict," in at least partial agreement with the French position that "there must be a reaction, a reaction that could take the form of a reaction with force." Gerges further claimed that "the international community is paralyzed," pointing out that "as the country becomes a playground for the merchants of death from near and far, its diverse social fabric is coming apart and extremism has taken hold of the traditionally tolerant Syrian soil." In spite of these dire assessments, he did not advocate military action (Gerges, 2013, Aug. 23, p. 36).

An opinion piece by *The Guardian*'s John Kampfner introduced what became a persistent and powerful argument regarding Britain's possible use of force: "the spectre of Iraq and Whitehall's inability to disentangle truth from wishful thinking over the contemporary tragedy in Syria." Following the debacle in Iraq, "accusations based on assertions alone, no matter how credible those assertions might be today," were no longer convincing. In this respect, Britain was not alone as Kampfner observed that the US "has a president, a body politic and public opinion scarred by Iraq and Afghanistan and largely averse to the use of military force." This, combined with an "international community [that] has been high on rhetoric and low on action," led the Syrian president "to have calculated that he can get away with gassing his civilian population." Kampfner hoped that the idea of "a rights-based approach" to intervention decision-making was not dead but that in the short run Assad "may be smiling, knowing that even if we hit back at him in a token gesture … he could be around for quite some time" (Kampfner, 2013, Aug. 26, p. 22). An editorial two days later confirmed Kampfner's assessment: "The British public remains … strongly opposed to British intervention or military aid to the Syrian rebels … [and] … the case has not yet been made authoritatively to the public." Moreover, Prime Minister Cameron "should be under no illusion that a post-Iraq public will be easily persuaded that another UK military engagement in the Middle East is necessary." In any event, the editorial pointed out that, as indisputably heinous as the use of poison gas was, "wars of choice are politically unrealistic without parliamentary authorization" (*Guardian*, 2013, Aug. 28, p. 30).

Guardian journalist Seumas Milne presented another strong argument against the military response in Syria, which he said was "now being planned by the US and its allies." As it was with Iraq, "intelligence about weapons of mass destruction is once again at the centre of the case made for a western missile strike." Milne claimed, first, that it was "hard to see a rational motivation" for the attack on the part of the Assad government and, second, that it was easy to see one for the opposition—to provoke an intervention by Western states, something for which they had long been striving. He pointed out that the opposition was untrustworthy in other respects as well, having engaged in "ethnically cleansing tens of thousands of Kurds from north east Syria across the border into Iraq." Mr. Obama was seen as moving from a position of caution, based on the argument that "'difficult, costly interventions … actually breed more resentment,'" to one where he was "back[ing] a direct military attack"—an attack that Milne stressed would lack Security Council authorization. This was seen as "a dangerous gamble, which British MPs have a responsibility to oppose" (Milne, 2013, Aug. 28, p. 29).

A day later, former UN weapons inspector Hans Blix made much the same argument in favour of requiring UN Security Council approval of any military action: "A quick punitive action in Syria ... without UN authorization ... [would suggest] ... that great military powers can intervene militarily when they feel politically impelled to do so." As for what the international community should do in response to the chemical attack, Blix implied, but did not specifically argue, that "global indignation" might be enough. He did not deny that the use of chemical weapons was a "moral obscenity" but pointed out that so too was the civil war itself. To bring it under control, he suggested that "supplier countries" to both sides (Russia, Iran, Saudi Arabia, Qatar, and Turkey) had leverage to stop it and should use it to that end (Blix, 2013, Aug. 29, p. 30).

Pro- and anti-use-of-force positions were presented, respectively, by Malcolm Rifkind, chairman of the Parliamentary Joint Committee on Intelligence and Security, and Martin Kettle, *Guardian* journalist. Rifkind acknowledged that it would be preferable for the Security Council to authorize military action against Syria. However, because this was unlikely, he maintained that "the international community ... cannot be paralyzed by such a failure to act." He then cited "the UN doctrine of 'responsibility to protect,'" noting that it had been accepted by all. Moreover, "if there is consensus among most of the international community—including the Arab League countries—that action is necessary, then it should go ahead." Any such response of course should be "limited, proportional and targeted on Syrian government military sites." Rifkind maintained that Assad had to pay a price for his behaviour, as failure to act "would not only be disastrous for the Syrian people,... it would also condemn the United Nations to the same fate as the League of Nations" (Rifkind, 2013, Aug. 29, p. 30). Martin Kettle, on the hand, focused on the role of Parliament in dealing with "David Cameron's needlessly precipitate Syria policy" and urged MPs to stop it "dead in tracks." He argued that any response to the chemical weapons attack needed "to have as much support and legitimacy as possible [and] this means letting the UN process take its course." [3] Kettle noted an interesting point on the side of British restraint, which we will address further in the Conclusion: "Significantly, there's little tabloid jingoism over Syria" (Kettle, 2013, Aug. 29, p. 31).

The last editorial immediately prior to the parliamentary vote shifted focus to the US, beginning with a quote from the chairman of the US Joint Chiefs of Staff: "'Once we take action, we should be prepared for what comes next. Deeper involvement is hard to avoid.'" On this point, the editorial argued that "skeptical generals and a hostile western public-at-large are entitled to answers"—answers that were not portrayed as forthcoming. In that Assad was seen to be gaining in strength, continued insistence by the West on his departure as a precondition for negotiations made little sense. More importantly, in that one air strike was unlikely to be sufficient to dislodge him, rebels might get "the impression that if the US could be prevailed upon to strike once, they could be called upon to strike again." The editorial called for a return to talks in Geneva, with participation from both Russia and Iran. It also suggested the idea of having "a permanent UN presence in Syria monitoring Mr. Assad's stocks of chemical weapons" (*Guardian*, 2013, Aug. 29, p. 32).

The first commentary following the parliamentary "no vote" came in the form of an opinion piece by Simon Jenkins. He focused on the government's resort to R2P, which was described as an attempt to circumvent the need for UN Security Council authorization. Jenkins argued that because UN resolution 1647 specifically required that any application of R2P be "'through the security council in accordance with the charter,'" any alternative authorization would lack legitimacy, as did the military operations in Iraq in 2003. In addition, he noted that public opinion was unsympathetic to military operations, and this meant that any strike would be just strong enough "to assuage the cries of the do-something lobby" and, therefore, unlikely to be decisive. The use of military force would also "be certain to increase the refugee flow, alienate Russia ... and infuriate a newly moderate Iran." Jenkins concluded with the observation that "sometimes it takes courage to conclude of foreign conflicts that we can only do harm by meddling" and that in this case the proper course would also be "extremes of diplomatic engagement and humanitarian relief" (2013, Aug. 30, p. 31). Another *Guardian* journalist, Polly Toynebee, added to distance framing by again commenting on the legacy of past failures of liberal interventionism: "Between that vision and the reality falls the long dark shadow of 12 years of war, in countries that don't thank us, doing more harm than good, killing many and sending home hundreds of our soldiers in coffins" (Toynebee, 2013, Aug. 30, p. 30).

Two editorials and five opinion pieces performed what might be termed a post-mortem examination on the parliamentary no vote and its consequences for Prime Minister Cameron as well as for Britain's place in the world. An editorial on August 30 described Mr. Cameron as "the principal loser," noting that "for a prime minister to lose control of a key issue of foreign policy ... is an almost unprecedented failure." The ill-fated decision to invade Iraq played a key role in this failure, and the message from that venture was "evidence first, verdict afterward—not the reverse." The spin that the editorial placed on the vote was that some lessons, in fact, had been learned from Iraq:

If all this results in a different kind of British approach to conflict, more measured and more respectful of the international order, though no less determined to uphold humanitarian and legal values, then perhaps some good can come from the dilemmas with which our politicians have wrestled this week." (*Guardian*, 2013, Aug. 30, p. 32)

Radio 4's Steve Richards also saw the vote as "a huge blow to Mr. Cameron personally … [placing him] … in the humiliating position of phoning Obama to tell him he could not take part," especially because the president "wanted him to act and … [Cameron] … sought to be with him, shoulder to shoulder as Tony Blair would have put it." Cameron's case for military strikes was described as "unconvincing," and Richards saw the outcome as "unequivocal. There would be no British military intervention in Syria." In terms of Britain's future role in the world, Richards pointed to critical changes in public attitudes toward conflict in general: "After Suez and until Iraq, the default political calculation of prime ministers was that British voters would support war and victory would make them stronger." That era was seen as "becoming increasingly distant," and he did not lament that "MPs and voters dare ask whether firing a few missiles is the appropriate response to a situation of multilayered complexity, and why the UK feels the need yet again to be at forefront of such open-ended, vaguely defined military ventures" (Richards, 2013, Aug. 31, p. 43).

An article by the leader of the Labour opposition, Ed Miliband, also focused on the lessons learned from Iraq and came to the same conclusion: that "evidence should always precede decision, not decision preceding evidence." He stressed the importance of "hard-headed but full-hearted engagement with the UN … [pointing out that] … seeking to work through the UN must be the essential precondition of any action" (Miliband, 2013, Aug. 31, p. 42).

The Guardian's final editorial in August dealt with Britain's place in the world: would it be "free at last" from its role as "'a plaything of the US military,'" or would it be a country with "'the international credibility of Luxembourg?'" The editorial argued that neither would result. Mr. Cameron was wounded but not mortally so. It was also unclear whether "British policy towards Syria had done a total U-turn" because the issue of military strikes could come back to parliament for another vote should Assad use chemical weapons again. The editorial went on to make a nuanced case that there was "no evidence that British public opinion has turned isolationist." Rather, the British people were described as "fed up," with the causes ranging from "post-9/11 years of national sacrifice,… humiliating excesses of US national security policy,… and above all with the failure of policy." With respect to the last, the editorial noted that "Iraq casts a very long, very dark shadow." The result was that when Mr. Obama, "a respected American president," issued a call for help in responding to "clearly intolerable war crimes—the answer was a clear one. Enough" (*Guardian*, 2013, Aug. 31, p. 44). Whether this constituted isolationism or something else might be open to debate, but the consequence was not: the British leadership had

> something tough to absorb about public tolerance for dangerous military engagement in hostile environments which, ever since Iraq, have felt variously precipitate, illegitimate, excessive, costly, unfocused and even, in the end, not really our fight either. (*Guardian*, 2013, Aug. 31, p. 44)

On the same topic, journalist John Harris questioned whether Britain any longer had "a political establishment that can credibly speak to the public—or even their own parties—about the gravest affairs of state, and take the people with them." To blame was a combination of a more "presidential style" in British politics and the fact that "people at the top have become less and less convincing." Harris placed a good deal of blame for this on former prime minister Tony Blair: "This is what Tony Blair bequeathed to British politics and it needs to be binned for good" (Harris, 2013, Sept. 2, p. 25).

Following the negative British vote, attention shifted to the United States and Mr. Obama's decision to seek congressional approval for the use of force against Syria. Whereas opinion content on the British vote had overwhelmingly favoured restraint, initially at least, it was more mixed regarding military action on the part of its transatlantic ally. A *Guardian* editorial outlined the difficult options:

> Do nothing effective, and the world would be averting its gaze from a type of warfare which has always triggered a special repugnance from countries which regard themselves as upholding moral standards. Do something forceful, and the human and military impact on Syria and beyond might be hard either to control or justify. (*Guardian*, 2013, Sept. 2, p. 26).

The editorial acknowledged that "Mr. Obama is right to be cautious," at least in part because "public opinion is war-weary." Relying on democratic process to reach a decision on the use of force was applauded, but at the same time the editors stressed that "democracies have international responsibilities as well as domestic ones." With respect to how to end the war, the editorial sent a mixed message. What was described as "Western nervousness" was not seen as helpful. Rather, "a considered approach" was the right one ... [but at the same time] ... the need for an engaged strategy is as urgent as ever, and is neglected at our collective peril" (*Guardian*, 2013, Sept. 2, p. 26).

Guardian journalist Jonathan Steele argued strongly against a US resort to force, calling it "a case of breathtaking arrogance, a call for recognition that the US is not only the world's policeman but the world's enforcer." Even though the planned strikes were to be "limited and narrow," he argued that "war is still war, and the dangers of unintended consequences, mission creep and cracking on for the sake of cracking on lurk behind every sand hill." Steele hoped that after "the futility of eight years of fighting in Iraq," the American people were placing "the very concept of empire under scrutiny" (Steele, 2013, Sept. 2, p. 24).

Former al-Jazeera executive Wadah Khanfar listed a number of reasons why a US intervention would not be supported by the Syrian population, the most important of which was "fears that American airstrikes will open the way for future US meddling in Syrian affairs." At the same time, he criticized the US for "prevent[ing] the delivery of advanced weaponry, especially anti-aircraft missiles, to the Free Syrian Army … on the pretext that such weapons could fall into the hands of extremists." While rejecting American military action, Khanfar maintained that "the international community needs to take a strong stand over the Syrian regime's use of chemical weapons against its people." In the final analysis, he argued that "the US and western countries should allow Syrians to accomplish their revolutionary objectives by themselves—to eradicate the regime with their own hands." However, to accomplish this "the West should not prevent them acquiring the means to decide the struggle militarily" (Khanfar, 2013, Sept. 3, p. 32).

Jonathan Freedland's opinion article put the focus on President Barack Obama, the "reluctant interventionist," and claimed that "hesitation and ambivalence … [had] … defined his approach to Syria." However, following the declaration of a chemical weapons red line and then its breach, "he had to act…. He cannot close his eyes to the violation of what has been the world's most enduring prohibition on weapons of mass destruction, the convention against chemical weapons." Freedland framed the issue in terms of maintaining presidential credibility: "If he is to succeed in those areas where many would want him to succeed—say on Israeli-Palestine peace talks—he needs to be heeded" (Freedland, 2013, Sept. 4, p. 35).

Journalist Jenni Russell reviewed the history of US decision making on Syria and concluded that in spite of "obsessively modeling what various interventions or non-interventions in Syria might achieve … nothing has developed as they expected." Specifically, options such as arming the opposition and creating a no-fly zone were found wanting. Anticipating events, Russell broached the possibility of "attempting to concentrate … on the securing of Bashar al-Assad's chemical and biological weapons so that neither he nor any rebel groups can use them." In the final analysis, realism prevailed: "The unpalatable truth is that there is no safe, morally pure solution." Russell "reluctantly concluded that Obama's conviction—that the world must not rule out military action—is right" (Russell, 2013, Sept. 6, p. 36).

British historian and Harvard professor Niall Ferguson criticized the humanitarian left, offered a history lesson on the Middle East, and prodded the American president to take long overdue action on Syria. On the first of these, he argued that "American military power is the best available means of preventing crimes against humanity … [and that as the US] … retreats from global hegemony, we shall see more not less violence"—a reality that he charged "leftists" had difficulty accepting. On the second, he saw the Middle East, as created by the British and French during WWI, as fragmenting, offering as examples both Iraq and Syria. Likening the process at work in the region to what happened in Yugoslavia in the 1990s, Ferguson saw "no obvious reason why … [Jordan, Lebanon, and Israel] … should all survive in their present form." On the third, he criticized President Obama for his "tendency to defer difficult decisions to Congress and a lack of coherent strategy in the Middle East." For Syria, this meant "an addiction to half- and quarter measures … anything rather than risk 'another Iraq.'" According to Ferguson, the situation clearly called for American intervention, which he suggested might not occur until Hillary Clinton assumed the presidency in 2017. Such a delay would not be helpful, though, as "the longer the US dithers, the bigger the sectarian conflicts in the region are likely to become" (Ferguson, 2013, Sept. 7, p. 54).

An editorial on September 5 shifted the focus from the US to the enigmatic Russian president Vladimir Putin and what could be expected from him regarding Syria in the upcoming meeting of the G20 in St. Petersburg. The editorial's answer was "not all that much." It described Putin as "a child of the cold war, and his foreign policy as entirely instrumental. His enemies' enemies are his friends … [and] … he doubtless enjoy[ed] David Cameron's humiliation by the House of Commons." He still maintained that "the 21 August attack was the work of anti-Assad forces." However, if the Syrian government were proven to be responsible, the possibility that Putin would agree to a response including military action could not be ruled out. Given "Russia's generally obstructionist approach to international moves over Syria … the prospects for progress at or in the margins of the G20 seem poor" (*Guardian*, 2013, Sept. 5, p. 34). This pessimism was confirmed in an editorial two days later that asserted that "world leaders … [are] … palpably losing faith in the very process of international diplomacy that they are meant to be driving forward." Indeed, the problem transcended Syria: the G20 meeting confirmed "that the Bush wars and then the subprime crisis have effectively ended that … moment of uncontested [American] supremacy … [and] … its chance to reshape the world without resistance from the old Soviet Union" (*Guardian*, 2013, Sept. 7, p. 56).

As the US Congressional vote neared, opinion commentary shifted decidedly toward opposing President Obama's declared intention to use of force. For example, *Guardian* journalist Gary Younge argued that because the US had little credibility left in the Middle East, there was no need to maintain that the region would be endangered if the US backed out of Obama's red line commitment. He pointed out as well that those who advocated intervention based on "principles of human solidarity and internationalism … [cannot] … claim, with any integrity, that they have a plan that will soon stem the bloodshed" (Younge, 2013, Sept. 9, p. 37). A day later, *Guardian* columnist and political activist George Monbiot accused the US of being the most serious abuser of the UN Security Council veto—casting 83 vetoes, 42 of which were cast to protect Israel from condemnation. In light of this, who was the United States to claim that the UN system was "illegitimate" when Russia and China had exercised the veto "to obstruct its attempt to pour petrol on another Middle Eastern fire?" In addition, Monbiot cited what he described as an unsatisfactory US record in dealing with its own chemical weapons, as well as in providing cover "for Israel's weapons of mass destruction." Monbiot further argued that the US was on shaky ground in pursuing military action:

> Obama's failure to be honest about his nation's record of destroying international norms and undermining international law, his myth-making about the role of the US in world affairs, and his one-sided interventions in the Middle East, all render the crisis in Syria even harder to resolve. (Monboit, 2013, Sept. 10, p. 35)

The chemical weapons agreement was generally supported in a *Guardian* editorial appearing on September 11. The proposal, it acknowledged, "could be a significant breakthrough. For the first time in two and a half years, everyone in the Syrian crisis—except the rebels—appears to be on the same page." According to the editorial, the proposal was also useful because "the closer Mr. Obama comes to pulling the trigger, the more difficulty his advisers and spokesmen have in defining the mission." In addition, the agreement was seen as a way to get "back to the negotiating table at Geneva." Diplomacy was portrayed as increasingly necessary because "as the war drags on, an Assad defeat looks unlikely" (*Guardian*, 2013, Sept. 11, p. 34). On the same day, journalist John Pilger had little positive to say about the proposed agreement and even less positive to say about the US and its role in Syria. R2P fared no better. Described as a tool of "liberal realists," he saw it as playing "a vital propaganda role in urging the 'international community' to attack countries where 'the security council rejects a proposal or fails to deal with it'" (Pilger, 2013, Sept. 11, p. 34).

An editorial on September 13 revisited a theme introduced a week earlier—the consequences of changes in how world leaders viewed appropriate strategies for dealing with conflict. On this point, "crisis management" was seen as replacing "the pursuit of grand designs." The public mood of "war-weariness" obviously played a role in this but so too did "a judgment that most foreign policy problems fell into the 'too hard' category." The key question remained: "What grand design should international policymakers be pursing?" Strategies of the past were found wanting: "Democracy promoting and state-building are debased currencies ... and responsibility to protect is following a similar trajectory in Syria." No answer to the question was forthcoming, but the problem was stark: "If indeed we are bidding farewell to a world where the global policeman is no longer up to walking the beat, to whom does the task now fall?" (*Guardian*, 2013, Sept. 13, p. 44).

Simon Jenkins continued to take stock of where the world stood in terms of the future of military intervention and saw little hope for the concept of R2P. Acknowledging that in some cases intervention appeared to work (for example, Bosnia, Kosovo, Libya, and Mali), there were others where it didn't (e.g., Lebanon, Somalia, Iraq, and Afghanistan). In any event, Jenkins noted that "seldom is there any audit of intervention, let alone much in the way of aftercare." R2P, in particular, came in for harsh criticism:

> A concept so noble in the drawing rooms of Manhattan has degenerated into a sickening prelude to more bloodshed. It has become a diplomatic Babel of grandstanding, war-mongering, neo-imperialism and general half-heartedness, its signatures the missile strike and punitive sanctions.... What remains of 'responsibility to protect' should be properly humanitarian." (2013, Sept. 18, p. 29)

For civil wars in general, Jenkins believed that the best course is to leave combatants "to fight to a standstill." As for Syria, Vladimir Putin was now the "dominant player" and the pressure on him was described as "intense.... He and Iran have become the power brokers of this war" (Jenkins, 2013, Sept. 18, p. 29).

Lord Michael Williams, UN special coordinator for Lebanon, saw the chemical weapons agreement as helpful in banning their use, noting that "Syria has already taken the first step by signing the chemical weapons agreement," but in terms of ending the conflict, "it would do little." However, in that Assad's position had been strengthened and that "Russia has clearly taken a dramatic diplomatic lead," a new round of realistic diplomacy, leaving out possible Chapter VII action, was called for. This, in turn, would further damage "American deterrence capability." Lord Williams pointed out that "there is now considerable doubt in Israel that Obama would ever authorize a strike against Iran ... [with the consequence that] ... chances of an Israeli strike are likely to grow" (Williams, 2013, Sept.14, p. 51). For Williams, Iranian participation in any Syrian peace talks was essential, although admittedly difficult for Washington to endorse.

The Guardian's final editorial in our study period appeared in mid-September and reiterated a generally positive, although measured, view of the chemical weapons agreement, which was characterized as "probably the best framework solution that anyone could have hoped for in the circumstances." It also endorsed Lord Williams's view that Israel would likely feel endangered by US abandonment and that "Israel's prime minister may be about to talk himself into launching ... [an attack against Iran] ... which he has already postponed on at least one occasion." Likewise, the Free Syrian Army would view "the failure to come good on air strikes as nothing short of a betrayal ... giving up any hope that America wants to help it." Russia and Iran were now the key players in the conflict. Russia rose to that position due to "the vacillations of a war-weary US ... and a president who has yet "to devise a credible strategy for stopping this war." For its part, Iran needed to be convinced that just as chemical weapons became a liability for Assad, so too must support for Syria be seen as a liability to Iran—namely "a roadblock to a sanctions-free future" (*Guardian*, 2013, Sept. 16, p. 30).

The final two opinion pieces in September continued to focus on the implications of the chemical weapons agreement on Iran—both its role in ending the war and its alleged pursuit of nuclear weapons. Hans Blix praised the agreement for taking "the US off a military course that appeared to go against American public opinion, might have been rejected by Congress, and could have led to the loss of many lives in Syria and dragged Washington into further armed conflict." Blix also set the conditions for "a conference to bring about a transitional government," arguing that "the US now seems fully aware that Iran is central to this challenge ... [because] ... President Obama made clear that Iran will have a place at the conference about peace in Syria." Blix believed, however, that more was possible. In light of Iran's new president, described as "intent on entering into a calmer dialogue about its nuclear program and reducing the concerns about it," progress on this most important issue was possible as well. Blix emphasized that in any such discussions Iran's "pride and dignity" needed to be respected (Blix, 2013, Sept.19, p. 36).

Alastair Crooke described the chemical weapons agreement as a "tipping point" in the conflict that could either lead "toward new solutions, or into a new phase of conflict." In deciding which would prevail, Crooke asked, "Why should the possibility of US talks with Iran hold out such potential?" In answering, he outlined the regional struggle for hegemony between Shia Iran and Sunni Gulf States, most notably Saudi Arabia, with the strategy of the latter the overthrow of Bashar al-Assad. The US acceptance of the chemical weapons agreement in lieu of a military attack had signalled victories for both Assad and Iran. Stemming from this, Crooke envisioned a possible rapprochement between Iran and Saudi Arabia: "'The Persians and the Sunni sheiks quarrel all the time, but also can patch up without outside help.'" He went on to argue that if the big quarrel could be settled, "Syria is likely to be a key part of this" (Crooke, 2013, Sept. 30, p. 26).

The Globe and Mail's Opinion Narrative

The brazen use of chemical weapons by what was assumed to be the Syrian regime occasioned an immediate *Globe* editorial that argued strongly for a military response that went well beyond earlier calls for the creation of a no-fly zone: "The message needs to be made clear that the world will not tolerate the use of chemical weapons." While the US was seen as justifiably concerned about extreme Islamists among opposition forces, "Britain and France are open to a military response." In any event, it was clear that "Syria must pay a price" (*Globe*, 2013, Aug. 23, p. 10).

Presidents of the University of Winnipeg and the University of Ottawa, Lloyd Axworthy and Allan Rock, respectively, championed the 1999 NATO mission in Kosovo "as an appropriate precedent ... to be used as the basis for action in Syria." In that Russia would veto any Security Council authorization for the use of force, the mission would of necessity fall to "a coalition of countries prepared to take action," and President Obama was reportedly "looking to Kosovo as a model in Syria." They called upon "friends, allies, all those who seek a world of justice to urge him on, and offer their support" (Axworthy & Rock, 2013, Aug. 27, p. 13).

A second *Globe* editorial appeared to be not quite as enthusiastic in its endorsement of military action. First, it noted that "the consensus is that this monstrous act must not go unanswered." It also pointed to Prime Minister Harper's statement that "the situation demanded a 'firm response' ... [and that] ... the US and Britain will lead the response." As well, a government spokesperson had indicated that Canada "will continue to work with its allies 'in lockstep.'" Not so fast, the editorial cautioned. What was missing was a Parliamentary debate to consider "the full range of options available to Canada and its allies, not to mention the degree of Canada's participation in what now appears to be an inevitability" (*Globe*, 2013, Aug. 29, p. 12).

In early September, Jeffrey Simpson joined the debate on the side of caution. He questioned why the US, in particular, would want to be drawn into "a civil conflict of almost unfathomable complexity." Moreover, because the Syrian government "had plenty of warning to disperse its assets," he called into question the effectiveness of air strikes. He also questioned whether there was in fact "another coalition of the willing" ready to step up and contended that, if there were, it certainly would not be NATO. Most notably, Simpson dismissed the Kosovo analogy: "By bombs alone Syria's hellish war will not end." Finally, Simpson challenged the argument that failing to act would undermine US leadership: "The United States remains the world's undisputed military leader. It can act whenever it wants. Reluctance to do so in one case—this one—is not a test case for its leadership" (Simpson, 2013, Sept. 4, p. 13).

In his analysis of President Obama's decision to seek Congressional approval for a military strike, another of the paper's columnists, Konrad Yakabuski, took the opposite side. He saw air strikes as necessary "to alter the extreme, immoral behaviour of the Assad regime." The goal of military force was to get Assad to the negotiating table, and to make this happen Russia's Vladimir Putin was again named the go-to man. In seeking Congressional approval for the use of force, Mr. Obama was described as "rolling dice": the Senate was likely to vote yes; the House, probably no. In any event, Yakabuski predicted that the president would go ahead on his own, even if this meant going without traditional allies at his side (2013, Sept. 5, p. 17). On the same day, a *Globe* editorial agreed with Yakabuski, arguing that "Obama's present strategy toward Syria appears to be well thought out and should be acted upon." It also pointed to Russia as likely to push Syria toward negotiations as "there is no reason to suppose that ... [Mr. Putin] ... wants an expanded war in the Middle East" (*Globe*, Sept. 5, p. 16).

Campbell Clark analyzed the political climate in Washington in terms of support for possible air strikes. He emphasized that Mr. Obama "does not want to get the United States involved in Syria's civil war" but that his commitment to punish the Syrian government for its use of chemical weapons against the civilian population had forced his hand. Also, to get support in Congress, Clark argued that Obama might have to mount "a serious strike ... to degrade the Assad regime's [military capability]." In terms of what would follow, he cited Washington Institute for Near East Policy analyst Andrew Tabler's suggestion that after such military strikes the US should initiate a policy of "'discriminate support and arming'—funding the secular-nationalist rebels they know the best, to help increase their stature" (Clark, 2013, Sept. 5, p. 12).

Two days later, Jeffrey Simpson again weighed in on the side of restraint, maintaining that "the United States, with support from Canada, is about to enter [a civil war] with only the vaguest ideas of what intervention will or should bring." According to Simpson, what was likely to follow was increased involvement on the part of Iran and Hezbollah and increased internal repression. Intervention would, in any case, "not change the balance in the war." Diplomacy was also complicated by the fact that the US and Russia differed on whether "a political solution" should exclude or include Assad. On the feasibility of arming reliable rebels, Simpson was skeptical, pointing out that "figuring out how to provide weapons to the 'moderates' without having some of them fall into the hands of the militants is easier said than done" (Simpson, 2013, Sept. 7, p. F2).

Another opinion article by Axworthy and Rock appeared between Mr. Obama's decision to seek Congressional approval for military action and the proposal for destroying Syria's chemical weapons. It referred to "'*our' collective failure*," and no one, with the exception of Canada, escaped scathing condemnation. The UN led the list, both its "dysfunctional Security Council," crippled by the veto given the P5, and its weapons inspectors, who were not tasked with finding out who used chemical weapons but only if they had been used. In addition, the secretary-general was criticized because "his recent statements fail to reflect the underlying principle of R2P." Ban Ki-moon was described as having chosen "to wring his hands and leave the immense moral authority of his office untapped" (Axworthy & Rock, 2013, Sept. 10, p. 13; italics added).

Axworthy and Rock further criticized British Prime Minister David Cameron for "not effect[ively] whipping the vote" on a mandate to use military force. As well, President Obama's "legendary caution ... [was beginning] ... to look more like chronic indecision." The two authors also took to task their fellow "opinion leaders" who argued against intervention: "Abhorring war, preferring diplomacy and hoping for a negotiated settlement, they seem unaware that such a possibility has never been more remote." Canada was portrayed as having "laudably supported intervention," and Mr. Harper was praised for his statement "that leaving Mr. Assad's war crimes unanswered established a precedent that will haunt the world for generations." The authors ended with the observation that "when the history of the Syrian war is written, it will chronicle massive suffering that the world allowed to go on far too long" (Axworthy & Rock, 2013, Sept. 10, p. 13).

The Globe's first editorial following the proposal for the destruction of Syria's chemical weapons did not focus primarily on the agreement itself but on President Obama's "escape" from a Congressional rejection: "He could easily have hobbled himself from being able to make any serious response" to a further use of chemical weapons by the Syrian government. The weapons agreement was obviously not what *The Globe* had in mind when it had earlier called for Mr. Putin's input to resolve the conflict; and the editorial at best reflected a wait-and-see attitude. The agreement was described as "confirm[ing] the extent to which Syria is a client state of Russia" as well as demonstrating "Russia's ability to restrain—and to protect" the Syrian government. While Secretary of State Kerry acknowledged that the agreement was "entirely worth pursuing," the editorial ended on a skeptical note, praising France for insisting on "serious consequences, including air strikes, if the process bogs down" (*Globe*, Sept. 12, p. 14).

Campbell Clark's column published on the same day focused on the views of Assad's opponents and offered a similarly unenthusiastic evaluation of the agreement. Players who opposed a Western air strike—the Syrian government in particular—would benefit; but so too would Mr. Obama, who was "grasping … [the deal] … because it helps him stay out [of Syria]." Those who clamoured for air strikes, chiefly Assad's opposition at home and abroad, "expected more … [but] … Western nations have decided to leave Syrians to their fate" (Clark, 2013, Sept. 12, p. 6).

Globe columnist Margaret Wente launched a sharp attack at Barack Obama for agreeing to the chemical weapons proposal: "It just makes him look gullible. The President has allowed himself to be hog-tied and hornswoggled by Lilliputians." Russia and Mr. Putin were presented as untrustworthy, while Mr. Assad was seen as using the agreement "to obfuscate, delay, prevaricate and continue killing people." On the personal level, Wente described Mr. Obama as confused, prone to over-thinking, not really meaning what he said, and "let[ting] himself get rolled by the biggest bully on the block." As a consequence, his "Middle East policy is in ruins" (Wente, 2013, Sept. 14, p. F2).

The Globe's final editorial in our study period remained skeptical over whether the agreement "will prove effective." In any event, "Western powers must remain tenacious in pressing Russia and the Syrian government to fulfill their end of the chemical-weapons bargain." In that there was "a real possibility that this latest round of diplomacy will lead absolutely nowhere," the editorial counselled the West to keep its powder dry. And, if there were signs of "bad faith" in carrying out the agreement, the use of force in the form of "limited military air strikes should be revisited" (*Globe,* Sept. 17, p. 12).

Lewis MacKenzie presented the interesting argument (later confirmed) that the Russian proposal to destroy Syria's chemical weapons had in fact been the result of US–Russian negotiations. For MacKenzie, the agreement was "just a little too slick and well-coordinated over a very short period and multiple time zones" to have been "spontaneous."[4] On the actual agreement, he was only somewhat more positive than *The Globe's* editorial board, describing it as "mildly encouraging regarding the continued use of chemical weapons in the 2½-year civil war." There were, however, two problems. First, the agreement shifted the focus away from the actual conflict that at that point had "killed more than 100,000 on both sides" and would likely kill more irrespective of the agreement. Second, MacKenzie described the agreement as very difficult to carry out, both in terms of getting the weapons out of Syria under wartime conditions (a task that "stretches the imagination") and the ability of the West to destroy them. As for the conflict itself, MacKenzie foresaw a long stalemate "ultimately leading to tired participants who ultimately agree to negotiate." This he described as "a pretty embarrassing best-case scenario" (MacKenzie, 2013, Sept. 17, p. 13).

DISCUSSION

The major chemical weapons attack in the third week of August opened the floodgates for commentary in *The New York Times*: Was a response necessary? What should it entail? Who should authorize it? Should more have been done earlier on? And, finally, was the agreement to dispose of Syria's chemical weapons a reasonable response to the atrocity? *The Times* editorial board struggled with these issues and moved from support of Mr. Obama's prior cautious approach to acknowledgement that something had to be done. However, that something was seen to be limited: first, in terms of legitimacy (either authorized by a Security Council resolution or a Congressional vote); and second, by the need to punish Assad but to do so in a way that would not further involve the US in the civil war itself. The chemical weapons agreement, while by no means perfect, was framed as a reasonable step forward. Finally, the agreement, while clearly not a solution to ending the war and the ongoing humanitarian crisis it had produced, was seen as an unexpected way for the American president to extricate himself (and a skeptical US public) from his commitment to respond to Assad's breach of international norms and laws. Ian Hurd and Michael Ignatieff discussed R2P and its associated problems, but by the end of September even Nicholas Kristof had abandoned hope of any "humanitarian intervention" (the "responsibility to protect" doctrine long since having been jettisoned), calling instead for greater access to help the victims of the ongoing killing.

The chemical weapons attack also prompted extensive commentary in *The Guardian*, and while some pro–use-of-force arguments were presented, by and large (as was the case throughout the study), strong distance framing predominated in the British newspaper. The use of force, even in response to what was clearly an egregious violation of international law, was not seen as a good option. As to why it was not, the so-called "lessons of Iraq" stood front and centre, with numerous references to the need for evidence to precede decisions, as well as to war weariness (if not isolationism) on the part of British and American mass publics. The UN Security Council was repeatedly identified as the sole body entrusted to authorize the use of force, and attempts by Britain and the US to bypass that body with votes authorizing the use of force were not supported, although some opposite views on this question were also presented. *The Guardian* generally applauded the defeat of Mr. Cameron on the use-of-force vote in Parliament, but the paper was not nearly as firm in its opposition to a US military response. The chemical weapons agreement whereby Syria's chemical weapons were to be removed and destroyed was greeted at best with cautious optimism.

The Globe and Mail had supported greater levels of military commitment in Syria earlier in 2013 and, following the chemical weapons attack, called for a military response, with Lloyd Axworthy and Alan Rock proposing a Kosovo-type R2P mission led by the US. Other opinion contributors, however, such as Jeffrey Simpson, argued against a military response. Thus, there was no consistent position with respect to whether the use of force would be beneficial or harmful. *The Globe* also ended up deeply suspicious of the chemical weapons agreement that took US air strikes (which the paper supported) off the table, with Margaret Wente's column especially critical of the actions of the US president. As was the case with editorials, none of the opinion articles pinned much hope on the success of the September chemical weapons agreement.

CONCLUSION

Several general observations are suggested by material presented in the pre-ceding chapters. First, the Syrian situation was an immediate and ongoing serious concern for the three newspapers examined. Second, there was a remark-able degree of consistency in the *issues* they presented to their readerships, if not in the *solutions* they advocated. Third, though none of them mounted a sustained campaign for any type of military intervention in the tragedy, they all weighed the wisdom and the feasibility of a variety of strategies to bring the conflict to an end. Finally, the international Responsibility to Protect, an idea incorporated into the UN peacekeeping arsenals a scant six years earlier (and much celebrated thereafter by at least the Western academic world), was rarely mentioned directly. With respect to these limited references, however, there were differences in emphasis and evaluation from paper to paper (and over time) that need to be recognized, as well as implications for how future Syria-type crises might be approached by the international community that need to be explored.

QUANTITATIVE SUMMARY

During the two and a half years covered by our quantitative content analysis, opinion-leading elites did not agree on whether or how to respond to disturbing events in Syria. However, in the balance of these views, arguments advocating non-involvement clearly predominated; as a result, there was no media "push" that might have given rise to a public campaign on behalf of international intervention.

As we noted in Chapter 3, Piers Robinson suggested an interaction between media and government in the process of intervention decision mak-ing and that in certain conditions media coverage could provide an important input to such decisions. However, while the *issue of international involvement* grew in importance as the conflict dragged on, opinion-leading elites in the US, Britain, and Canada did not ever come close to a critical mass that favoured an international response to the Syria crisis, much less a military one. Commentators who approached the matter primarily from a national interest point of view and those who were mainly concerned about humanitarian imperatives were equally divided in this respect. Overall, during the first 31 months of the conflict, opinion-leading material favouring a military response was challenged by over four times as much material that discouraged such a response (5 per cent in favour vs. 22 per cent opposed). Opinion-leading material in *The Guardian* was especially opposed to the idea of military action (32 per cent), while only 2 per cent favoured such a response. In *The Globe*, 23 per cent of opinion content opposed military action, and in *The Times* 12 per cent opposed the use of force. In the latter two newspapers, only 7 per cent of content favoured military action (data consolidated from chapters 4–7, not shown in tabular form).

On the broader question of whether the international community "should do something" (including non-military options), opposition was less pronounced. Nonetheless, over our study period just over twice as great a percentage of opinion-leading content was opposed to such involvement as favoured it (29 per cent to 13 per cent). Opinion leaders writing in *The Guardian* were the most negative, with 36 per cent of material opposing international involvement and only 7 per cent supporting it. In *The Times* and *The Globe*, support for international involvement hovered around 15 per cent (18 per cent and 14 per cent, respectively), with anti-involvement positions reflected in 25 per cent and 21 per cent of content, respectively (data consolidated from chapters 4–7, not shown in tabular form). Added to these two indicators of anti-intervention framing was the growing belief among virtually all opinion leaders that Syria was on the path to turn out badly, regardless of what the West did or did not do. Significantly, these pessimistic views regarding Syria's future peaked just prior to the only serious consideration of a resort to force in the late summer of 2013.

Ironically, the two main groups in the US that pressed for greater military involvement on the side of Assad's opponents occupied very different positions on the ideological spectrum. On the right were neo-conservative hawks (e.g., senators John McCain and Lindsey Graham), whose calls for arming the opposition, creating a no-fly zone, and launching air strikes against Syrian military targets were echoed by various journalists, think-tank spokespersons, and academics. On the left were "liberal internationalists" (academics and journalists), who focused on the human-security dimension of the conflict and urged greater Western intervention based on the humanitarian *principles* behind the Responsibility to Protect, although not necessarily on the specific doctrine itself. (We will return to R2P below.) Not even this surprising coalition succeeded, of course, in changing the dominant frame that there were *no good options* for Syria and significant downsides for the West, the Middle East, and perhaps the configuration of world order, should outside forces become directly involved in a conflict characterized by multi-layered complexity.

While it is not possible to say with certainty whether anti-intervention framing merely reflected public opinion or was the creator of that dominant view (question 2, Chapter 3), it is clear that media opinion and what there was of public opinion marched in lock-step (see poll material presented below). However, as Thomas Friedman pointed out with respect to the US, the debate over Syria was conducted largely at the elite level—there was little public engagement with the matter as had occurred, for example, in the case of the "Save Darfur" movement (2013, Sept. 18). In the UK, Jonathan Freedland similarly noted that public opinion appeared "utterly disengaged, unbothered by the slaughter" (2012, Oct. 20, p. 45). The one partial exception was the British Stop the War Coalition, which appeared more concerned with keeping the US out of the conflict than with the fate of endangered Syrians. As mentioned earlier, Martin Kettle also observed that there was little "tabloid jingoism over Syria," suggesting that the bloodshed there had not engaged the interest of the mass population (2013, Aug. 29, p. 31), despite substantial media preoccupation with it—or perhaps more correctly with the political situation created by it. One wonders whether mass publics might have been more "engaged" with Syria had media campaigned loudly for plunging headlong into it, and also whether in that circumstance outcomes such as the rejection of military intervention by the British Parliament might have been different; but at this stage these can only be intriguing speculations. However, the fact remains that neither a popular nor a sustained media movement advocating an R2P humanitarian intervention developed in any of the three countries studied.

NARRATIVE SUMMARY

All three newspapers tended to see the conflict, especially in its early months, as another chapter in the Arab Spring (although it was not necessarily called that), with the North American papers emphasizing a more or less clear divide between the forces of repression and those of liberty or reform, and with the latter deserving of strong support (see Friedman, 2011, Apr. 13, Apr. 15; *NYT*, 2011, Apr. 29; *Globe*, 2011, Mar. 31, Apr. 25).

In *The Globe* in 2011, doubt arose, but only gradually, concerning the composition and the trustworthiness of the anti-government forces (see Bell, 2011, Aug. 12). It was not, however, until its editorial on January 12, 2012, that *The Globe* began to distance itself from Assad's opponents by referring to them as "armed insurgents" rather than "protesters." This was followed shortly afterward by General Lewis MacKenzie's warning that it was unwise to divide the combatants into "good guys" and "bad guys" and that some care had to be taken lest the West end up supporting extremists (2012, Feb. 22, p. 17).

The Guardian differed from the two North American papers during the early months of the struggle and, to a lesser degree, thereafter, in appearing more committed to the rebel cause. One measure of this is the strong positions the paper adopted editorially, and another is the much greater attention it devoted to background analyses of the political and sectarian situations in the Middle East and to the implications of these for various possible outcomes to the conflict. A significant number of the latter were written by analysts of Middle Eastern origin, who often had a passionate interest in Syria per se and a deep, but not necessarily unbiased, knowledge of the region as a whole; by contrast, *Times* coverage tended to be more dispassionate and more narrowly focused on Syria as a two-sided issue.

All three papers nonetheless exhibited strong anti-Assad postures. They struggled with the means by which he could be forced to accept reform or, as his tactics came to be considered less and less tolerable, forced to relinquish his office. With the exception of *The Guardian's* Simon Jenkins (2013, May 29), all commentators agreed that Assad had to be disposed of in one way or another and that the international community should encourage that result to the furthest extent possible. The form that encouragement should take, however, was quite another matter, as the three newspapers quickly realized that the Syrian situation was far more complex, for instance, than that unfolding in Libya.

All three papers made frequent references to the plight of Syria's citizens, both those within the country and those who were refugees in neighbouring countries. However, what appeared to concern many Western observers was how this dictator could be "brought to justice" as others had been during the Arab Spring (a desire that was only partially and indirectly humanitarian). But there was also a concern about the effects of the conflict on bordering nations (Israel prominent among them) and on Shia–Sunni balances within the region. In addition, there was an issue of "face saving" for those in position of world leadership; no one wanted to appear powerless to deal with outrageous behaviour by the tyrannical ruler of a small state. The last applied particularly to the American president with respect to Assad's use of chemical weapons, in defiance of his declared "red line."

The tendency to put political- and national-interest considerations ahead of humanitarian ones was abundantly illustrated by Michael Doran and Max Boot's opinion piece in *The New York Times* of September 27, 2012. They listed five reasons in support of a Libya-style intervention in Syria by the US. Only the last, and obviously least significant, of these was that intervention might end "a terrible human rights disaster." On the opposite side, one might also recall that former Canadian diplomat Derek Burney and academic Fen Osler Hampson later came close to suggesting that what was going on in Syria was not "our" business, or at least not Canada's. They too offered five reasons for what they considered to be a proper response to the Syrian morass—that is, staying as far away from it as possible. All of their reasons were political and self-interested, and they counselled Canada to refrain from "stoking the fires" of the conflict or "trying to pick winners" (2013, June 19, p. 29). These views tended to be extreme, however. Most commentators considered that the conflict could not be ignored and that international involvement in it was inevitable in one way or another (see in particular articles by Thomas Friedman).

It should be noted that more than a year before the Doran and Boot article, *The Times*, after some hesitation, had editorially declared that "a foreign military intervention is out of the question" (2011, July 19, p. 22). But it did continue to present its readers with a variety of opinions on both sides of the issue. (For the "anti" side of the debate, see articles by Keller, 2012, Mar. 19; Bali & Rana, 2012, Apr. 11; and an *NYT* editorial, 2012, Apr. 10. In addition to Doran & Boot, pro-intervention arguments were presented by Friedman, 2012, Apr. 29; Maleh, 2012, May 31; Bull, 2012, Aug. 15.)

Indeed, openness to a variety of approaches was characteristic of all three papers' treatment of the problem. With the exception of *The Guardian*'s consistent opposition to any form of military intervention, no position was ever completely ruled out. Syria was a major and ongoing irritant, a boil that would not heal and for which political doctors had no cure. The same issues and suggested responses tended to reappear again and again, particularly following major developments within the country and in the region. Hence, *The Guardian* came out in opposition to a Libya-type no-fly zone fairly early on, arguing that it was not a good model because that operation had not proved effective in protecting lives in Libya (2011, Nov. 1). But the newspaper later presented at least one tentatively favourable commentary on that line of action by former foreign secretary Lord David Owen (2012, June 9) and a highly debatable argument by Marko Hoare on June 19, 2013, to the effect that a no-fly zone, along with providing arms to the anti-government forces, would be widely supported in the Middle Eastern region and thus was desirable on a number of grounds.

In contrast, *The Globe* took no editorial position with respect to a possible no-fly zone or other military intervention prior to the 2013 use of chemical weapons. It did, however, print four op-ed articles strongly suggesting the establishment of a no-fly zone (Segal, 2012, June 22; Wark, 2012, July 19; and Heinbecker, 2013, Mar. 15, June 8) and a curious one by Princeton University professor Anne-Marie Slaughter that argued that since "killing always begets killing" it was necessary to take "decisive action" (at least a credible threat of force) in order to "create space for peace" (2013, May 29, p. 15). There was only one word of caution in this respect, and it was offered by General Lewis MacKenzie (2012, June 25).

The use of chemical weapons in August 2013, which was widely assumed (but never conclusively confirmed) to have been carried out by government forces, interjected new life into the "should we" or "shouldn't we" debate, giving strength to the pro-intervention contingent, particularly in the US. On the grounds that Assad had to be punished for violating long-established international norms, the editors of *The Times*, for example, were moved to endorse a military response on the Libyan model for the first time, although with the somewhat curious proviso that "deep involvement" in the civil war should be avoided (2013, Aug. 27, p. 20). Some commentators agreed (Kristof, 2013, Aug. 29, Sept. 5, Sept. 8; Keller, 2013, Sept. 9), although not all thought there would be sufficient international support for such an undertaking, and no one advocated unilateral action by the US. However, some disagreed that it would be appropriate in any case (Friedman, 2013, Sept. 4; Hathaway & Shapiro, 2013, Sept. 4; De Waal & Conley-Zilkic, 2013, Sept. 5), and the paper's editors backed away from their August 27, 2013, position in a series of editorials: August 29, August 31, and September 7. Overall, then, the chemical weapons attack seemed only temporarily to stimulate inclinations to deploy arms.

The Guardian, it will be recalled, was less moved to action by the use of chemical weapons than its American counterpart, *The New York Times*. *The Guardian* declared editorially on August 23 that force was not a good response to the use of such weapons and somewhat pointedly avoided the assumption that Assad was necessarily responsible for using them. Seven editorials and op-ed articles followed throughout the remainder of August, almost all strongly agreeing with the paper's editorial position. Only one commentator quibbled somewhat with this stance by arguing that failure to respond to the atrocity in some fashion would be disastrous for Syria and for the United Nations (Rifkind, 2013, Aug. 29).

The Globe and Mail, on the other hand, came close to being the mirror image of *The Guardian*. It began editorially on August 23 by proclaiming that Syria "must pay a price" and followed that pronouncement on August 29 by asserting that Assad's "monstrous act must not go unanswered" and on September 5 by the more strategic argument that decisive action against Assad would push Russia to push the Syrian leader into negotiations. To these were added several contributions by former minister of foreign affairs Lloyd Axworthy and former ambassador to the United Nations Allan Rock, who maintained that unless righteous retribution were exacted, Assad's war crimes would "haunt the world for generations" (2013, Aug. 27, Sept. 10). Konrad Yakabuski also claimed that air strikes were needed to force the Syrian president to negotiate (2013, Sept. 5). Jeffrey Simpson, however, counselled caution and warned that forceful intervention would not alter the balance of the civil war, in any case (2013, Sept 4, Sept 7).

Accordingly, it may be argued that after Syria used chemical weapons, pressure toward launching a military strike of some kind was gaining the upper hand in the US. Moreover, given Obama's previously declared "red line," that stance probably would have carried the day had it not been for the agreement that would see Syria allowing its stockpile of such weapons destroyed under international supervision.[1] Interestingly, not everyone was happy at this retreat from the brink. Recall, for instance, that *The Globe*'s Campbell Clark expressed disappointment over the chemical weapons agreement—it meant the West had "decided to leave Syrians to their fate" (2013, Sept. 12, p. 6); and columnist Margaret Wente, although not usually a commentator on international issues, denounced the agreement as a means by which Assad could "obfuscate, delay, and continue killing people" and cast Obama as "gullible" for agreeing to it (2013, Sept. 14, p. F2).

There were those who were convinced that morality demanded support of some kind for those who were fighting for justice and democracy. For those who were either disillusioned (for a variety of different reasons) with Libya-like operations or persuaded that insufficient public support made such an exercise unlikely, there was a fallback position. This was to supply the Syrian rebels with arms—or, to take one step back, at least with communications equipment, intelligence, and training. No such suggestions were made during 2011, but they began to appear in *The Times* early in 2012, apparently in response to discussions of the possibility in Washington circles, or perhaps in response to agitation by the British and French governments for lifting the ban on arms supplies imposed by the European Union. These suggestions in *The Times*, however, found no echo in either *The Guardian* or *The Globe* until 2013.

What is surprising is that even by 2011 the disparate and fragmented nature of the groups making up the anti-government forces in Syria was well known, but some interventionists nonetheless clung to the hope that the balance could be tipped in favour of the "good rebels" by sending them arms (up to and including surface-to-air missiles), which would be kept out of the hands of the "bad rebels." (See for example, *The Times* article by Senator Bob Corker, 2012, Apr. 24; and *The Globe*, 2013, Jan. 2.) However, the majority of commentators in both *The Times* and *The Guardian* rejected this possibility, and both newspapers ran editorials criticizing Obama's June 2012 decision to send "small arms" to the rebels (*NYT*, 2013, June 15; *Guardian*, 2013, June 15). *The Guardian*, it should be noted, was particularly vehement in opposing the entry of further arms of any kind into Syria, with Jonathan Steele going so far as to argue that Britain had "blood on its hands" for supplying even non-lethal equipment to the opposition forces (2013, Feb. 1, p. 34). Of nine references to the idea in the British paper between February 1 and June 19, 2013, only the last, by Marko Hoare, thought it had any merit. However, the fact that the idea was not only seriously suggested but acted upon—openly by some governments and covertly by others—was an indication of the extent to which some felt a responsibility to try to influence the conflict's outcome.

Three other aspects of the newspapers' treatment of the Syrian crisis are worthy of attention: (1) their respective concepts of the role that the US and Russia were playing in it; (2) the roles that those states should be playing to resolve it; and (3) the impact of Jon Western's (2005) suggestion regarding the importance of "latent public opinion," especially on British and American decisions regarding the use of force.

Russia was, of course, generally considered to be the primary barrier to achieving the "right thing" in Syria, although it was often unclear what the right thing was and, therefore, what sort of policy was appropriate to get to it. Both *The Times* and *The Guardian* denounced the obstructivism of Russia (and, more or less incidentally, of China) in the Security Council, with the latter describing the country editorially as the "global protector of tyrants" (*Guardian*, 2012, Feb. 7, p. 32; see also the less graphic references in *The Times* editorials of Sept. 1 and Dec. 23, 2011, and Feb. 7, 2012). In general, though, criticism was not particularly severe, and all three papers recognized that, as General Lewis MacKenzie put it in a *Globe* opinion piece on February 22, 2012, "the only solution to the Syrian conflict goes through Moscow" (p. 17) (see also *The Times* editorial of March 1, 2013, which used very similar language). There were several suggestions that the US and Russia needed to work more closely to cobble together a solution, which implied that this was not altogether out of the question (in *The Times* see Halevy, 2012, Feb. 8; Kristof, 2012, Nov. 15; Simes & Saunders, 2012, Dec. 22; and in *The Guardian* see Manna, 2013, Apr. 19).

In contrast, *The Guardian* in particular was bitterly critical of practically every aspect of the US response to the crisis and, especially, of its early adoption of positions that the paper felt had effectively closed the door to co-operation with Russia and compromises with Assad. Its initial complaint was that the US would not support reform in Syria if that were contrary to its national interests (2011, May 20), as if Britain or other countries could be expected to act with greater altruism. On the other hand, Simon Tisdall complained that the US talked a lot but did nothing, although he was unclear as to what he would have liked the country to do (2011, Oct. 4). The chief, and probably most valid, criticism, however, was that President Obama had ruined diplomatic efforts undertaken by former secretary-general Kofi Annan by insisting from the outset that the Syrian president had to go before anything else could be considered. This meant, *The Guardian* argued, that Assad had no reason to negotiate; and Russia, no reason to pressure him to do so (*Guardian*, 2012, July 28; see also Glass, 2013, June 7, and *Guardian*, 2013, July 19).

At the same time, *The Guardian* cited a "yawning lack of direction from Barack Obama" (*Guardian*, 2013, May 5), and, following the use of chemical weapons, it claimed that the British people were fed up with the "humiliating excesses of US security policy" and had a right to tell Obama "enough" despite the "intolerable" Syrian war crimes (*Guardian*, 2013, Aug. 31, p. 44). The only grudging approval that US policy received from *The Guardian* was for refraining from any immediate military response following the use of the chemical weapons (*Guardian*, 2013, Sept. 2). However, that was followed by the assessment that the chemical weapons agreement had catapulted Russia into the driver's seat because of US failure to "devise a credible strategy for stopping the war" (*Guardian*, 2013, Sept. 16, p. 30). It is tempting to wonder if *The Guardian*, like Margaret Wente, would have preferred to not have the agreement and to wonder what the consequences of that might have been. Without wishing to suggest that US reactions to the crisis were always the most desirable, it is also tempting to wonder what overall strategy *Guardian* editors would have recommended to deal with what was internationally "intolerable," apart from wishing any actions to be peaceful and nonintrusive.

Neither *The Globe* nor *The Times*, it will be recalled, refrained from voicing some criticisms of the leadership that they assumed only the US could provide. *The Globe* was least directly critical, choosing to assess issues primarily in "we" terms rather than point fingers in any particular direction prior to 2013. However, Anne-Marie Slaughter charged that Obama was being "timid" (2013, May 29), and an editorial a month earlier implied much the same thing by urging the American president to give some "practical substance to his words" about red lines and chemical weapons; however, the editorial did not elaborate on what it would have preferred that to be (Globe, 2013, Apr. 28, p. 14). When the use of those weapons became a reality and there was no immediate retaliation, Lloyd Axworthy and Allan Rock also observed that Obama's "legendary caution" was beginning to look "more like chronic indecision" (2013, Sept. 10, p. 13). Again, the writers did not specify exactly what sort of decision they thought would have been appropriate, although presumably, given the same writers' earlier observations, it would of necessity have involved the use of force of some kind.

The Times did not so much disagree with what its government was doing as worry that it wasn't enough. Contrary to the position taken by *The Guardian*, for instance, the paper tacitly agreed with Obama's stated insistence that Assad must go but criticized him for doing too little to rally international support to achieve that outcome (2011, June 18). The paper also offered the suggestion that the US urge the Security Council to refer the Syrian president to the International Criminal Court. In view of the fact that the US was not a member of the court and had strongly pressured its allies and dependants to refrain from such membership, this was a very curious suggestion (*NYT*, 2011, Apr. 29, Nov. 17). Nicholas Kristof similarly complained of a lack of resolve on the part of the US and a failure to supply weapons to those rebels "who pass our vetting" (2012, Aug. 9, p. 23). But only Roger Cohen offered really hard criticisms. In his view the country was not only not showing the kind of leadership expected of it but was, in addition, demonstrating "growing isolationism" (2013, Sept. 13, p. 25).

The impact of such growing isolationism, imbedded in "latent public opinion" (especially in Britain and the US), was identified by Jon Western as a major input to intervention decision making. (See discussion in Chapter 3.) Moreover, it was clear from the arguments of opinion leaders that one of the reasons contributing to this isolationist mood was a series of perceived international intervention failures, beginning at least as far back as Afghanistan in 2001, and continuing through to the contemporary Arab Spring uprising in Libya. (See, for example, Kettle, 2012, Mar 15; Keller, 2012, Mar. 19; and Friedman, 2012, July 25.) For Great Britain, Iraq occupied pride of place on the list of problematic ventures. In any event, justifiable disillusionment over the lack of success of these interventions, no doubt combined with uncertainties related to the Great Recession that began in 2008, appear to have resulted in a general mood of isolationism, or at least a latent public opinion that was decidedly anti-interventionist.

To say that this isolationist mood determined the policy choices of American and British leaders would be to overstate the case, but as Bill Keller noted, "public opinion puts a thumb on the scale" (2012, Mar. 19, p. 21). And in this case we believe that there is ample evidence that it did serve to place restraints on decisions, especially in Great Britain.

REVIEW OF POLL DATA

In that there were few references to actual poll data in the opinion commentaries we have reviewed, we believe that it is useful to recount here just how heavy the "thumb of public opinion" may have been as far as intervention in Syria was concerned.

American Poll Data

An early September 2013 poll conducted by the Pew Research Center for the People and the Press pointed to problems for President Obama in going forward with air strikes against the Syrian government. It reported that "by a 48% to 29% margin, more Americans oppose than support" such operations. The poll also revealed that "74% believe airstrikes ... are likely to create a backlash against the United States ... [while] ... 61% think [they] would be likely to lead to a long-term military commitment there." Neither was the "democratic legitimacy" strategy pursued by the president viewed favourably: 59 per cent of respondents indicated that the US should "first get a United Nations resolution before taking military action in Syria," while only 28 per cent indicated that such authorization was not necessary (Pew Research Center, 2013, Sept. 3). A *New York Times*/CBS News poll conducted between September 6 and 8, 2013 (just prior to the announcement of the Russian-brokered chemical weapons agreement), reported that only 33 per cent of respondents approved of the president's handling of Syria, while 56 per cent disapproved. Fully 60 per cent specifically disapproved of planned US airstrikes (Landler & Thee-Brenan, 2013, Sept. 8).

More generally, since the beginning of the Iraq war a decade earlier, a growing isolationist mood appeared to have developed among the American mass public. Note the responses to the following questions:

- Should the US "take a leading role in trying to solve foreign conflicts?"
  April 2003: 48% Yes / 43% No; as opposed to
  2013: 34% Yes / 62% No

- Should the US "intervene to turn dictatorships into democracies?"
  "At the start of the Iraq war": 29% Yes / 48% No; as opposed to
  2013: 15% Yes / 72% No

Surprisingly, the survey also revealed that the American public appeared less than outraged by Assad's alleged use of chemical weapons: while 75 per cent believed that Assad had used them, roughly the same percentage was opposed to even "supplying rebel forces with conventional arms" as a response (Landler & Thee-Brenan, 2013, Sept. 8).

British Poll Data
A poll done by Britain's Channel 4 News in March 2013 showed that "half ... [of those surveyed] ... opposed sending defensive military supplies such as anti-aircraft guns to anti-Assad troops ... [while 64 percent] ... were against supplying full-scale military equipment such as tanks and heavy artillery." Reporter Lindsey Hilsum pointed to a disconnect between public opinion and government policy: the survey "highlights the unpopularity of deeper involvement in the conflict ... [despite the government's belief that] ... further intervention, short of sending British troops, is essential" (Hilsum, 2013, Mar. 21).

On the issue of a direct combat role, a poll taken four days after the chemical weapons attack reported that "only 9% of the public support sending British troops to fight in Syria, while 74% oppose it." Following the rejection of the use of force by Parliament, David Cameron further signalled the importance of public opinion to the British decision: "'It is very clear to me that the British parliament reflecting *the views of the British people*, does not want to see British military action. I get that and the government will act accordingly'" (as quoted in "Public opinion drove Syria debate," 2013, Aug. 30; italics in original).

We judge that polling results such as those reported above would have presented a challenge for governments that wanted to pursue policies of military intervention in Syria. However, the fact that both British and American leaders went ahead to schedule legislative votes on the issue would also lead us to believe that neither appeared to have considered lack of public support to be an insurmountable obstacle to a military response. Of course, in Britain the parliamentary rejection put an immediate stop to the prime minister's chosen policy, while in the US unfolding events offered an option other than air strikes (the agreement calling for the removal and destruction of Syria's chemical weapons), which was quickly deemed to be an adequate response.[2]

In sum, it would be incorrect to say that opinion material demonstrated a lack of concern about the Syrian situation or an absolute rejection of the *principle* of international responsibility in such situations. But there was very healthy skepticism about both the efficacy and the safety of any method of physical intervention that could reasonably be imagined to address the harm caused by the civil war. Such calculations would be entirely consistent with the criteria the ICISS report on R2P had laid down for determining when humanitarian military missions should be undertaken (see discussion in Chapter 2)—although we have found no evidence that any such calculations based on R2P criteria actually took place in either British or American decision making.[3] Thus, with respect to question 3 raised in Chapter 3, while evidence suggests that public opinion (most likely only partially media inspired) played a significant role in the British decision to reject force, as President Obama's interview with Jeffrey Goldberg reveals, any such link with respect to a similar American decision to abandon any military action appears weak (Goldberg, 2016, April). In concluding the book, we look more closely at what the three papers had to say about the most recent guideline for good conduct in the international realm and speculate on what their treatment of the R2P doctrine might mean for responses to future humanitarian crises.

THE NEWSPAPERS' EXAMINATION OF THE RESPONSIBILITY TO PROTECT

As we pointed out in the opening paragraph of this chapter, R2P received little specific attention in opinion-leading material overall, but there were significant differences in both the amount and the nature of the papers' evaluation of it. It was mentioned least in the pages of *The Times*. Nicholas Kristof observed in

April of 2011 that he hoped the Libyan intervention would "put teeth in R2P," although he stopped short of specific recommendations with respect to Syria (2011, Apr. 3, p. 12). But the concept was not mentioned specifically again in *The Times* until after the sarin gas attack more than two years later. At that point, two opinion articles spoke approvingly of what were assumed to be the principles underlying the doctrine but maintained that (1) it lacked the force of law (Hurd, 2013, Aug. 28), and (2) circumstances did not provide sufficient justification for resorting to military means in Syria (Hathaway & Shapiro, 2013, Sept. 4).[4] Michael Ignatieff added that R2P had been misused to achieve regime change in Libya and that public support was needed for the rebuilding of its "humanitarian protection" component. He continued to maintain, as did many R2P supporters, that R2P missions could be implemented through a process of "democratic legitimacy," such as had been initiated by the British and American leaders (2013, Sept. 14, p. 19). It is noteworthy that there were no editorial references to R2P in *The Times*.

In contrast, R2P was one of the earliest reference points for the editors of *The Globe*, probably at least partly because Canadians had been so prominently involved in initiating the ICISS and preparing its report. The paper editorialized on April 25, 2011, that Syria was "appropriate" for the "invocation" of the R2P doctrine but that there was no hope the UN could do so. That was because, the paper added on June 21, NATO's "overstretched interpretation of its mandate in Libya" left few willing to endorse another such venture in Syria (p. 10). Nevertheless, Lloyd Axworthy implied, but did not state outright, that after Libya, Syria would be the next test case for R2P (2011, Aug. 23).

In 2012, four more Syria-R2P commentaries appear in *The Globe*. First, Timothy Garton Ash claimed that any type of R2P intervention would make matters worse (2012, June 14). Then, Senator Hugh Segal argued that just such an intervention was nothing short of essential because "standing and watching is simply criminal" (2012, June 22, p. 13). In a third *Globe* commentary regarding R2P, Louise Arbour, former justice of the Supreme Court of Canada and former high commissioner for refugees among other distinguished legal posts, took the position that R2P was not sufficient when a government "embarked on a rampage against its own population" because, in those circumstances, only regime change would be adequate, and authorizing that was beyond possibility for the Security Council (2012, June 27, p. 13). Finally, Douglas Saunders seconded *The Globe*'s initial offering to the effect that Libya had effectively shelved R2P (2012, Sept. 22).

Somewhat surprisingly, 2013 produced only two R2P-related pieces. Garton Ash offered the puzzling conclusion that while R2P should apply, it didn't because it suffered from "a kind of subconscious racism" (2013, Apr. 25, p. 15). In the second piece, Axworthy and Rock lashed out at what they termed the general failure of the UN, and especially its secretary-general, to "reflect the underlying principles of R2P" (2013, Sept. 10, p. 13).

In keeping with the general opposition to military intervention in the Syrian tragedy, and its equation of R2P with that form of action (although it was not alone in that), *The Guardian* ignored the concept entirely until the use of sarin gas in 2013, save for three early pieces. The first two were by Simon Jenkins, in which he denounced what he perceived to be the tendency to take "up arms against every dictator" (2012, July 20, p. 39) and "to assume potency over other people's affairs that 'we' do not possess" (2013, May 29, p. 26), but the commentaries did not specifically mention R2P. The third piece was by Claire Spencer, in which she observed that Libya was likely "one of the last actions of a consensus-based 'international community'" (2013, Mar. 27, p. 38).

When chemical weapons made their appearance, however, the chairman of the Parliamentary Joint Committee on Intelligence and Security, Malcolm Rifkind, warned that since R2P had been accepted by all, failure to respond to that use would condemn the UN to the same fate as the League of Nations (2013, Aug. 29). A number of strenuous challenges to the "all" part of Rifkind's argument subsequently appeared. First of all, John Pilger described R2P as a propaganda instrument of "liberal realists" (2013, Sept. 11, p. 34), followed by Simon Jenkins, who maintained that R2P had become "a diplomatic Babel of grandstanding, war mongering, neo-imperialism, and general half-heartedness" (2013, Sept. 18, p. 29). Third, the paper added editorially that "democracy promoting and state-building are debased currencies … and the responsibility to protect is following a similar trajectory in Syria" (2013, Sept. 13). Clearly, R2P had not been accepted by "all."

What stands out most strongly in both the positive and the negative commentaries on R2P, even by those who were intimately involved in its creation, is that there was an automatic and unanimous interpretation of the doctrine as requiring the use of force. "Protection," in effect, could only come about by means of guns and bombs. This is particularly evident in the quotations from *The Guardian* cited immediately above. As we pointed out in Chapter 2, this interpretation is not what the ICISS report says, however, and is actually inconsistent with what it does say, as well as, one might add, with any realistic view of the world. Nevertheless, the old adage that if it waddles like a duck and quacks like a duck, it probably *is* a duck is relevant here. If the majority of political commentators believe and behave as if R2P equates to the use of force, then to all intents and purposes that is "the truth," and no amount of insistence that this is both simplistic and incorrect in terms of the written text and the intentions of its authors will alter that fact. Media references to the protection principle can therefore be expected to continue to focus on the dispatch of military might—that is, *if* media refer to it at all.

Our empirical data do not, of course, provide a firm basis for predicting how relevant the principle may be regarded when the next humanitarian outrage occurs. But those who remain committed to traditional concepts of national sovereignty, or those who are skeptical of the efficacy of proclaiming ethical standards for international behaviour, may be forgiven for seeing the scant attention that R2P was accorded during our study period as its well-deserved death knell. Aiden Hehir and Robert Murray, for instance, have described as "giddy" Secretary-General Ban Ki-moon's declaration that with the passage of Resolution 1973, sanctioning the use of force in Libya, "it should be clear to all that the responsibility to protect has arrived." The authors go on to argue that "R2P has demonstrably failed" because, among other reasons, "Russia's actions in Ukraine suggest that R2P's strategy of turning states into responsible human-rights-oriented actors ... is glaringly anachronistic" (Hehir & Murray, 2015, Mar. 17).[5] But is R2P really dead? Never to rise again? If so, can the cause of death be identified? Was it that it *was invoked* in Libya? Or that is *was not invoked* with respect to Syria?

Clearly, as the preceding chapters amply demonstrate, the Libyan and Syrian debacles are inextricably linked. First, the Libyan intervention disillusioned many people, including, in all probability, the leaders of some of the states that participated in the so-called no-fly-zone operation. What had seemed at the outset to be a simple military exercise with a straightforward and limited objective, duly authorized and in compliance with the latest enunciation of international principles of good behaviour, proved to be something else entirely. Quite apart from whether NATO powers deliberately engaged in trickery and deceit, the operation of an innocent-sounding no-fly zone seemingly required the application of far more force than most people had assumed it would. Moreover, as the operation continued, it became increasingly difficult, at least in the short term, to associate what was happening with the protection of anything beyond Western political values. When the Syrian conflict followed hard on the heels of Libya, then, there was a good deal of hesitation about launching a similar action under circumstances that were widely recognized as being far more difficult and complex on several different grounds.

What we may reasonably conclude from the above is that Libya poured some cold realism on the overheated idealism that bubbled up from R2P's near unanimous endorsement by the United Nations in 2005 and its adoption as policy by the Security Council in 2006. Libya demonstrated that protecting abused persons in far-flung parts of the world, in the sense of actually shielding them from harm, was not always possible; that trying to do so by military might, even when it was vastly superior to that of the abusers, and perhaps especially when it was deployed in the form of relatively low-risk aircraft and missile strikes, more often than not placed such people in even greater danger;

and that the costs of such efforts, both material and political, were significant even when shared among a coalition of those most able to bear them. Syria, in that it was commonly seen as a continuation of the Arab Spring reform movement sweeping the Middle East, was also a reminder that many people in many different places might have a legitimate claim for international protection, quite possibly at the same time, and it would simply not be possible to satisfy them all. In the best of circumstances, some selectivity would be necessary, as well as some recognition of the limits of what could be accomplished by external intervention.

In short, Libya made clear that the significant practical limits to the use-of-force interpretation of the R2P principle had to be recognized; for its part, Syria confirmed that they had been. For those who saw the doctrine as requiring the more or less automatic dispatch of military protectors whenever and wherever humanitarian emergencies arose, Syria did sadly mark the demise of that dream. But for those who take a less uncompromising view of possible responses to international conflict, R2P remains a guide to national and international human behaviour—an ideal for which to strive without the expectation of perfect achievement. We pointed out earlier that even those who were most staunchly opposed to military intervention in Syria nonetheless sought to find ways to end the bloodshed there, though not, admittedly, solely out of concern for issues of human security.

It would be naive to suggest, of course, that those efforts derived solely from R2P. There is, after all, nothing new about empathy for those in suffering or in efforts to alleviate that state, as two of the present authors tried to show with respect to ten humanitarian crises during the 1990s (Soderlund et al., 2008). But R2P did reinforce that empathy and gave it an important border-penetrating legitimacy that the international community had previously lacked. By endorsing the principle of R2P, the states of the world have agreed that state sovereignty is not absolute. They can still debate by how much and when it is limited, but it is doubtful that they can rescind that agreement in its entirety. R2P therefore provides, and we believe will continue to provide, an additional reason for political leaders to hesitate to behave badly and an additional reason for outside parties to hold them to account if they do. To some that may seem a small step forward, but we would argue that it is not an insignificant one given that small steps toward a more orderly and humane world are all that can realistically be expected.

Not everyone believes this necessarily adds up to the death of the R2P principle. Evan Cinq-Mars, for one, responded to the Hehir and Murray views quoted above by arguing that "boiling R2P down to the use and potential abuse of military force in 'hard cases' is as inaccurate as it is self-serving,... [and] ...

while there is much to be done to make R2P implementation more effective and consistent ... [it is] ... far from dead." For Cinq-Mars, "there's absolutely no need to scrap it all and start from scratch" (Cinq-Mars, 2015, Mar. 18).

In our view several points are important in this connection. First, there is no reason to think that human sympathy for those thought to be abused, or a desire to alleviate their suffering as far as possible, will cease. There was, it might be recalled, no shortage of compassion for endangered Syrians or anger directed against the source of their distress. Second, R2P is a strong enunciation of that natural human inclination and the first to give its active international pursuit a border-penetrating legitimacy. Third, that is no trivial development. In proclaiming that state sovereignty is not unlimited, R2P voiced the most fundamental alteration in thinking about the basis of interstate relations in the past 200 years. Fourth, and perhaps most important, despite the principle's near unanimous endorsement at the United Nations, we should not expect that such a new behavioural norm would be fully implemented instantly or consistently. R2P may, of course, never achieve that status at all, but we believe that it is somewhat premature to declare that it *will not*. We would argue that R2P will continue, at least for the foreseeable future, to be an accepted ideal of international conduct despite Syria and Libya, for the simple reason that once having been expressed and widely endorsed by the world, it cannot easily be rescinded. But only time will tell how often and under what circumstances the principle will be used as a genuine basis for the decisions of statesmen.

The Syrian civil war has of course morphed into the regional and indeed the international conflict that many commentators predicted it would, thanks largely to the brutal intervention of the radical terrorist group(s) known as the Islamic State of Iraq and Syria (ISIS), which proclaims widespread Islamic territorial ambitions. Various Western and regional powers are as of this writing engaged in what are so far limited forms of military confrontations with ISIS in both Syria and Iraq.[6] While it is likely that some of the components of ISIS began with more limited objectives focused on the ouster of the Assad government, the current conflict is more than a simple extension of that campaign, and Western military intervention is different from an effort to protect the innocents from tyrannical brutality. What is going on in that unfortunate part of the world now is not, therefore, an affirmation of R2P, but neither is it a denial. R2P is simply not relevant to a conflict where the enemy is intent on challenging the order of the modern world in favour of that of the seventh century. It is somewhat ironic, however, that since President Assad is also an opponent of ISIS, he and his long-time detractors, especially in the West, now find themselves facing a common enemy.

NOTES

INTRODUCTION

1 Based on an interview with President Obama, Jeffrey Goldberg reveals that it was the American president who had first

> told the Russian president 'that if he forced Assad to get rid of the chemical weapons, that would eliminate the need for us taking a military strike.' Within weeks,... [Secretary of State] ... Kerry, working with his Russian counterpart, Sergey Lavrov, would engineer the removal of most of Syria's chemical-weapons arsenal. (Goldberg, 2016, April, pp. 75–76)

2 December 2016 saw a potentially significant development in the war—the reported fall of Aleppo to Syrian government forces significantly bolstered by those of Russia. As we point out in Chapter 5, retired Canadian General Lewis MacKenzie argued in early 2012 that "the only solution to the Syrian conflict goes through Moscow" (2012). We suspect, however, that he could scarcely have envisioned the forceful manner with which Russian influence would be brought to bear.

CHAPTER 1

1 For a detailed and fascinating account of the political and military machinations with respect to the Middle Eastern portion of the war, see Scott Anderson's Pulitzer-winning *Lawrence in Arabia: War, Deceit, Imperial Folly and the Making of the Modern Middle East* (2014).

2 Syria's long-standing relationship as a client of Russia has paid dividends. Moscow has provided unwavering diplomatic and military support to the Assad regime throughout the current civil war.

3 It should be stressed, however, that by 2011 Syrian foreign relations became increasingly complex and problematic. Assad had managed to alienate much of the Sunni Muslim world, including Saudi Arabia and its Western backers, over his tight relationship with Iran (and its Shia client Hezbollah), the chief geo-strategic rival to Saudi and Western interests in the Middle East. Indeed, relations were so fraught that there is some credence to the argument that the Sunni Arab world and its allies had worked to undermine the Assad regime, including offering support to Assad's domestic opponents.

CHAPTER 2

1 President Obama showed no greater enthusiasm for R2P. When Samantha Power, who later was to become his ambassador to the United Nations and who was a firm believer in R2P, repeatedly urged him to endorse it, he eventually snapped, "'Samantha, enough, I've already read your book'" (quoted in Goldberg, 2016, p. 73).

2 A similar proposal for an independently recruited and organized rapid reaction force was the UN Emergency Peace Service (UNEPS). Its projected establishment and maintenance costs were considerably higher than those suggested by Hehir, however. Its functions were also significantly more modest and there was no thought of its operating independently of the Security Council (see Johansen, 2006b).

3 The Standby High-Readiness Brigade (SHIRBRIG), which operated between 1996 and 2008, was designed to perform much the same function—to provide a rapid-response force to dispatch to a crisis while the UN attempted to cobble together a peacekeeping mission. The plan was that SHIRBRIG'S member states would have troops earmarked for rapid deployment, with a capability to remain in the field for six months. Although not formally a part of the UN structure, SHIRBRIG'S only client was the UN Department of Peacekeeping Operations and, thus, would only be called upon for missions that had been authorized by the Security Council. Unfortunately, its success was limited (for details see Koops and Varwick, 2008; SHIRBRIG, 2009).

CHAPTER 3

1 Crises cases included in the 2008 study were Liberia (1990), Somalia (1992), Sudan (1992), Rwanda (1994), Haiti (1994), Burundi (1996), the Democratic Republic of Congo (1996), Sierra Leone (1997), Angola (1999), and East Timor (1999). Significantly, the only variable correlating with a robust international response was volume of media coverage. Spearman rank order correlations between *strength of international response* and *volume of media crisis reporting* for all 10 cases was +0.79, while for the eight African cases it was +0.81 (Soderlund et al., 2008, pp. 272–273). In contrast, for all cases the correlation between the *strength of international response* and the *severity of the crisis* was –0.18, with that for the African cases increasing only to +0.14 (2008, p. 264).

2 The cases studied by Western that resulted in non-intervention were Dien Bien Phu (1954) and Lebanon (1958) while those resulting in intervention were Grenada (1983), Somalia (1992), Bosnia (1992), and Iraq (2003).

3 This suggests an interesting possibility. If the chemical weapons agreement had not taken a possible U.S. military response off the table prior to a Congressional vote, the separation of executive and legislative powers *could* have resulted in a situation in which Mr. Obama went ahead with air strikes based on admittedly controversial presidential authority to do so, despite a non-supportive vote in Congress. In Britain, Mr. Cameron had no such option; faced with a negative vote, he had to accede to the will of Parliament on the issue.

4 The Facebook study was controversial not because of its findings (which tended to not be reported in popular accounts) but because of an alleged lack of "informed consent" on the part of Facebook users in the experiment. That issue hinged on the wording of the original agreement between Facebook and its users. Additionally, in that the study was "conducted by Facebook for internal purposes," the usual process of approval by a university ethics board was not followed. However, the editor of the *Proceedings of the National Academy of Sciences* (PNAS) added an "expression of concern" to the online version of the research paper: "It is nevertheless a matter of concern that the collection of the data by Facebook may have involved practices that were not fully consistent with the principles of obtaining informed consent and allowing participants to opt out" (Verma, 2014, June 17).

5 The process by which public opinion ultimately gets reflected in government policy lies beyond the scope of this study. However, we suggest that the process is far from automatic and involves much more than just a sustained media push. Organization and mobilization, such as seen in the activities of the "Save Darfur" group, documented by Rebecca Hamilton (2011) and Amanda Grzyb (2009), are needed. Even in the case of Darfur, however, results in the form of international intervention were painfully slow to materialize (Sidahmed,

Soderlund, & Briggs, 2010). Importantly, with respect to Syria the absence of "public engagement" was noted by opinion commentators in both Great Britain and the United States. Also, as suggested by Callaghan and Schnell (2001), even more important are the actions of governments "to shift public opinion." On this, studies of opinion manipulation by the Bush and Blaire governments prior to the 2003 invasion of Iraq are particularly revealing. (See, for example, Hiebert, 2003; Wheatcroft, 2004, June; Western, 2005; Miller, 2006; and Holsti, 2011.)

6   In a 2014 ranking of the top 200 newspapers in the world, *The New York Times* ranked first; *The Guardian,* second; and *The Globe and Mail,* twenty-fifth—making it the highest ranked Canadian newspaper ("2014 Newspaper Web Rankings," 2014).

7   Data for the study were accessed primarily from the *Factiva* electronic database beginning on March 1, 2011, and running through September 30, 2013. This period covers the beginning of protests against the al-Assad government up to a UN Security Council resolution endorsing the agreement to remove and destroy Syria's chemical weapons. The articles resulting from this search were catalogued into a database. *Globe and Mail* items were then cross-referenced with two other electronic databases—*Proquest* and *Canadian Newsstand,* while *New York Times* material was cross-referenced with the paper's own electronic index and that of the *Gale Group* to ensure completeness. Only articles that appeared in printed copies of the newspapers were included in the study. Doing so ensured consistency in data collection across the three papers, whose online presence was in constant flux and evolving in ways that made it difficult to offer reliable comparative data analysis. Further, in at least one of the papers we analyzed, payment to writers for articles that appear in the print versions of the paper is considerably higher than for pieces that appear solely online. As well, our understanding from speaking to authors of op-ed articles is that they have a strong preference to see their material appear in print. The discrepancy in the number of items in *The Globe and Mail* as opposed to the other two papers is partially explained by the fact that *The Globe* publishes only six days as opposed to seven days per week. Also, we suspect that the editors of *The New York Times* and *The Guardian* considered that their countries were likely to be primary responders to the crisis, while *Globe* editors had no such illusions about Canada.

At this point, editorials and opinion articles were read to ensure that the material dealing with the Syrian civil war was sufficient to merit coding. Those that dealt with Syrian topics unrelated to the war, those in which Syria was mentioned peripherally or as an example among a list of others—"false positives"—were excluded. Coding of the remaining material was done by Professors Soderlund and Najem. After three intensive sessions of joint coding and checks for inter-coder reliability, using Ole Holsti's percentage agreement method, inter-coder reliability was established at 84.7 per cent (Holsti, 1969, p. 140). Inter-coder reliability was reconfirmed at 87.9 per cent, at the point where approximately two-thirds of the coding had been done. In addition, following the completion of all coding, 10 per cent of items were thoroughly reviewed and coding was rechecked. Whatever coding discrepancies were found (and these were mainly between *positive* vs. *ambiguous* or *negative* vs. *ambiguous* judgments) were resolved to the satisfaction of both coders, and appropriate corrections were made.

8   Mark Jurkowitz and colleagues refer to Syria as a "mega story," and we agree. Their study for the Pew Research Journalism Project reported that in the six days between August 26 and August 31, 2013 (a time when possible US air strikes against Syria were being debated), six cable news networks in the US offered 321 stories aired over a total of 21 hours. CNN led the list with 381 minutes of coverage—over six and a half hours (Jurkowitz, Mitchell, & Matsa, 2013, Sept. 6). As well, the major TV broadcast networks (ABC, CBS, and NBC) all interrupted their scheduled daytime programming to air President Obama's remarks concerning a possible US military response to Syria's use of chemical weapons. On both

ABC and CBS, Obama's remarks were followed by "comments and analysis" by anchors and reporters (Steinberg, 2013, Aug. 30).

Newspapers as well gave Syria significant attention: the *Factiva* database indicated that in January 2012 *The Globe and Mail* ran twenty-five news stories and opinion pieces on Syria, and in September of 2012, fifty-one, for an average of well over one item per day. Moreover, an Ipsos poll released on October 9, 2013, confirmed widespread awareness of the Syrian conflict: 97 per cent of British respondents, 95 per cent of American respondents, and 91 per cent of Canadian respondents had "seen, heard or read about the current situation in Syria" (Ipsos, 2013, Oct. 9).

9   Opinion material from 2011 and 2012 are reported in chapters 4 and 5. For 2013 we analyzed two periods separately: material from January 1 to August 21 (the date of a government chemical weapons attack on a civilian neighbourhood) is reported in Chapter 6, while that from August 22 to September 30 (during which both Great Britain and the United States actively pursued military responses that ultimately were not carried out) is reported in Chapter 7.

CHAPTER 4

1   Throughout the period of our study, only in opinion material appearing in *The Globe and Mail* was a possible role for Canada in Syria mentioned.

2   There were problems with this suggestion. Because Syria had not ratified the Rome Statute creating the International Criminal Court (ICC), it would be necessary for the Security Council to refer the matter to the ICC (Axworthy, 2011, July 7, p. 17). Also, in that under international law rebels lacked belligerent status, "violence perpetrated against them would not constitute 'war crimes'" (Roff and Momani, 2011, p. 17).

In February 2012, *Globe* columnist Doug Saunders dismissed the idea that the ICC could play a useful role in Syria. Chief Prosecutor Luis Moreno Ocampo had been accused of overzealousness, with the result that "the court is no longer seen as a major international force." Saunders also advanced the argument that "threatening leaders with trials runs the risk of keeping them in power longer" (Saunders, 2012, Feb. 25, p. F9). However, in January of 2013, historian and author Erna Paris endorsed a Swiss proposal to get a Security Council referral of Syria to the ICC. Russia, however, declared the initiative to be "counterproductive" (Paris, 2013, Jan. 25, p. 11).

3   Early on in the conflict, Michael Bell made the perceptive assessment that "a reassertion of Mr. al-Assad's power, as distasteful as it is . . . [may be] . . . the lesser of evils in a situation where chaos seems the most likely alternative" (Bell, 2011, p. 13).

CHAPTER 5

1   Maleh did not address the issue that the way in which the NATO "no-fly zone" mission in Libya had been carried out far exceeded what might normally fall under a mandate of protecting the civilian population from air attacks. He was clearly calling for a military mission that was aimed at regime change rather than one that was designed primarily to protect civilians.

2   This of course was the justification for international intervention in domestic conflicts prior to the acceptance of R2P by the UN Security Council in 2006.

3   It should be noted that Segal and Wark supported the establishment of no-fly zones for different reasons: Segal, on the basis of humanitarian morality inherent in R2P; Wark, on the basis of calculations of national interest characteristic of *realpolitik*. That both the "liberal left" and the "hard right" advocated intervention without success will be addressed further in the book's conclusion.

CHAPTER 6

1 The attack on the US consulate in Benghazi in the fall of 2012 that killed the US ambassador definitively moved Libya from the "success" or "too early to tell" columns, where initially it had been placed, to the recognition that international intervention had failed to produce a democratic outcome. By mid-2013, Thomas Friedman confirmed that "the transition government has not been strong enough to bring order to Libya and the instability there has metastasized" (Friedman, 2013, June 23, p. 11).

2 In early September, *The Guardian* again dealt with the refugee issue in an editorial and opinion piece. These made very much the same case as had been presented in July—namely, that the refugee issue was a huge problem and that the limited international response left much to be done.

3 In a September opinion piece commenting on Mr. Obama's turn to Congress for approval of air strikes against Syria, Anne-Marie Slaughter appeared to argue the other side. In a lesson on the US Constitution, she praised a system that places constraints on executive powers to use force: "Turning to the legislature may prove inconvenient, frustrating and even counterproductive, but it is the right thing to do." In doing so, Mr. Obama has joined "a small class of leaders who actively seek to constrain their own power" (Slaughter, 2013, Sept. 19, p. 17).

CHAPTER 7

1 In light of events in Ukraine beginning in March 2014 and following, one has to question the sincerity of these remarks or at least concede that Mr. Putin favours a case-by-case application of the principles he appeared to support.

2 What Friedman did not mention was that in terms of "guiding" mass public opinion, policy elites overwhelmingly came down on the side of caution with respect to intervention, thus providing no support for popular mobilization behind Western involvement. This is a point we will revisit in our conclusion.

3 Interestingly, Kettle suggested that the United States might not be too unhappy in the event of a parliamentary rejection of force: "It is arguable that a vote in the UK parliament could stay Washington's hand from a politically controversial, premature strike that would raise massive issues of legitimacy" (Kettle, 2013, Aug. 29, p. 31).

4 Anne-Marie Slaughter was even more specific, referring to "a backroom deal" struck between the US secretary of state and the Russian foreign minister (Slaughter, 2013, Sept. 19, p. 17). Both MacKenzie and Slaughter were on the right track (see Goldberg, 2016, April).

CONCLUSION

1 As pointed out in the Notes to the Introduction (note 1) and in Chapter 7, the suggestion that removing Syria's chemical weapons would take US airstrikes off the table originated not from Russia but, rather, from the American president (Goldberg, 2016, April, pp. 75–76).

2 While comments by the British prime minister and foreign secretary that the Syrian situation needed to be addressed by the international community were noted (and strongly rejected in opinion commentary), there is little evidence to suggest that during the period of the study there were determined efforts by either the British or US government to shift the weight of the "thumb" of public opinion to favour a Syrian intervention. However, following the chemical weapons attack, at least one such effort by President Obama was identified in the article by *Times'* public editor Margaret Sullivan (2013, Sept. 15). Had the "democratic legitimacy" authorization votes for the use of force passed in Britain and gone forward in the US, no doubt there would have been various government-directed efforts to increase

public support for the planned air strikes against Assad, as we have indeed seen following the initiation of air attacks against ISIS forces.

3 We mentioned in Chapter 2 that initially the US had not been an enthusiastic supporter of R2P, and it is important to note that President Obama "declined" to follow the suggestion made by Samantha Power that he endorse R2P in his 2009 speech accepting the Nobel Peace Prize (Goldberg, 2016, April, pp. 72–73). In addition, the doctrine is not mentioned in Goldberg's account of how the president reached his decision to not employ force in Syria; in fact, American national interest lay at the heart of any military commitment.

4 Hurd advocated going ahead with an R2P "use of force response" without Security Council authorization, based on the argument that the widespread acceptance of the doctrine signalled that international law had evolved. Hathaway and Shapiro argued the opposite—that only the Security Council could authorize the use of force.

5 Janice Gross Stein agrees, arguing that "the old order, where governance solutions can be imposed from the outside, is gone for good. As a result the activist liberal order has come to an end" (Gross Stein, 2015, Sept. 26, p. F8). Mohammed Nuruzzaman is another in a list of critics of NATO's expansion of a humanitarian mandate to include regime change in Libya. He also cited the failure to apply R2P's "responsibility to rebuild" component: "In the post-NATO intervention period, Libya simply descended into a state of complete chaos and violence" (Nuruzzaman, 2015, p. 543).

6 In September 2015 Russia also entered the aerial war in the region, although most felt that protection of the Assad regime was a more important motivator than was the defeat of ISIS. In any case, in March 2016, President Putin announced a considerable withdrawal of Russian forces from Syria. Canadian participation in the aerial war against ISIS also terminated in March 2016.

REFERENCES

2014 newspaper web rankings. (2014). *4International Media & Newspapers*. Retrieved from http://www.4imn.com/top200/

Adams, Simon. (2012, November 16). The world's next genocide. *New York Times*, p. 35.

Aday, Sean. (2006). The framesetting effects of news: An experimental test of advocacy versus objectivist frames. *Journalism and Mass Communications Quarterly, 83*(4), 767–784.

Aita, Samir. (2012, July 23). Syria after Assad. *The Guardian*, p. 22.

Ajami, Fouad. (2012). *The Syrian rebellion*. Palo Alto, CA: Hoover Institution, Stanford University.

Al-Bayanouni, Ali. (2011, August 4). Assad's myth need busting: He's not defending Syria from sectarian tensions. *The Guardian*, p. 30.

Al-Bayanouni, Ali. (2012, August 7). A future for all Syrians. *The Guardian*, p. 24.

Al-Haj Saleh, Yassin. (2011, April 11). Prisoner of Damascus. *New York Times*, p. 25.

Al-Haj Saleh, Yassin (2013, September 10). A Syrian's cry for help. *New York Times*, p. 23.

Al Shami, Abdur Rahman. (2011, September 1). Intervention Syrians trust. *The Guardian*, p. 31.

Alexander, Douglas. (2013). Do not fan the flames: Offering support to rebels risks intensifying tragic conflict. *The Guardian*, p. 30.

Ali, Tariq (2011, April 30). Who will reshape the Arab world: Its people, or the US? Phase one of the Arab spring is over. Phase two—the attempt to crush or contain genuine popular movements—has begun. *The Guardian*, p. 36.

Allison, Graham, & Zelikow, Peter. (1999). *The essence of decision: Explaining the Cuban missile crisis* (2nd ed.). New York, NY: Addison, Wesley Longman.

Almond, Gabriel. (1960). *The American people and foreign policy*. New York, NY: Prager.

Anderson, Scott. (2014). *Lawrence in Arabia: War, deceit, imperial folly and the making of the modern Middle East*. Toronto, ON: Signal M & S.

Annan warns African leaders on undermining ICC. (2013, October 8). *Zimbabwe News Daily*. Retrieved from http://www.thezimbabwemail.com/world/18522 -annan-warns-african-leaders-on-undermining-icc

Arbour, Louise. (2012, June 27). For justice and civilians, don't rule out regime change; if a state launches a massive criminal enterprise against its people, why shouldn't leaders be removed? *Globe and Mail*, p. 13.

Atwan, Abdel Bari. (2012, February 29). Diplomacy may yet break the Syrian deadlock. *The Guardian*, p. 32.

Atwan, Abdel Bari. (2012, May 14). The Syrian peace plan has been blown out of the water. *The Guardian*, p. 24.

Axworthy, Lloyd. (2011, July 7). Refer Assad to the ICC. *Globe and Mail*, p. 17.

Axworthy, Lloyd. (2011, August 23). Toward a more humane, just world; by intervening to protect Libyan civilians, we are resetting the international order. *Globe and Mail*, p. 22.

Axworthy, Lloyd, & Rock, Allan. (2013, August 27). Intervene in Syria? Look to the "Kosovo model"; responsibility to protect, while not perfect, brought mass killing of civilians to an end in 1999 mission. *Globe and Mail*, p. 13.

Axworthy, Lloyd, & Rock, Allan. (2013, September 10). Syrians suffer "our" failure; an international cast of characters and institutions—starting with the United Nations— have been tested by crisis and found wanting. *Globe and Mail*, p. 13.

Ayoob, Mohammed. (2012, October 5). Sucked into the quagmire: Turkey risks being drawn into a conflict from which, unlike Saudi Arabia and the US, it cannot escape. *The Guardian*, p. 38.

Bali, Asliu, & Rana, Aziz. (2012, April 11). To stop the killing, deal with Assad. *New York Times*, p. 23.

Beaumont, Peter. (2012, August 11). Help with conditions: Britain must make it clear that human rights abuses by Syrian rebels will bring our support to an end. *The Guardian*, p. 33.

Bell, Michael. (2011, August 12). No happy ending to Syria's power struggle. *Globe and Mail*, p. 13.

Bell, Michael. (2012, February 3). After the fall, a sectarian struggle; the increasingly likely demise of Bashar al-Assad and the Baath Party would make a major loser of Tehran, which is reliant on Damascus in pursuit of a Shia crescent through Iraq and Lebanon. *Globe and Mail*, p. 19.

Bell, Michael. (2012, July 23). In Syria, the power's play hardball; with Damascus on the brink, sovereign interests are trumping multilateralism. But the international community must be ready to step up. *Globe and Mail*, p. 11.

Bellamy, Alex. (2009). *Responsibility to protect, the global effort to end mass atrocities.* Cambridge, UK: Polity Press.

Bellamy, Alex. (2011). Libya and the responsibility to protect: The exception and the norm. *Ethics and International Affairs, 25*(3), 263–269.

Berinsky, Adam, & Kinder, Donald. (2006). Making sense of issues through media frames: Understanding the Kosovo crisis. *Journal of Politics, 68*(3), 640–656.

Blix, Hans. (2013, August 29). The west has no mandate to act as a global policeman. *The Guardian*, p. 30.

Blix, Hans. (2013, September 19). A chance for an Iran deal. *The Guardian*, p. 36.

Blow, Charles. (2013, August 31). War-weariness. *New York Times*, p. 19.

Blow, Charles. (2013, September 7). Remembering all the children. *New York Times*, p. 23.

Brooks, David. (2011, June 3). The depravity factor. *New York Times*, p. 23.

Brooks, David. (2013, August 30). One great big war. *New York Times*, p. 19.

Bruni, Frank. (2013, September 15). What war means. *New York Times*, p. 3.

Bryce, Trevor. (2014). *Ancient Syria: A thousand year history.* Oxford, UK: Oxford University Press.

Bull, Bartle. (2012, August 15). What Syria's rebels need. *New York Times*, p. 23.

Burney, Derek, & Hampson, Fen. (2013, June 19). Five reasons to stay out Syria. *Globe and Mail*, p. 15.

Byman, Daniel. (2012). Regime change in the Middle East: Problems and prospects. *Political Science Quarterly, 127*(1), 25–47.

Byman, Daniel. (2013, May 5). Mr. Obama, don't draw that line. *New York Times*, p. 4.

Callaghan, Karen, & Schnell, Franke. (2001). Assessing the democratic debate: How news media frame elite policy discourse. *Political Communication, 18*(2), 183–212.

Campbell, Menzies. (2013, May 24). Syria needs help, but it doesn't need arms. *The Guardian*, p. 52.

Caspary, William. (1970). The "Mood Theory": A study of public opinion and foreign policy. *American Political Science Review, 64*, 536–547.

Chalk, Frank, Dallaire, Roméo, Matthews, Kyle, Barquerio, Carla, & Doyle, Simon. (2010). *Mobilizing the will to intervene: Leadership and action to prevent mass atrocities.* Montreal, QC: Montreal Institute for Genocide and Human Rights Studies. Retrieved from http://www4.carleton.ca/cfp/app/serve.php/1244.pdf

Chesterman, Simon. (2011). "Leading from behind": The Responsibility to Protect, the Obama Doctrine, and humanitarian intervention after Libya. *Ethics and International Affairs, 25*(3), 279–285.

Cinq-Mars, Evan. (2015, March 18). In support of R2P: No need to reinvent the wheel. OpenCanada.ORG. Retrieved from http://opencanada.org/features-in-support-of-r2p-no-need-to-reinvent-the-wheel/

Clark, Campbell. (2013, May 9). All urgency, no action in Syria debate. *Globe and Mail*, p. 8.

Clark, Campbell. (2013, September 5). A strike on al-Assad is one thing; what comes next is another. *Globe and Mail*, p. 12.

Clark, Campbell. (2013, September 12). Syrian-Canadians feel sense of betrayal. *Globe and Mail*, p. 6.

Clark, Wesley. (2013, June 18). To get a truce, be ready to escalate. *New York Times*, p. 25.

Cockburn, Patrick. (2015). *The rise of Islamic State: ISIS and the new Sunni revolution.* New York, NY: Verso.

Cohen, Bernard. (1963). *The press and foreign policy.* Princeton, NJ: Princeton University Press.

Cohen, Bernard. (1994). Introduction to media and foreign policy: A view from the academy. In W. L. Bennett & D. Paletz (Eds.), *Taken by storm: The media, public opinion, and US foreign policy in the Gulf War* (pp. 8–11). Chicago, IL: University of Chicago Press.

Cohen, Roger. (2013, September 13). An anchorless world. *New York Times*, p. 25.

Cooper, Richard, & Kohler, Juliette (Eds.). (2009). *Responsibility to protect: The global moral compact for the 21st century.* New York, NY: Palgrave Macmillan.

Cooper, Richard, & Kohler, Juliette. (2009). Moving from military intervention to judicial enforcement: The case for an international marshals service. In R. Cooper and J. Kohler (Eds.), *Responsibility to protect: The global moral compact of the 21st century* (pp. 243–262). New York, NY: Palgrave Macmillan.

Corker, Bob. (2013, April 24). Dithering while Damascus burns. *New York Times*, p. 23.

Crooke, Alastair. (2011, November 5). The great Syria game. *The Guardian*, p. 42.

Crooke, Alastair. (2013, June 17). The red line is not crossed: Syria is already awash with weapons which are at the limit of what can be safely given to the rebels. *The Guardian*, p. 26.

Crooke, Alastair. (2013, September 30). The strategy has backfired: The Gulf states' plans to undermine Iran and Syria are in tatters. *The Guardian*, p. 26.

Deutsch, Karl, & Merritt, Richard. (1965). Effects of events on national and international images. In H. Kelman (Ed.), *International behavior: A social–psychological analysis* (pp. 132–187). New York, NY: Holt, Rinehart and Winston.

De Waal, Alex, & Conley-Zilkic, Bridget. (2013, September 5). What Sir William would do in Syria. *New York Times,* p. 25.

Doran, Michael, & Boot, Max. (2012, September 27). 5 reasons to intervene in Syria now. *New York Times,* p. 29.

Douthat, Ross. (2013, September 1). War, what is it good for? *New York Times,* p. 11.

Douthat, Ross. (2013, September 8). Gambling with the presidency. *New York Times,* p. 12.

Dowd, Maureen. (2013, June 16). Bill schools Barry on Syria. *New York Times,* p. SR11.

Dowd, Maureen. (2013, September 4). Shadow of a doubt. *New York Times,* p. 23.

Dowd, Maureen. (2013, September 8). Barry's war within. *New York Times,* p. 11.

Dowd, Maureen. (2013, September 11). Who do you trust? *New York Times,* p. 27.

Droz-Vincent, Phillippe. (2014). "State of barbary" (take two): From the Arab Spring to the return of violence in Syria. *Middle East Journal, 68*(1), 33–58

Dwomoh, Richard. (2015). *The international community and the Responsibility to Protect.* Saarbrucken, Germany: Lambert Academic Publishing.

Entman, Robert. (2007). Framing bias: Media in the distribution of power. *Journal of Communication, 57*(1), 163–173.

Evans, Gareth. (2008). *The Responsibility to Protect, ending mass atrocity crimes once and for all.* Washington, DC: Brookings Institution Press.

Evans, Gareth. (2009). The Responsibility to Protect: From an idea to an international norm. In R. Cooper and J. Kohler (Eds.), *Responsibility to Protect: The global moral compact for the 21st century* (pp. 15–29). New York, NY: Palgrave Macmillan.

Fennimore, Martha, & Sikkink, Katherine. (1998). International norm dynamics and political change. *International Organization, 52*(4), 887–917.

Ferguson, Niall. (2013, September 7). The left's blind spot: In Syria, as elsewhere, US military might is the best means of preventing crimes against humanity. *The Guardian,* p. 54.

Forsythe, David. (2002). The United States and international criminal justice. *Human Rights Quarterly, 24*(4), 974–991.

Little agreement for Canadian, International intervention in Syria. (2013, September 4). Forum Research. Retrieved from http://www.forumresearch .com/...4092013%29_Forum_

Freedland, Jonathan. (2011, Aug, 31). Why wait for politicians to oust foreign tyrants. *The Guardian,* p. 27.

Freedland, Jonathan. (2012, February 11). Syria is not Iraq. *The Guardian,* p. 45.

Freedland, Jonathan. (2012, July 21). The battle for Syria is a battle for the entire Middle East. *The Guardian,* p. 43.

Freedland, Jonathan. (2012, October 20). We condemn Israel. So why the silence on Syria? *The Guardian,* p. 45.

Freedland, Jonathan. (2013, September 4). Enough of playing Hamlet: Obama needs to act now. *The Guardian,* p. 35.

Friedman, Thomas. (2011, March 30). Looking for luck in Libya. *New York Times,* p. 26.

Friedman, Thomas. (2011, April 13). Pray, hope, prepare. *New York Times,* p. 25.

Friedman, Thomas. (2011, May 15). "I am a man." *New York Times,* p. 10.

Friedman, Thomas. (2011, May 22). They shoot horses don't they? *New York Times,* p. 8.

Friedman, Thomas. (2011, November 27). In the Arab world, it's the past vs. the future. *New York Times,* p. 11.

Friedman, Thomas. (2012, February 5). Russia, sort of, but not really. *New York Times,* p. 11.

Friedman, Thomas. (2012, February 29). There be dragons. *New York Times,* p. 27.

Friedman, Thomas. (2012, April 29). Words of the prophets. *New York Times,* p. SR1.

Friedman, Thomas. (2012, July 25). Syria is Iraq. *New York Times,* p. 25.

Friedman, Thomas. (2012, November 14). Obama's nightmare. *New York Times,* p. 29.

Friedman, Thomas. (2012, December 2). Letter from Syria. *New York Times,* p. SR11.

Friedman, Thomas. (2012, December 5). Iron empires, iron fists, iron dome. *New York Times,* p. 31.

Friedman, Thomas. (2013, February 10). Any solution to Syria? *New York Times,* p. SR11.

Freidman, Thomas. (2013, March 27). Caution, curves ahead. *New York Times,* p. 23.

Friedman, Thomas. (2013, May 22). Tell me how this ends. *New York Times,* p. 27.

Friedman, Thomas. (2013, June 23). Syria scorecard. *New York Times,* p. 11.

Friedman, Thomas. (2013, September 4). Arm and shame. *New York Times,* p. 23.

Friedman, Thomas. (2013, September 11). Threaten to threaten. *New York Times,* p. 27.

Friedman, Thomas. (2013, September 18). The man with pink hair. *New York Times,* p. 23.

Funk, Kevin, & Fake, Steve. (2009). R2P: Disciplining the mice, freeing the lions. *Foreign Policy in Focus.* Retrieved from http://www.fpif.org_r2p_disciplining_the_mice_freeing_the_lions/

Gagnon, Lysiane. (2013, June 5). Why amplify Syria's arms race? *Globe and Mail,* p. 13.

Gamson, William, & Modigliani, Andre. (1989). Media discourse and public opinion on nuclear power: A constructivist approach. *American Journal of Sociology, 95*(1), 1–37.

Garcia, J. Malcolm. (2013, February 15). Why Syria's Islamists are gaining. *New York Times,* p. 27.

Garton Ash, Timothy. (2012, April 12). Turkey's neo-Ottoman game plan; the fate of Syria's resisters and civilians depends on the old-fashioned regional competition of diverse sovereign powers. *Globe and Mail,* p. 15.

Garton Ash, Timothy. (2012, June 14). How to stop the slaughter in Syria? We in the West have to consider if there are any larger carrots and sticks we can still show Russia, even at some cost to ourselves. *Globe and Mail,* p. 19.

Garton Ash, Timothy. (2013, April 25). Glimpse the ghost of things to come; how different things would have been if Syria were Europe and Serbia in the Middle East. *Globe and Mail,* p. 15.

Gause III, F. Gregory. (2011). Why Middle East studies missed the Arab spring. *Foreign Affairs, 90*(4), 81–90.

Gelb, Leslie, & Simes, Dimitri. (2013, July 7). A new anti-American axis. *New York Times,* p. 5.

Gerges, Fawaz. (2012, July 26). This is not a house of glass: The authoritarian state in Syria will remain in place regardless of when Assad departs. *The Guardian,* p. 30.

Gerges, Fawaz. (2013, August 23). On Assad's shoulders. *The Guardian,* p. 36.

Ghalioun, Burhan. (2011, May 31). The endgame for Syria's bloody junta. *The Guardian,* p. 28.

Glass, Charles. (2013, March 5). With friends like these. *The Guardian,* p. 32.

Glass, Charles. (2013, June 7). What are your chances if you're a Syrian citizen now? *The Guardian;* p. 42.

Globe. [Editorial]. (2011, March 31). Resorting to a plot. *Globe and Mail*, p. 22.

Globe. [Editorial]. (2011, April 25). The Turkish model. *Globe and Mail*, p. 10.

Globe. [Editorial]. (2011, June 21). Too little and too much. *Globe and Mail*, p. 16.

Globe. [Editorial]. (2011, August 4). Democrats disavow their own. *Globe and Mail*, p. 14.

Globe. [Editorial]. (2011, August 29). No easy exit. *Globe and Mail*, p. 10.

Globe. [Editorial]. (2011, November 17). Blood ties. *Globe and Mail*, p. 18.

Globe. [Editorial]. (2011, November 29). In a league of its own. *Globe and Mail*, p. 16.

Globe. [Editorial]. (2012, January 3). The Arab League's phony mission. *Globe and Mail*, p. 12.

Globe. [Editorial]. (2012, January 12). A dangerous delusion. *Globe and Mail*, p. 12.

Globe. [Editorial]. (2012, May 29). Syrian peace begins in Moscow. *Globe and Mail*, p. 14.

Globe. [Editorial]. (2012, July 19). Avoiding a messy end in Syria. *Globe and Mail*, p. 12.

Globe. [Editorial]. (2013, January 2). Pitfalls, chaos and terrorism. *Globe and Mail*, p. 12.

Globe. [Editorial]. (2013, April 28). The reddening line. *Globe and Mail*, p. 14.

Globe. [Editorial]. (2013, August 23). Red line, crossed. *Globe and Mail*, p. 10.

Globe [Editorial]. (2013, August 29). Parliament needs to debate war. *Globe and Mail*, p. 12.

Globe [Editorial]. (2013, September 5). Imposing a cost for chemical warfare. *Globe and Mail*, p. 16.

Globe [Editorial]. (2013, September 12). Close call for Obama. *Globe and Mail*, p. 14.

Globe [Editorial]. (2013, September 17). Chemical weapons and hard diplomacy. *Globe and Mail*, p. 12.

Goldberg, Jeffrey. (2016, April). The Obama Doctrine: The US president talks through his hardest decisions about America's role in the world. *The Atlantic*, 72–90.

Goldstone, Jack. (2011). Understanding the revolutions of 2011. *Foreign Affairs*, *90*(3), 8–16.

Goodman, Peter, Hasan, Mehdi, & Boudet, Alexander. (2013, September 6). Public opinion sharply opposed to Syria strikes. *The World Post* (a Partnership of Huffington Post and Berggruen Institute of Governance). Retrieved from http://www.huffingtonpost.com/2013/09/05/world-public-opinion-syrian3876187.html?view=print&commref=false

Grayson, Alan. (2013, September 7). On Syria vote, trust but verify. *New York Times*, p. 23.

Greenstock, Jeremy. (2013, May 16). The civil war is still to come. *The Guardian*, p. 38.

Groom, A. J. R., & Taylor, Paul. (2000). The United Nations system and the Kosovo crisis. In A. Schnabel and R. Thakur (Eds.), *Kosovo and the challenge of humanitarian intervention: Selective indignation, collective action, and international citizenship* (pp. 291–318). New York, NY: United Nations University Press.

Gross, Kimberly. (2008). Framing persuasive appeals: Episodic and thematic framing, emotional responses, and public opinion. *Political Psychology*, *29*(2), 169–192.

Gross Stein, Janice. (2015, September 26). The next debate. *Globe and Mail*, p. F8.

Grzyb, Amanda. (2009). Media coverage, activism, and creating public will for intervention in Rwanda and Darfur. In A. Grzyb (Ed.), *The world and Darfur: International response to crimes against humanity in Western Sudan* (pp. 61–91). Montreal, QC, and Kingston, ON: McGill-Queen's Press.

Guardian. [Editorial]. (2011, March 23). Arab revolution: Unstoppable force. *The Guardian*, p. 34.

Guardian. [Editorial]. (2011, March 31). Syria: A lost opportunity. *The Guardian*, p. 34.

Guardian. [Editorial]. (2011, April 21). Syria: States of emergency. *The Guardian*, p. 40.

Guardian. [Editorial]. (2011, May 20). Middle East: Obama weaves an uncertain path. *The Guardian*, p. 36.

Guardian. [Editorial]. (2011, June 2). Syria: Truth will out. *The Guardian*, p. 32.

Guardian. [Editorial]. (2011, June 13). Syria: Butchery, while the world watches. *The Guardian*, p. 26.

Guardian. [Editorial]. (2011, June 21). Syria: The national monologue. *The Guardian*, p. 30.

Guardian. [Editorial]. (2011, August 2). Syria: Under the hammer. *The Guardian*, p. 28.

Guardian. [Editorial]. (2011, August 9). Syria: King's speech. *The Guardian*, p. 28.

Guardian. [Editorial]. (2011, August 19). The Syrian impasse: Assad at bay. *The Guardian*, p. 36.

Guardian. [Editorial]. (2011, November 1). Syria: Delaying the inevitable. *The Guardian*, p. 32.

Guardian [Editorial]. (2011, December 14). Syria: Back to the future. *The Guardian*, p. 32.

Guardian. [Editorial]. (2011, December 24). Syria: Bloodshed in Damascus. *The Guardian*, p. 36.

Guardian. [Editorial]. (2012, January 24). Syria: A plan with no resolution. *The Guardian*, p. 30.

Guardian. [Editorial]. (2012, February 1). Soviet hangover turned headache: Syria and Russia. *The Guardian*, p. 30.

Guardian. [Editorial]. (2012, February 7). Syria: Russia on the wrong side. *The Guardian*, p. 32.

Guardian. [Editorial]. (2012, March 10). Syria: Staring into a sectarian abyss. *The Guardian*, p. 38.

Guardian. [Editorial]. (2012, March 28). Syria: A devious diplomacy. *The Guardian*, p. 32.

Guardian. [Editorial]. (2012, April 13). Syria: The only plan in town. *The Guardian*, p. 36.

Guardian. [Editorial]. (2012, May 29). Syria: Horror of Houla. *The Guardian*, p. 32,

Guardian. [Editorial]. (2012, June 8). Syria: No peace, no plan. *The Guardian*, p. 36.

Guardian. [Editorial]. (2012, July 7). Syria: Long, hard slog. *The Guardian*, p. 38.

Guardian. [Editorial]. (2012, July 28). Syria: Destruction and a death of diplomacy. *The Guardian*, p. 40.

Guardian. [Editorial]. (2012, August 22). Syria: A long war lies ahead. *The Guardian*, p. 30.

Guardian [Editorial]. (2012, Oct. 25). Syria: Brahimi makes his move. *The Guardian*, p. 34.

Guardian. [Editorial]. (2012, December 14). Syria: Russian writing on the wall. *The Guardian*, p. 44.

Guardian. [Editorial]. (2013, March 26). Syria: It only gets worse. *The Guardian*, p. 34.

Guardian. [Editorial]. (2013, April 27). Chemical weapons: Inspection time in Syria. *The Guardian*, p. 40.

Guardian. [Editorial]. (2013, May 5). Syria: civil war turns regional crisis. *The Guardian*.

Guardian. [Editorial]. (2013, May 11). Syria: The ugly choice ahead. *The Guardian*, p. 44.

Guardian. [Editorial]. (2013, May 21). Syria: No place for back-seat drivers. *The Guardian*, p. 32.

Guardian. [Editorial]. (2013, June 6). Syria: A town fall, talks falter. *The Guardian*, p. 34.

Guardian. [Editorial]. (2013, June 15). Syrian civil war: A one-way street. *The Guardian*, p. 52.

Guardian. [Editorial]. (2013, June 19). Lost in translation: Syria and the G8. *The Guardian*, p. 32.

Guardian. [Editorial]. (2013, July 19). Middle East: A wall of difficulties. *The Guardian*, p. 34.

Guardian. [Editorial]. (2013, July 25). Syrian refugees: No way home. *The Guardian*, p. 30.

Guardian. [Editorial]. (2013, August 9). Syria: There is worse to come. *The Guardian*, p. 30.

Guardian. [Editorial]. (2013, August 23). Syria: Chemical weapons with impunity. *The Guardian,* p. 38.

Guardian. [Editorial]. (2013, August 28). In the shadow of Iraq: MPs and Syria. *The Guardian,* p. 30.

Guardian. [Editorial]. (2013, August 29). Syria: Feeding the fire. *The Guardian,* p. 32.

Guardian. [Editorial]. (2013, August 30). Two cheers for parliament: The Syria debate. *The Guardian,* p. 32.

Guardian. [Editorial]. (2013, August 31). Britain's new mood: The Syria vote. *The Guardian,* p. 44.

Guardian. [Editorial]. (2013, September 2). US and Syria: Gambling with engagement. *The Guardian,* p. 26.

Guardian. [Editorial]. (2013, September 5). G20 and Syria: Putin's show. *The Guardian,* p. 34.

Guardian. [Editorial]. (2013, September 7). A forlorn display: G20 and Syria. *The Guardian,* p. 56.

Guardian. [Editorial]. (2013, September 11). Syria: A path worth exploring. *The Guardian,* p. 34.

Guardian. [Editorial]. (2013, September 13). International order: Drifting without an anchor. *The Guardian,* p. 44.

Guardian. [Editorial]. (2013, September 16). Syria: The deal that only goes so far. *The Guardian,* p. 30.

Hain, Peter. (2012, October 22). A diplomatic catastrophe. *The Guardian,* p. 24.

Halevy, Ephraim. (2012, February 8). Iran's Achilles' heel. *New York Times,* p. 27.

Hall, Benjamin. (2012, October 19). Among the snipers of Aleppo. *New York Times,* p. 31.

Hamilton, Rebecca. (2011). *Fighting for Darfur: Public action and the struggle to stop genocide.* New York, NY: Palgrave Macmillan.

Harkin, James. (2012, November 21). Syrians may be better off without cheerleaders. *The Guardian,* p. 32.

Harris, John. (2013, September 2). Westminster's posturing elite can't engage the public. *The Guardian,* p. 25.

Hathaway, Oona, & Shapiro, Scott. (2013, September 4). On Syria, a UN vote isn't optional. *New York Times,* p. 23.

Hearst, David. (2011, October 14). One region, four players. *The Guardian,* p. 41.

Hehir, Aidan. (2012). *The Responsibility to Protect; rhetoric, reality and the future of humanitarian intervention.* New York, NY: Palgrave Macmillan.

Hehir, Aidan, & Murray, Robert. (2015, March 17). The need for post-R2P humanitarianism. OpenCanada.ORG. Retrieved from http://opencanada.org/features/the-need-for-post-r2p-humanitarianism/

Heinbecker, Paul. (2011, November 22). Think twice, Canada; we need fewer exclamation points and more question marks while discussing Tehran's nuclear program and Syria's crackdown—especially when it comes to preemptive action. *Globe and Mail,* p. 15.

Heinbecker, Paul. (2013, March 15). Heed the lessons of Iraq; Canada was right not to march off to war in 2003. But the warning signs that pointed to that fiasco now point to Iran. *Globe and Mail,* p. 15.

Heinbecker, Paul. (2013, June 18). Every day, the costs of inaction grow; the strategic and humanitarian rationales for intervention have overwhelmed the counterarguments. *Globe and Mail,* p. 15.

Herzog, Michael. (2013, May 8). An act of defence: Israel has no interest in getting drawn into the Syrian quagmire. *The Guardian*, p. 26.

Hiebert, Ray. (2003). Public relations and propaganda in framing the Iraq war: A preliminary review. *Public Relations Review, 29*(3), 243–255.

Hill, Christopher. (2013, May 16). When to talk to monsters. *New York Times*, p. 27.

Hilsum, Lindsey. (2013, March 21). UK public opposes government's aim to arm Syrian rebels. Channel 4 News. Retrieved from http://www.channel4.com

Hinnebusch, Raymond. (2001). *Syria: Revolution from above*. London, UK: Routledge.

Hirst, David. (2011, March 22). Even anti-western Syria is not immune to revolution: President Assad claims his country is stable, but unrest is gathering pace—and any uprising will be more like Libya's. *The Guardian*, p. 36.

Hirst, David. (2012, August 16). Lebanon's fate also hangs in the balance. *The Guardian*, p. 34.

Hoare, Marko. (2013, June 19). Dangerous dithering: Western reluctance to back the Free Syrian Army demoralizes its soldiers and strengthens al-Qaida. *The Guardian*, p. 30.

Holsti, Ole. (1969). *Content analysis for the social sciences and humanities*. Reading, MA: Addison-Wesley.

Holsti, Ole. (2011). *American public opinion on the Iraq War*. Ann Arbor, MI: University of Michigan Press.

Hopwood, Derek. (1969). *The Russian presence in Syria and Palestine 1843–1914*. Oxford, UK: Clarendon Press.

Hurd, Ian. (2013, August 28). Bomb Syria, even if it is illegal. *New York Times*, p. 27.

International Commission on Intervention and State Sovereignty (ICISS). (2001). *The Responsibility to Protect: Report of the International Commission on Intervention and State Sovereignty*. Ottawa, ON: International Development Research Centre. Retrieved from http://www.iciss.ca.pdf/Commission-Report.pdf

Ignatieff, Michael. (2012, March 20). The parallel universe of Bashar al-Assad; the Syrian dictator's gamble depends on convincing everyone that his tyranny is the better option—and on the loyalty of his tank commanders. *Globe and Mail*, p. 13.

Ignatieff, Michael. (2013, September 14). The duty to protect, still urgent. *New York Times*, p. 19.

Institute for Strategic Studies. (2013, October 9). *Africa must strengthen the International Criminal Court for its own sake*. Retrieved from http://www.polity.org.za/article/africa-must-strengthen-the-international -criminal-court-for-its-own-sake

Ismail, Salwa. (2011, April 29). Syria and the sectarian "plot": Assad's regime has been fostering fears of a religious divided in order to undermine protesters. *The Guardian*, p. 36.

Iyengar, Shanto, & Simon, Adam. (1993). News coverage of the gulf crisis and public opinion: A study of agenda-setting, priming, and framing. *Communication Research, 20*(3), 365–383.

Jackson, Patrick. (2006). Relational constructivism: A war of words. In J. Sterling-Folker (Ed.), *Making sense of international relations theory* (pp. 139–155). Boulder, CO: Lynne Rienner.

Jenkins, Simon. (2012, July 20). This language of war won't help Syria escape its agony. *The Guardian*, p. 39.

Jenkins, Simon. (2012, December 7). If only saying nothing were an option for Hague of the FO: As Britain's experiment in nation-building goes up in flames, our foreign minister still lectures other states. How dare he? *The Guardian*, p. 44.

Jenkins, Simon. (2013, May 29). The greatest miscalculation since the rise of fascism. *The Guardian*, p. 26.

Jenkins, Simon. (2013, August 30). It takes more courage to say there is nothing we can do. *The Guardian*, p. 31.

Jenkins, Simon. (2013, September 18). Putin preens himself but the pressure on him is intense. *The Guardian*, p. 29.

Johansen, Robert. (2006a). The impact of US policy toward the international criminal court on the prevention of genocide, war crimes, and crimes against humanity. *Human Rights Quarterly*, 28(2), 301–331.

Johansen, Robert. (2006b). A United Nations peace service to prevent genocide and crimes against humanity. Unitar. Retrieved from http://unitar.org/ny/sites/unitar.org.ny.files/UNEPS_proposal.pdf

Jurkowitz, Mark, Mitchell, Amy, & Matsa, Katerina Eva. (2013, September 6). How Al Jazeera tackled the crisis over Syria. *Pew Journalism Research Project*. Retrieved July 3, 2014, from http://www/Journalism.org/2013/09/06/how-al-jazeera-tackled-the-crisis-over-syria/

Kabbani, Rana. (2011, March 30). From the Turks to Assad: To us it is all brutal colonialism. *The Guardian*, p. 30.

Kabbani, Rana. (2011, August 10). Can Syrians dare to hope? *The Guardian*, p. 26.

Kampfner, John. (2013, August 26). Britain can't act on Syria till it faces up to the spectre of Iraq. *The Guardian*, p. 22.

Keller, Bill. (2012, March 19). Falling in and out of war. *New York Times*, p. 21.

Keller, Bill. (2012, October 22). Presidential Mitt. *New York Times*, p. 23.

Keller, Bill. (2013, May 6). Syria is not Iraq. *New York Times*, p. 27.

Keller, Bill. (2013, September 9). Our new isolationism. *New York Times*, p. 21.

Kettle, Martin. (2012, March 15). Yes we are all war-weary. But it may come at a price. *The Guardian*, p. 35.

Kettle, Martin. (2013, August 29). Today Ed Miliband can speak for Britain on Syria. *The Guardian*, p. 31.

Khanfar, Wadah. (2012, February 7). The Syrian street is wise. *The Guardian*, p. 30.

Khanfar, Wadah. (2012, August 31). This may be the best chance to exit the Syrian quagmire. *The Guardian*, p. 34.

Khanfar, Wadah. (2013, March 16). Break this stalemate: The west's policy in Syria has been to let neither side win. It's time to take sides, and arm the rebels. *The Guardian*, p. 42.

Khanfar, Wadah. (2013, May 7). In place of strife: The Middle East stands on the brink of sectarian disaster. Instead in should embrace economic union. *The Guardian*, p. 26.

Khanfar, Wadah. (2013, September 3). Syrians want rid of Assad, but without US bombs. *The Guardian*, p. 32.

Khouri, Rami. (2011, July 26). Sectarianism starts at home; when citizens are denied political participation and accountability by their own governments, they turn to ethnic or religious groups for identity, services and protection. *Globe and Mail*, p. 13.

Khouri, Rami. (2011, November 16). The Arab League awakening. *Globe and Mail*, p. 23.

Khouri, Rami. (2012, January 26). Arab regime change? Leave it to the Arabs. *The Guardian*, p. 34.

Khouri, Rami. (2012, February 15). Is Bashar al-Assad listening? A diplomatic offensive indicates that politics, rather than fighting on the ground, will determine the outcome of what's a low-intensity civil war. *Globe and Mail*, p. 17.

Khouri, Rami. (2012, April 10). Syria's key to real change. *The Guardian*, p. 30.

King, Gary, & Zeng, Langche. (2001). Improving forecasts of state failure. *World Politics*, *53*(4), 623–658.

Kingston, Paul. (2011, June 23). EU must target merchant class. *Globe and Mail*, p. 21.

Kodmani, Bassma. (2011, August 1). To topple Assad, it takes a minority. *New York Times*, p. 21.

Koops, Joachim, & Varwick. Johannes. (2008). *Ten years of SHIRBRIG: Lessons learned development prospects and strategic opportunities for Germany.* GPPI Research Paper Series No. 11. Berlin, Germany: Global Public Policy Institute. Retrieved from http://www .academia.edu/449213/Ten_Years_of_SHIRBRIG_Lessons_Learned_and_Strategic_ Opportunities_for_Germany

Kramer, Adam, Guillory, Jamie, & Hancock, Jeffrey. (2014, June 17). Experimental evidence of massive-scale emotional contagion through social networks. *Proceeds of the National Academy of Sciences USA* (*PNAS*), *111*(24), 8788–8790. Retrieved from http:// www.pnas.org/content/111/24/8788.full.pdf

Kristof, Nicholas. (2011, April 3). Is it better to save no one? *New York Times*, p. 12.

Kristof, Nicholas. (2012, August 9). Obama AWOL in Syria. *New York Times*, p. 23.

Kristof, Nicholas. (2012, November 15). The men are vanishing here. *New York Times*, p. 35.

Kristof, Nicholas. (2012, November 18). Inside Syria, a grandma faces down war. *New York Times*, p. SR11.

Kristof, Nicholas. (2013, August 29). Reinforce a norm In Syria. *New York Times*, p. 27.

Kristof, Nicholas. (2013, September 5). The right question on Syria. *New York Times*, p. 25.

Kristof, Nicholas. (2013, September 8). Pulling the curtain back on Syria. *New York Times*, p. 1.

Kristof, Nicholas. (2013, September 12). That threat worked. *New York Times*, p. 31.

Kristof, Nicholas. (2013, September 15). Hearing you out. *New York Times*, p. 11.

Kristof, Nicholas. (2013, September 19). Fawzia's choice. *New York Times*, p. 31.

Kristof, Nicholas. (2013, September 22). The boy who stood up to Syrian injustice. *New York Times*, p. 11.

Kuperman, Alan. (2006). Suicidal rebellions and the moral hazard of humanitarian intervention. In T. Crawford and A. Kuperman (Eds.), *Gambling on humanitarian intervention; moral hazard, rebellion and civil* war (pp. 1– 25). New York, NY: Routledge.

Kuperman, Alan (2015). Obama's Libya debacle: How a well-meaning intervention ended in failure. *Foreign Affairs*, *94*(2), 66–77.

Landler, Mark, & Thee-Brenan, Megan. (2013, September 8). Survey reveals scant backing for Syria strike. *New York Times*. Retrieved from http://www.nytimes.com

Lesch, David. (2005). *The new lion of Damascus: Bashar al-Assad and modern Syria.* New Haven, CT: Yale University Press.

Lesch, David. (2011, March 30). The Syrian president I know. *New York Times*, p. 27.

Lesch, David. (2012). *Syria: The Fall of the House of Assad.* New Haven, CT: Yale University Press.

Leverett, Flynt. (2005). *Inheriting Syria: Bashar's trial by fire.* Washington, DC: Brookings Institution.

Lippmann, Walter. (1922). *Public opinion.* New York, NY: Macmillan Co.

Luttwak, Edward. (2013, August 25). In Syria, American loses if either side wins. *New York Times*, p. 4.

Lynch, Marc. (2006). Critical theory: Dialogue, legitimacy, and justifications for war. In J. Sterling-Folker (Ed.), *Making sense of international relations theory* (pp. 182–197). Boulder, CO: Lynne Rienner.

Lynch, Marc, Freelon, Deen, & Aday, Sean. (2014). Syria in the Arab spring: The integration of Syria's conflict with the Arab uprisings, 2011–2013. *Research and Politics*, October–December, 1–7.

Macfarlane, S. Neil, Thiekling, Carolin, & Weiss, Thomas. (2004). The responsibility to protect: Is anyone interested in humanitarian intervention? *Third World Quarterly*, 25(5), 977–992.

MacKenzie, Lewis. (2012, February 22). The road to Damascus goes through Moscow: The Western proclivity for anointing good and bad sides has been hasty as usual—instead of rattling sabers and sending toothless observer missions, we should be enlisting the Kremlin. *Globe and Mail*, p. 17.

MacKenzie, Lewis. (2013, June 25). Why this strategy won't fly in Syria; Iraq, Kosovo and Libya offer lessons in "mission creep" and other distortions. *Globe and Mail*, p. 13.

MacKenzie, Lewis. (2013, September 17). Chemical weapons deal changes little on the battlefield; the challenge of securing, removing and destroying stockpiles is daunting. *Globe and Mail*, p. 13.

Mahmood, Mona, Letsch, Constance, Smith, Helena, Kingsley, Patrick, & Chulov, Martin. (2013, July 25). Special report: Syria refugees. *The Guardian*, p. 19.

Maleh, Haitham. (2012, May 31). A peace plan in name only. *New York Times*, p. 29.

Manna, Haytham. (2011, March 31). Change, or be changed: The young protesters in Syria will not be put off by President Bashar al-Assad's refusal to listen. *The Guardian*, p. 31.

Manna, Haytham. (2012, June 23). Led astray by violence: Foreign influence and arms have split Syria's civil movement, making peace ever more remote. *The Guardian*, p. 38.

Manna, Haytham. (2012, December 18). After Assad, what then? *The Guardian*, p. 28.

Manna, Haytham. (2013, April 19). Syrians can be reconciled: Regional interventions have failed and the SNC's in turmoil. The solution is negotiation, not violence. *The Guardian*, p. 30.

Mardini, Ramzy. (2013, February 4). After Assad, chaos? *New York Times*, p. 19.

Mardini, Ramzy. (2013, June 16). Bad idea, Mr. President. *New York Times*, p. SR5.

McCombs, Maxwell. (2005). A look at agenda-setting: Past, present and future. *Journalism Studies*, 6(4), 543–557.

McCombs, Maxwell, & Shaw, Donald. (1972). The agenda-setting function of mass media. *Public Opinion Quarterly*, 36(3), 176–187.

McCombs, Maxwell, & Shaw, Donald. (1993). The evolution of agenda-setting research: Twenty-five years in the marketplace of ideas. *Journal of Communication*, 43(2), 58–67.

McCombs, Maxwell, Shaw, Donald, & Weaver, David. (1997). *Communication and democracy: Exploring the intellectual frontiers in agenda-setting theory*. Mahwah, NJ: Lawrence Erlbaum Associates.

McCombs, Maxwell, & Reynolds, Amy. (2002). News influence on our pictures of the world. In J. Bryant and D. Zillmann (Eds.), *Media effects: Advances in theory and research* (2nd ed.) (pp. 1–18). Mahwah, NJ: Lawrence Erlbaum Associates, 1–18.

Miles, Oliver. (2012, September 4). The patient peacemaker. *The Guardian*, p. 30.

Miliband, Ed. (2013, August 31). I believe Britain can still make a difference in Syria. *The Guardian*, p. 42.

Miller, David. (2006). Propaganda managed democracy: The UK and lessons of Iraq. *Socialist Register*, 134–145. Retrieved from http://strathprints.ac.uk/1376/1/strathprints001376.pdf

Mills, Kurt. (2012). Bashir is dividing us. *Human Rights Quarterly, 34*(2), 1–29.

Milne, Seumas. (2012, February 8). Intervention in Syria will escalate not stop the killing. *The Guardian,* p. 29.

Milne, Seumas. (2012, June 6). Foreign intervention will only shed more Syrian blood. *The Guardian,* p. 30.

Milne, Seumas. (2012, August 8). Intervention is now driving Syria's decent into darkness. *The Guardian,* p. 27.

Milne, Seumas. (2012, December 19). Intervention in Syria risks blowback and regional war. *The Guardian,* p. 27.

Milne, Seumas. (2013, May 8). Cynical to the end, the west bleeds Syria to weaken Iran. *The Guardian,* p. 26.

Milne, Seumas. (2013, August 28). An attack on Syria will only spread the war and killing. *The Guardian,* p. 29.

Mohamed, Feisal. (2013, May 12). The tyrant as target. *New York Times,* p. 3.

Molloy, Mike, & Bell, Michael. (2012, October 29). A team Canada plan for Syria. *Globe and Mail,* p. 11.

Momani, Bessma. (2011, August 4). Unintended consequences. *Globe and Mail,* p. 15.

Monbiot, George. (2011, September 20). Damned if we do impose sanctions on Syria. And damned if we don't. *The Guardian,* p. 31.

Monbiot, George. (2013, September 10). Obama's rogue state breaks every law it claims to uphold. *The Guardian,* p. 35.

Najem, Tom Pierre, Walter C. Soderlund, E. Donald Briggs, & Sarah Cipkar. (2016, September). Was R2P a viable option for Syria? Opinion content in the *Globe and Mail* and the *National Post*, 2011–2013. *International Journal, 71*(3), 433–449.

Nasr, Vali. (2011, August 28). If the Arab Spring turns ugly. *New York Times,* p. 4.

Nasr, Vali. (2012, July 29). Syria after the fall. *New York Times,* p. 22.

Nelson, Thomas, Oxley, Zoe, & Clawson, Rosalee. (1997). Toward a psychology of framing effects. *Political Behavior, 19*(3), 221–246.

Nuruzzaman, Mohammed. (2015). Rethinking foreign military interventions to promote human rights: Evidence from Libya, Bahrain and Syria. *Canadian Journal of Political Science, 48*(3), 531–552.

NYT. [Editorial]. (2011, April 29). President Assad's crackdown: Too much of the world is mute as Syria's president slaughters those who dare protest. *New York Times,* p. 26.

NYT. [Editorial]. (2011, May 10). They should be condemning Syria. *New York Times,* p. 26.

NYT. [Editorial]. (2011, May 20). Peace and change: President Obama said many right things about the Arab Spring, but he can't stop there. *New York Times,* p. 22.

NYT. [Editorial]. (2011, June 4). President Assad's bloody hands: The Security Council needs to do its job and condemn the brutality and impose sanctions. *New York Times,* p. 20.

NYT. [Editorial]. (2011, June 18). Syria's nightmare: It is past time for President Assad to "get out of the way." *New York Times,* p. 18.

NYT. [Editorial]. (2011, July 19). Syria's struggle: The opposition isn't giving up and needs clearer support from Washington and its allies. *New York Times,* p. 22.

NYT. [Editorial]. (2011, August 4). Who will help the Syrians? Tougher sanctions, and a united front, are the only hope of ending the killing. *New York Times,* p. 24.

NYT. [Editorial]. (2011, August 9). The Arab States and Syria: Arab monarchies, repressive themselves, finally speak out on Syrian crackdowns. *New York Times,* p. 22.

NYT. [Editorial]. (2011, September 1). Isolating Assad: The world is rightly fed up with Syria's brutal leader, but he still has powerful enablers. *New York Times,* p. 28.

NYT. [Editorial]. (2011, October 11). Enabling Mr. Assad: Instead of denouncing the killing in Syria, Russia and China have ensured it will continue. *New York Times,* p. 26.

NYT. [Editorial]. (2011, November 9). Syria and the Arab League. *New York Times,* p. 30.

NYT. [Editorial]. (2011, November 17). The killing in Syria goes on. *New York Times,* p. 30.

NYT. [Editorial]. (2011, December 23). Get tougher on Assad. *New York Times,* p. 30.

NYT. [Editorial]. (2012, January 20). Syria's rising toll. *New York Times,* p. 26.

NYT. [Editorial]. (2012, February 2). Russia's bad bet on Syria. *New York Times,* p. 26.

NYT. [Editorial]. (2012, February 7). Killing in Syria. *New York Times,* p. 30.

NYT. [Editorial]. (2012, February 15). The enablers. *New York Times,* p. 24.

NYT. [Editorial]. (2012, February 25). Syria's horrors. *New York Times,* p. 18.

NYT. [Editorial]. (2012, March 3). Crushing Homs. *New York Times,* p. 18.

NYT. [Editorial]. (2012, April 10). President Assad's latest bluff. *New York Times,* p. 22.

NYT. [Editorial]. (2012, April 21). Assad's lies. *New York Times,* p. 20.

NYT. [Editorial]. (2012, June 9). Assad, the butcher. *New York Times,* p. 20.

NYT. [Editorial]. (2012, July 19). Assassination in Damascus. *New York Times,* p. 28.

NYT. [Editorial]. (2012, August 7). If Assad falls in Syria. *New York Times,* p. 22.

NYT. [Editorial]. (2012, August 29). A refugee disaster in the making. *New York Times,* p. 26.

NYT. [Editorial]. (2012, December 1). Measured approach to the Syrian crisis. *New York Times,* p. 24.

NYT. [Editorial]. (2012, December 11). Al Qaeda in Syria. *New York Times,* p. 30.

NYT. [Editorial]. (2013, January 21). The Syrian refugee crisis. *New York Times,* p. 20.

NYT. [Editorial]. (2013, Mar, 1). Help for Syrian rebels. *New York Times,* p. 22.

NYT. [Editorial]. (2013, Apr, 23). More help for Syrian rebels. *New York Times,* p. 30.

NYT. [Editorial]. (2013, April 25). Were chemical weapons used in Syria? *New York Times,* p. 30.

NYT. [Editorial]. (2013, April 30). Ill-considered advice on Syria. *New York Times,* p. 18.

NYT. [Editorial]. (2013, May 9). Diplomatic stirrings on Syria. *New York Times,* p. 28.

NYT. [Editorial]. (2013, May 21). Why is Russia still arming Syria? *New York Times,* p. 24.

NYT. [Editorial]. (2013, June 7). The new security team. *New York Times,* p. 26.

NYT. [Editorial]. (2013, June 15). After arming the rebels, then what? *New York Times,* p. 20.

NYT. [Editorial]. (2013, August 23). The corpses in Syria. *New York Times,* p. 26.

NYT. [Editorial]. (2013, August 27). Responding to Syrian atrocities. *New York Times,* p. 20.

NYT. [Editorial]. (2013, August 29). More answers needed on Syria. *New York Times,* p. 26.

NYT. [Editorial]. (2013, August 31). Absent on Syria. *New York Times,* p. 18.

NYT. [Editorial]. (2013, September 3). Debating the case for force. *New York Times,* p. 24.

NYT. [Editorial]. (2013, September 4). Britain's Syria vote in perspective. *New York Times,* p. 22.

NYT. [Editorial]. (2013, September 5). The stakes in Congress. *New York Times,* p. 24.

NYT. [Editorial]. (2013, September 7). Can Mr. Obama avoid mission creep? *New York Times,* p. 22.

NYT. [Editorial]. (2013, September 10). A diplomatic proposal for Syria. *New York Times,* p. 22.

NYT. [Editorial]. (2013), September 12). Diplomacy as deterrent. *New York Times,* p. 30.

NYT. [Editorial]. (2013, September 16). The Syrian pact. *New York Times,* p. 22.

NYT. [Editorial]. (2013, September 27). Some progress on Syria. *New York Times,* p. 22.

Ovenden, Kevin. (2012, February 17). Playing with fire in Syria: After decades of selling arms to tyrants, western talk of humanitarian intervention rings hollow. *The Guardian,* p. 32.

Owen, David. (2012, June 9). We can intervene in Syria—and with Russia's blessing. *The Guardian,* p. 43.

Owen, David. (2013, May 4). Syria: the solution: Syria needs a regional settlement that is owned by the region. The UN must make than happen. *The Guardian,* p. 42.

Oxenreider, Tsh. (2015, September 7). A brief history of Syria. *The Art of Simple.* Retrieved from theartofsimple.net/

Page, Benjamin, & Shapiro, Robert. (1983). Effects of public opinion on policy. *American Political Science Review, 77*(1), 175–190.

Pape, Robert. (2012, February 3). Why we shouldn't attack Syria (yet). *New York Times,* p. 25.

Paris, Erna. (2013, January 25). Referring Syria to the ICC is worth a try. *Globe and Mail,* p. 11.

Pattison, J. (2008). Humanitarian intervention and a cosmopolitan UN force. *Journal of Political Theory, 4*(1), 126–145.

Pew Research Center. (2013, September 3). Public opinion runs against Syrian airstrikes. *Pew Research Center for the People & the Press.* Retrieved from http://www.people-press .org

Pilger, John. (2013, September 11). The silent military coup that took over Washington. *The Guardian,* p. 34.

Polk, William. (2013, December 10). Understanding Syria: From pre-civil war to post Assad. *The Atlantic.* Retrieved from http://www.theatlantic.com/international/archive/2013/ understanding-syria-from-pre-civil-war-to-post-assad/281989

Pollock, David. (2103, April 16). Syria's forgotten front. *New York Times,* p. 2.

Price, Vincent, Tewksbury, David, & Powers, Elizabeth. (1997). Switching trains of thought: The impact of news frames on readers' cognitive responses. *Communication Research, 24*(5), 481–506.

Public opinion drove Syria debate. (2013, August 30). YouGov.co. Retrieved from http:// www.yougov.co/uk

Pukhov, Ruslan. (2012, July 7). Why Russia is backing Syria. *New York Times,* p. 17.

Puley, Greg. (2005). *The Responsibility to Protect: East, West, and Southern Africa perspectives on preventing and responding to humanitarian crises.* Waterloo, ON: Project Plowshares Working Paper 05–5.

Putin, Vladimir. (2013, September 12). A plea for caution from Russia. *New York Times,* p. 31.

Quilliam, Neil. (1999). *Syria and the new world order.* Reading, UK: Ithaca Press.

Rabinovich, Itamar. (2012, August 2). Syria, viewed from Israel. *The Guardian,* p. 30.

Reinold, Theresa. (2010). The responsibility to protect—much ado about nothing? *Review of International Studies, 36*(Supplement S1), 55–78.

Richards, Steve. (2013, August 31). For a fragile leader, the past can be a treacherous guide. *The Guardian,* p. 43.

Richards, Steve. (2013, September 7). Miliband's tormentors forget the constraints of leadership. *The Guardian,* p. 55.

Rifkind, Malcolm. (2013, August 29). Stand up to Assad. *The Guardian,* p. 30.

Robinson, Piers. (2000). The policy-media interaction model: Measuring media power during humanitarian crisis. *Journal of Peace Research, 37*(5), 613–633.

Robinson, Piers. (2002). *The CNN effect: The myth of news, foreign policy and intervention.* New York, NY: Routledge.

Roff, Heather, & Momani, Bessma. (2011, October 25). The tactics of intervention: Why Syria will never be Libya; unless the West is prepared to invade, we can merely deplore what the regime is doing against its own people. *Globe and Mail,* p. 17.

Rogers, Everett, & Dearing, James. (1988). Agenda-setting research: Where has it been, where is it going? In J. Anderson (Ed.), *Communication yearbook* (Vol. 11) (pp. 555–594). Beverley Hills, CA: Sage Publications.

Rogers, Everett, Dearing, James, & Bergman, Dorine. (1993). The anatomy of agenda-setting research. *Journal of Communication, 43*(2), 68–84.

Rosenau, James. (1966). Pre-theories and theories of foreign policy. In R. B. Farrell (Ed.), *Approaches to comparative and international politics* (pp. 27–92). Evanston, IL: Northwestern University Press.

Roth, Kenneth. (2013, February 4). The new Syria will need rights, not reprisals. *The Guardian,* p. 26.

Rubin, Barry. (2013, May 7). Israel's motive in Syria was pure self-defence; in 2006 a red line was laid down that any attempt to transport advanced weapons would be stopped by force. *Globe and Mail,* p. 15.

Russell, Jenni. (2013, September 6). There is no safe, morally pure solution for Syria. *The Guardian,* p. 36.

Ruthven, Malise. (2013, June 28). Syria is not alone in its descent into sectarianism. *The Guardian,* p. 46.

Sands, Philippe. (2013, January 17). A justified gamble. *The Guardian,* p. 32.

Saunders, Doug. (2012, February 4). Obama, Merkel and Putin are at war with reason. *Globe and Mail,* p. F9.

Saunders, Doug. (2012, February 25). Ocampo's crusades tainted the idea of international justice. *Globe and Mail,* p. F9.

Saunders, Doug. (2012, September 22). Stopping Syria's slaughter: What do you mean "we"? *Globe and Mail,* p. F9.

Scheufele, Dietram, & Iyengar, Shanto. (2011). The state of framing research: A call for new directions. In Kate Kenski & Kathleen Hall Jamieson (Eds.), *The Oxford handbook of political communication.* Retrieved from https://www.researchgate.net/publication/224818492_The_state_of_framing_research_A_call_for_new_directions

Seale, Patrick. (1988). *Assad of Syria: The struggle for the Middle East.* Berkeley, CA: University of California Press.

Seale, Patrick. (2011, April 12). If Assad fails, we will see all the region's alliances unravel. *The Guardian,* p. 28.

Seale, Patrick. (2012, April 14). Syria needs Annan's plan. *The Guardian,* p. 40.

Seale, Patrick. (2012, May 28). This is no plan for peace. *The Guardian,* p. 27.

Sebag Montefiore, Simon. (2011, March 27). Every revolution is revolution in its own way. *New York Times,* p. 11.

Segal, Hugh. (2012, June 22). We must act now in Syria or pay later. *Globe and Mail,* p. 13.

Seigneurie, Ken. (2012). Discourses of the 2011 Arab revolutions. *Journal of Arabic Literature, 43,* 484–509.

SHIRBRIG. (2009). *SHIRBRIG: Lessons learned report.* Hovelte Barracks, Denmark: SHIRBRIG Headquarters. Retrieved from http://www.operationspaix.net/DATA/ DOCUMENT/556_v_Shirbrig_lessons_learned_report_pdf

Sidahmed Abdel Salem, Soderlund, Walter, & Briggs, E. Donald. (2010). *The Responsibility to Protect in Darfur: The role of mass media.* Lanham, MD: Lexington Books.

Simes, Dimitrik, & Saunders, Paul. (2012, December 22). To save Syria, we need Russia. *New York Times*, p. 25.

Simpson, Jeffrey. (2012, October 24). Obama's edge: Muscularity with restraint. *Globe and Mail*, p. 15.

Simpson, Jeffrey. (2013, June 7). Before intervening in Syria, check hubris at the door. *Globe and Mail*, p. 15.

Simpson, Jeffrey. (2013, September 4). Syria is not a test of US leadership. *Globe and Mail*, p. 13.

Simpson, Jeffrey. (2013, September 7). Intervention is easier said than done. *Globe and Mail*, p. F2.

Slaughter, Anne-Marie. (2012, February 24). How to halt the butchery in Syria. *New York Times*, p. 27.

Slaughter, Anne-Marie. (2013, May 29). Going to school in Syria: Tens of thousands are dead and a cradle of civilization has been laid to waste. *Globe and Mail*, p. 15.

Slaughter, Anne-Marie. (2013, September 19). Muzzling the dogs of war; Obama has entered a small class of leaders who actively seek to constrain their own power. *Globe and Mail*, p. 17.

Snyder, Richard, Bruck, Henry, & Sapin, Burton. (1962). *Decision making as an approach to the study of international politics.* New York, NY: Free Press of Glencoe.

Soderlund, Walter, Briggs, E. Donald, Hildebrandt, Kai, & Sidahmed, Abdel Salam (2008). *Humanitarian crises and intervention: Reassessing the impact of mass media.* Sterling, VA: Kumarian Press.

Soderlund, Walter, E. Briggs, Donald, Najem, Tom, & Roberts, Blake. (2012). *Africa's deadliest conflict: Media coverage of the humanitarian disaster in the Congo and the United Nations' Response, 1997–2008.* Waterloo, ON: Wilfrid Laurier University Press.

Soderlund, Walter, & Briggs, E. Donald. (2014). *The independence of South Sudan: The role of mass media in the responsibility to prevent.* Waterloo, ON: Wilfrid Laurier University Press.

Soroka, Stuart. (2003). Media, public opinion and foreign policy. *International Journal of Press/Politics, 8*(1), 27–48.

Spencer, Claire. (2013, March 27). Syria's strange bedfellows: The west needs to face up to the fact that its alliance against Assad is riddled with contradictions. *The Guardian*, p. 38.

Steele, Jonathan. (2011, November 18). Without an amnesty, Assad will not step down peacefully. *The Guardian*, p. 47.

Steele, Jonathan. (2012, January 18). Most Syrians back Assad. But we never hear about it. *The Guardian*, p. 32.

Steele, Jonathan. (2012, March 20). Syria might need its own Mandela to end this war. *The Guardian*, p. 34.

Steele, Jonathan. (2012, July 10). Only an arms embargo can break Syria's deadlock. *The Guardian*, p. 28.

Steele, Jonathan. (2012, August 6). Why Annan had enough. *The Guardian*, p. 20.

Steele, Jonathan. (2012, October 29). What hope for Syria? *The Guardian*, p. 28.

Steele, Jonathan. (2013, February 1). End this bloodshed: Israel's attack on Syria shows how volatile this conflict is. *The Guardian*, p. 34.

Steele, Jonathan. (2013, February 26). Kerry's problem: The new secretary of state should resist the SNC and US hawks and push for talks, not arms. *The Guardian*, p. 28.

Steele, Jonathan. (2013, May 21). Syria's chance for change. *The Guardian*, p. 30.

Steele, Jonathan. (2013, September 2). The American people face a reality TV choice over Syria. *The Guardian*, p. 24.

Steinberg, Brian. (2013, August 30). Broadcast nets interrupt programs for Syria coverage. *Variety*. Retrieved from http://variety.com/tv/news/broadcast-program-for-syria-coverage-1200593371/#

Stevenson, Jonathan. (2013, July 19). To oust Assad, pressure Hezbollah. *New York Times*, p. 25.

Sullivan, Margaret. (2013, September 15). The delicate handling of images of war. *New York Times*, p. 12.

Takeyh, Ray. (2013, May 28). In Syria, go big or stay home. *New York Times*, p. 19.

Taking sides on Syria. (2013, October 9). Ipsos. Retrieved from http://ipsos-na.com/news-polls/pressrelease.aspx?id=6279

Thompson, Allan. (2007). The Responsibility to Report: A new journalistic paradigm. In A. Thompson (Ed.), *The media and the Rwandan genocide* (pp. 433–445). Ottawa, ON: International Development Research Centre.

Tisdall, Simon. (2011, October 4). On the world state, Obama the idealist has taken fright. *The Guardian*, p. 28.

Toynebee, Polly. (2013, August 30). No 10 curses, but Britain's illusion of empire is over. *The Guardian*, p. 30.

Van Dam, Nikolaos. (1979). *The struggle for power in Syria*. New York, NY: St. Martin's Press.

Verma, Inder. (2014, June 17). Expression of concern. *PNAS*. Retrieved from http://www.pnas.org/content/111/24/8788.full.pdf

Wark, Wesley. (2012, July 19). How to end the fighting in Syria; whether we support the rebels covertly or impose a no-fly zone, we must act now. *Globe and Mail*, p. 13.

Weaver, David. (2007). Thoughts on agenda setting, framing, and priming. *Journal of Communication*, *57*(1), 142–147.

Weiss, Thomas. (2012). *Humanitarian Intervention* (2nd ed.). Cambridge, UK: Polity Press.

Weiss, Michael, & and Hassan, Hassan. (2015). *Isis: Inside the army of terror*. New York, NY: Regan Arts.

Wente, Margaret. (2013, September 14). Barack Obama, the 90-pound weakling; he doesn't mean what he says, and he got rolled by the biggest bully on the block. Why would anyone take him seriously now? *Globe and Mail*, p. F2.

Western, Jon. (2005). *Selling intervention and war: The presidency, the media, and the American public*. Baltimore, MD: Johns Hopkins University Press.

Wheatcroft, Geoffrey. (2004, June). The tragedy of Tony Blair. *The Atlantic*. Retrieved from http://www.theatlantic.com/past/docs/issues/2004/06/wheatcroft.htm

Williams, Michael. (2013, September 14). The best hope for Syria: If the diplomacy is to progress, one day the US will have to sit down at the same table as Iran. *The Guardian*, p. 51.

Wolfsfeld, Gadi. (1997). *Media and political conflict: News from the Middle East*. Cambridge, UK: Cambridge University Press.

Wright, Robin. (2013, September 29). Imagining a remapped Middle East. *New York Times*, p. 7.

Yakabuski, Konrad. (2013, September 5). A long week in American politics. *Globe and Mail*, p. 17.

Yakabuski, Konrad. (2015, September 10). Ending Syria's civil war is now the world's business. *Globe and Mail*, p. 15.

Yassin-Kassab, Robin. (2011, June 17). After all this bloodshed, there is no going back for Syrians. *The Guardian*, p. 36.

Younge, Gary. (2013, September 9). The US has little credibility left: Syria won't change that. *The Guardian*, p. 37.

ABOUT THE AUTHORS

E. DONALD BRIGGS (Ph.D., University of London, 1961) is Professor Emeritus of Political Science at the University of Windsor, where he taught international relations and African politics from 1963 until his retirement in 1999. His interest in intervention and mass media dates back to his Ph.D. dissertation, *The Anglo-French Incursion into Suez, 1956*, which analyzed press opinion regarding the legality of the 1956 Suez invasion. Among his publications are *Media and Elections in Canada* (1984), "The Zapatista Rebellion in Chiapas, 1994" (2003), *Humanitarian Crises and International Intervention: Reassessing the Role of Mass Media* (2008), *The Responsibility to Protect in Darfur: The Role of Mass Media* (2010), *Africa's Deadliest Conflict: Media Coverage of the Congo and the United Nations Response, 1997–2008* (2012), and *The Independence of South Sudan: The Role of Mass Media in the Responsibility to Prevent* (2014). For many years he was the coordinator of the World University Service Canada (WUSC) program at the University of Windsor, in which capacity he was responsible for sponsoring fifteen refugee students from conflict-ridden countries in Africa to Canada.

TOM PIERRE NAJEM (Ph.D., University of Durham, 1997) is Professor of Political Science at the University of Windsor (where he served as Department Head from to 2002 to 2012), and is Project Manager of The Jerusalem Old City Initiative. He is a specialist in the field of international relations and comparative politics of the developing world, with a concentration in the Middle East and North Africa. He has also lived and worked in the Middle East and North Africa and held previous academic appointments in Morocco and at the University of Durham, UK. His latest publications include the following: *Track Two Diplomacy and Jerusalem* (co-editor, Routledge, 2017); *Governance and Security in Jerusalem* (co-editor, Routledge, 2017); *Contested Sites in Jerusalem* (co-editor, Routledge, 2017); *Africa's Most Deadly Conflict: Media Coverage of the Humanitarian Disaster in the Congo and the United Nation's Response,*

1997–2008 (co-author, Wilfrid Laurier University Press, 2012), and *Lebanon: the Politics of a Penetrated Society* (Routledge, 2011).

WALTER C. SODERLUND (Ph.D., University of Michigan, 1970) is Professor Emeritus in the Department of Political Science at the University of Windsor. He has a long-standing interest in intervention, beginning in the late 1960s with research for his Ph.D. dissertation, *The Functional Roles of Intervention in International Politics*. He has also worked extensively in the area of international communication, where his focus has been on the Caribbean, especially the way in which events in Cuba and Haiti have been portrayed in North American media and the possible impact of this coverage on US foreign policy. He is the author of *Media Definitions of Cold War Reality* (2001) and *Mass Media and Foreign Policy* (2003) and co-author of *Humanitarian Crises and Intervention: Reassessing the Role of Mass Media* (2008), *The Responsibility to Protect in Darfur: The Role of Mass Media* (2010), *Cross-Media Ownership and Democratic Practice in Canada: Content-Sharing and the Impact of New Media* (2012), *Africa's Deadliest Conflict: Media Coverage of the Congo and the United Nations Response, 1997–2008* (2012) and *The Independence of South Sudan: The Role of Mass Media in the Responsibility to Prevent* (2014).

INDEX

Books in the Studies in International Governance Series
Published by Wilfrid Laurier University Press

Irrelevant or Indispensable? The United Nations in the 21st Century edited by Paul Heinbecker and Patricia Goff | 2005 | xii + 196 pp. | ISBN 978-0-88920-493-5

Haiti: Hope for a Fragile State edited by Yasmine Shamsie and Andrew S. Thompson | 2006 | xvi + 131 pp. | ISBN 978-0-88920-510-9

Canada and the Middle East: In Theory and Practice edited by Paul Heinbecker and Bessma Momani | 2007 | ix + 232 pp. | ISBN 978-1-55458-024-8

Exporting Good Governance: Temptations and Challenges in Canada's Aid Program edited by Jennifer Welsh and Ngaire Woods | 2007 | xx + 343 pp. | ISBN 978-1-55458-029-3

Critical Mass: The Emergence of Global Civil Society edited by James W. St.G. Walker and Andrew S. Thompson | 2008 | xxviii + 302 pp. | ISBN 978-1-55458-022-4

Afghanistan: Transition under Threat edited by Geoffrey Hayes and Mark Sedra | 2008 | xxxiv + 314 pp. | ISBN 978-1-55458-011-8

Emerging Powers in Global Governance: Lessons from the Heiligendamm Process edited by Andrew F. Cooper and Agata Antkiewicz | 2008 | xxii + 370 pp. | ISBN 978-1-55458-057-6

Can the World Be Governed? Possibilities for Effective Multilateralism edited by Alan S. Alexandroff | 2008 | vi + 438 pp. | ISBN 978-1-55458-041-5

From Civil Strife to Peace Building: Examining Private Sector Involvement in West African Reconstruction edited by Hany Besada | 2009 | xxiii + 287 pp. | ISBN 978-1-55458-052-1

The Global Food Crisis: Governance Challenges and Opportunities edited by Jennifer Clapp and Marc J. Cohen | 2009 | xviii + 270 pp. | ISBN 978-1-55458-192-4

Implementing WIPO's Development Agenda edited by Jeremy de Beer | 2009 | xvi + 188 pp. | ISBN 978-1-55458-154-2

Redesigning the World Trade Organization for the Twenty-first Century edited by Debra P. Steger | 2009 | xx + 478 pp. | ISBN 978-1-55458-156-6

Backpacks Full of Hope: The UN Mission in Haiti by Eduardo Aldunate, translated by Alma Flores | 2010 | xx + 232 pp. | ISBN 978-1-55458-155-9

From Desolation to Reconstruction: Iraq's Troubled Journey edited by Mokhtar Lamani and Bessma Momani | 2010 | xi + 246 pp. | ISBN 978-1-55458-229-7

Africa's Deadliest Conflict: Media Coverage of the Humanitarian Disaster in the Congo and the United Nations Response, 1997–2008 by Walter C. Soderlund, E. Donald Briggs, Tom Pierre Najem, and Blake C. Roberts | 2012 | xix + 237 pp. | ISBN 978-1-55458-835-0

The Independence of South Sudan: The Role of Mass Media in the Responsibility to Prevent by Walter C. Soderlund and E. Donald Briggs | 2014 | xvi + 166 pp. | ISBN 978-1-77112-117-0

Syria, Press Framing, and the Responsibility to Protect by E. Donald Briggs, Walter C. Soderlund, and Tom Pierre Najem | 2017 | xii + 228 pp. | ISBN 978-1-77112-307.5